ABOUT THIS PUBLICATION

FOR SERVICE ASSISTANCE

Customer Service
1.704.898.0770

North Carolina General Statues is published by The Muliti-Media Group of Greater Charlotte in Charlotte, North Carolina. Copyright 2015 by the Multi-Media Group of Greater Charlotte. This book or parts thereof may not be reproduced in any form, stored in a retrieval system, or transmitted in any form by any means—electronic, mechanical, photocopy, recording or otherwise—without prior written permission of the publisher, except as provided by United States of America copyright law.

The records required by U.S. Code 2257(a) through (c) and the pertinent regulations 28 C.F.R. Cli. 1, Part 75 with respect to this publication and all materials associated with such records are maintained by The Multi-Media Group of Greater Charlotte, Publisher and available for review by Attorney General.

www.visionbooks.org

Copyright © 2015 by MMGGC
All rights reserved!

TID: 5064448
ISBN (10) digit: 1502934477
ISBN (13) digit: 978-1502934475

123-4-56789-01239-Paperback
123-4-56789-01239-Hardback

First Edition

090520140547

Printed in the United States of America

2015 EDITION

North Carolina Criminal Law And Procedure-Pamphlet # 60

Printed In conjunction with the Administration of the Courts

North Carolina Criminal Law and Procedure
Pamphlet Reference Guide

Chapters	Pamphlet
Chapter 1 Civil Procedure	1
Chapter 1 Civil Procedure (Continue)	2
Chapter 1A Rules of Civil Procedure	2
Chapter 1B Contribution.	2
Chapter 1C Enforcement of Judgments.	2
Chapter 1D Punitive Damages.	2
Chapter 1E Eastern Band of Cherokee Indians.	2
Chapter 1F North Carolina Uniform Interstate Depositions and Discovery Act.	2
Chapter 2 - Clerk of Superior Court [Repealed and Transferred.]	3
Chapter 3 - Commissioners of Affidavits and Deeds [Repealed.]	3
Chapter 4 - Common Law	3
Chapter 5 - Contempt [Repealed.]	3
Chapter 5A - Contempt	3
Chapter 6 - Liability for Court Costs	3
Chapter 7 - Courts [Repealed and Transferred.]	3
Chapter 7A – Judicial Department	3
Chapter 7A – Continuation (Judicial Department)	4
Chapter 7A – Continuation (Judicial Department)	5
Chapter 7B - Juvenile Code	5
Chapter 8 - Evidence	6
Chapter 8A - Interpreters for Deaf Persons [Recodified.]	6
Chapter 8B - Interpreters for Deaf Persons	6
Chapter 8C - Evidence Code	6
Chapter 9 - Jurors	6
Chapter 10 - Notaries [Repealed.]	6
Chapter 10A - Notaries [Recodified.]	6
Chapter 10B - Notaries	6
Chapter 11 - Oaths	6
Chapter 12 - Statutory Construction	6
Chapter 13 - Citizenship Restored	6
Chapter 14 - Criminal Law	7
Chapter 14 –Criminal Law (Continuation)	8
Chapter 15 - Criminal Procedure	9
Chapter 15A - Criminal Procedure Act (Continuation)	10
Chapter 15A - Criminal Procedure Act (Continuation)	11
Chapter 15B - Victims Compensation	11
Chapter 15C - Address Confidentiality Program	11
Chapter 16 - Gaming Contracts and Futures	11
Chapter 17 - Habeas Corpus	11

Chapter 17A - Law-Enforcement Officers [Recodified.]	11
Chapter 17B - North Carolina Criminal Justice Education and Training System [Recodified.] Chapter 17C - North Carolina Criminal Justice Education and Training Standards Commission	11 11
Chapter 17D - North Carolina Justice Academy	11
Chapter 17E - North Carolina Sheriffs' Education and Training Standards Commission	11
Chapter 18 - Regulation of Intoxicating Liquors [Repealed.]	12
Chapter 18A - Regulation of Intoxicating Liquors [Repealed.]	12
Chapter 18B - Regulation of Alcoholic Beverages	12
Chapter 18C - North Carolina State Lottery	12
Chapter 19 - Offenses against Public Morals	12
Chapter 19A - Protection of Animals	12
Chapter 20 - Motor Vehicles	13
Chapter 20 - Motor Vehicles (Continuation)	14
Chapter 20 - Motor Vehicles (Continuation)	15
Chapter 20 - Motor Vehicles (Continuation)	16
Chapter 21 - Bills of Lading	17
Chapter 22 - Contracts Requiring Writing	17
Chapter 22A - Signatures	17
Chapter 22B - Contracts Against Public Policy	17
Chapter 22C - Payments to Subcontractors	17
Chapter 23 - Debtor and Creditor	17
Chapter 24 – Interest	17
Chapter 25 – Uniform Commercial Code	18
Chapter 25 – Uniform Commercial Code (Continuation)	19
Chapter 25A – Retail Installment Sales Act	20
Chapter 25B - Credit	20
Chapter 25C - Sales of Artwork	20
Chapter 26 - Suretyship	20
Chapter 27 - Warehouse Receipts [Repealed.]	20
Chapter 28 - Administration [Repealed.]	20
Chapter 28A - Administration of Decedents' Estates	20
Chapter 28B - Estates of Absentees in Military Service	20
Chapter 28C - Estates of Missing Persons	20
Chapter 29 - Intestate Succession	21
Chapter 30 - Surviving Spouses	21
Chapter 31 - Wills	21
Chapter 31A - Acts Barring Property Rights	21
Chapter 31B - Renunciation of Property and Renunciation of Fiduciary Powers Act	21
Chapter 31C - Uniform Disposition of Community Property Rights at Death Act	21
Chapter 32 - Fiduciaries	21
Chapter 32A - Powers of Attorney	21
Chapter 33 - Guardian and Ward [Repealed and Recodified.]	21

Chapter 33A - North Carolina Uniform Transfers to Minors Act	21
Chapter 33B - North Carolina Uniform Custodial Trust Act	21
Chapter 34 - Veterans' Guardianship Act	22
Chapter 35 - Sterilization Procedures	22
Chapter 35A - Incompetency and Guardianship	22
Chapter 36 - Trusts and Trustees [Repealed.]	22
Chapter 36A - Trusts and Trustees	22
Chapter 36B - Uniform Management of Institutional Funds Act [Repealed.]	22
Chapter 36C - North Carolina Uniform Trust Code	22
Chapter 36D - North Carolina Community Third Party Trusts, Pooled Trusts	23
Chapter 36E - Uniform Prudent Management of Institutional Funds Act	23
Chapter 37 - Allocation of Principal and Income [Repealed.]	23
Chapter 37A - Uniform Principal and Income Act	23
Chapter 38 - Boundaries	23
Chapter 38A - Landowner Liability	23
Chapter 39 - Conveyances	23
Chapter 39A - Transfer Fee Covenants Prohibited	23
Chapter 40 - Eminent Domain [Repealed.]	23
Chapter 40A - Eminent Domain	23
Chapter 41 - Estates	23
Chapter 41A - State Fair Housing Act	23
Chapter 42 - Landlord and Tenant	23
Chapter 42A - Vacation Rental Act	23
Chapter 43 - Land Registration	23
Chapter 44 - Liens	24
Chapter 44A - Statutory Liens and Charges	24
Chapter 45 - Mortgages and Deeds of Trust	24
Chapter 45A - Good Funds Settlement Act	24
Chapter 46 - Partition	24
Chapter 47 - Probate and Registration	25
Chapter 47A - Unit Ownership	25
Chapter 47B - Real Property Marketable Title Act	25
Chapter 47C - North Carolina Condominium Act	25
Chapter 47D - Notice of Settlement Act [Expired.]	25
Chapter 47E - Residential Property Disclosure Act	25
Chapter 47F - North Carolina Planned Community Act	25
Chapter 47G - Option to Purchase Contracts	25
Chapter 47H - Contracts for Deed	25
Chapter 48 - Adoptions +	26
Chapter 48A - Minors	26
Chapter 49 - Bastardy	26
Chapter 49A - Rights of Children	26
Chapter 50 - Divorce and Alimony	26
Chapter 50A - Uniform Child-Custody Jurisdiction and	

Enforcement Act	26
Chapter 50B - Domestic Violence	26
Chapter 50C - Civil No-Contact Orders	26
Chapter 51 - Marriage	26
Chapter 52 - Powers and Liabilities of Married Persons	27
Chapter 52A - Uniform Reciprocal Enforcement of Support Act [Repealed.]	27
Chapter 52B - Uniform Premarital Agreement Act	27
Chapter 52C - Uniform Interstate Family Support Act	27
Chapter 53 - Banks	27
Chapter 53A - Business Development Corporations and North Carolina Capital Resource Corporations	28
Chapter 53B - Financial Privacy Act	28
Chapter 54 - Cooperative Organizations	28
Chapter 54A - Capital Stock Savings and Loan Associations [Repealed.]	28
Chapter 54B - Savings and Loan Associations	29
Chapter 54C - Savings Banks	29
Chapter 55 - North Carolina Business Corporation Act	30
Chapter 55A - North Carolina Nonprofit Corporation Act	31
Chapter 55B - Professional Corporation Act	31
Chapter 55C - Foreign Trade Zones	31
Chapter 55D - Filings, Names, and Registered Agents for Corporations, Nonprofit Corporations, and Partnerships	31
Chapter 56 - Electric, Telegraph and Power Companies [Repealed.]	31
Chapter 57 - Hospital, Medical and Dental Service Corporations [Recodified.]	31
Chapter 57A - Health Maintenance Organization Act [Recodified.]	31
Chapter 57B - Health Maintenance Organization Act [Recodified.]	31
Chapter 57C - North Carolina Limited Liability Company Act.	31
Chapter 58 - Insurance.	32
Chapter 58A - North Carolina Health Insurance Trust Commission [Recodified.]	32
Chapter 58A - North Carolina Health Insurance Trust Commission [Recodified.] (Continuation)	33
Chapter 58A - North Carolina Health Insurance Trust Commission [Recodified.] (Continuation)	34
Chapter 58A - North Carolina Health Insurance Trust Commission [Recodified.] (Continuation)	35
Chapter 58A - North Carolina Health Insurance Trust Commission [Recodified.] (Continuation)	36
Chapter 58A - North Carolina Health Insurance Trust Commission [Recodified.] (Continuation)	37
Chapter 58A - North Carolina Health Insurance Trust	

Commission [Recodified.] (Continuation)	38
Chapter 59 - Partnership.	39
Chapter 59B - Uniform Unincorporated Nonprofit Association Act.	39
Chapter 60 - Railroads and Other Carriers [Repealed and Transferred.]	39
Chapter 61 - Religious Societies	39
Chapter 62 - Public Utilities	39
Chapter 62 - Public Utilities (Continuation)	40
Chapter 62A - Public Safety Telephone Service And Wireless Telephone Service	40
Chapter 63 - Aeronautics	40
Chapter 63A - North Carolina Global TransPark Authority	40
Chapter 64 - Aliens	40
Chapter 65 – Cemeteries	40
Chapter 66 - Commerce and Business	41
Chapter 67 - Dogs	41
Chapter 68 - Fences and Stock Law	41
Chapter 69 - Fire Protection	41
Chapter 70 - Indian Antiquities, Archaeological Resources and Unmarked Human Skeletal Remains Protection	42
Chapter 71 - Indians [Repealed.]	42
Chapter 71A - Indians	42
Chapter 72 - Inns, Hotels and Restaurants	42
Chapter 73 - Mills	42
Chapter 74 - Mines and Quarries	42
Chapter 74A - Company Police [Repealed.]	42
Chapter 74B - Private Protective Services Act [Repealed.]	42
Chapter 74C - Private Protective Services	42
Chapter 74D - Alarm Systems	42
Chapter 74E - Company Police Act	42
Chapter 74F - Locksmith Licensing Act	42
Chapter 74G - Campus Police Act	42
Chapter 75 - Monopolies, Trusts and Consumer Protection	42
Chapter 75A - Boating and Water Safety	43
Chapter 75B - Discrimination in Business	43
Chapter 75C - Motion Picture Fair Competition Act	43
Chapter 75D - Racketeer Influenced and Corrupt Organizations	43
Chapter 75E - Unlawful Activities in Connection With Certain Corporate Transactions	43
Chapter 76 - Navigation	43
Chapter 76A - Navigation and Pilotage Commissions	43
Chapter 77 - Rivers, Creeks, and Coastal Waters	43
Chapter 78 - Securities Law [Repealed.]	43
Chapter 78A - North Carolina Securities Act	43
Chapter 78B - Tender Offer Disclosure Act [Repealed.]	43
Chapter 78C - Investment Advisers	43
Chapter 78D - Commodities Act	43

Chapter 79 - Strays [Repealed.]	43
Chapter 80 - Trademarks, Brands, etc.	44
Chapter 81 - Weights and Measures [Recodified.]	44
Chapter 81A - Weights and Measures Act of 1975.	44
Chapter 82 - Wrecks [Repealed.]	44
Chapter 83 - Architects [Recodified.]	44
Chapter 83A - Architects	44
Chapter 84 - Attorneys-at-Law	44
Chapter 84A - Foreign Legal Consultants	44
Chapter 85 - Auctions and Auctioneers [Repealed.]	44
Chapter 85A - Bail Bondsmen and Runners [Recodified.]	44
Chapter 85B - Auctions and Auctioneers	44
Chapter 85C - Bail Bondsmen and Runners [Recodified.]	44
Chapter 86 - Barbers [Recodified.]	44
Chapter 86A - Barbers	44
Chapter 87 - Contractors	44
Chapter 88 - Cosmetic Art [Repealed.]	44
Chapter 88A - Electrolysis Practice Act	44
Chapter 88B - Cosmetic Art	45
Chapter 89 - Engineering and Land Surveying [Recodified.]	45
Chapter 89A - Landscape Architects	45
Chapter 89B - Foresters	45
Chapter 89C - Engineering and Land Surveying	45
Chapter 89D - Landscape Contractors	45
Chapter 89E - Geologists Licensing Act	45
Chapter 89F - North Carolina Soil Scientist Licensing Act	45
Chapter 89G - Irrigation Contractors	45
Chapter 90 - Medicine and Allied Occupations	45
Chapter 90 - Medicine and Allied Occupations (Continuation)	46
Chapter 90 - Medicine and Allied Occupations (Continuation)	47
Chapter 90 - Medicine and Allied Occupations (Continuation)	48
Chapter 90A - Sanitarians and Water and Wastewater Treatment Facility Operators	48
Chapter 90B - Social Worker Certification and Licensure Act	48
Chapter 90C - North Carolina Recreational Therapy Licensure Act	48
Chapter 90D - Interpreters and Transliterators	48
Chapter 91 - Pawnbrokers [Repealed.]	48
Chapter 91A - Pawnbrokers Modernization Act of 1989	48
Chapter 92 - Photographers [Deleted.]	48
Chapter 93 - Certified Public Accountants	48
Chapter 93A - Real Estate License Law	49
Chapter 93B - Occupational Licensing Boards	49
Chapter 93C - Watchmakers [Repealed.]	49
Chapter 93D - North Carolina State Hearing Aid Dealers and Fitters Board.	49
Chapter 93E - North Carolina Appraisers Act	49

Chapter 94 - Apprenticeship	49
Chapter 95 - Department of Labor and Labor Regulations	49
Chapter 95 - Department of Labor and Labor Regulations (Continuation)	50
Chapter 96 - Employment Security	50
Chapter 97 - Workers' Compensation Act	50
Chapter 97 - Workers' Compensation Act (Continuation)	51
Chapter 98 - Burnt and Lost Records	51
Chapter 99 - Libel and Slander	51
Chapter 99A - Civil Remedies for Criminal Actions	51
Chapter 99B - Products Liability	51
Chapter 99C - Actions Relating to Winter Sports Safety and Accidents	51
Chapter 99D - Civil Rights	51
Chapter 99E - Special Liability Provisions	51
Chapter 100 - Monuments, Memorials and Parks	51
Chapter 101 - Names of Persons	51
Chapter 102 - Official Survey Base	51
Chapter 103 - Sundays, Holidays and Special Days	51
Chapter 104 - United States Lands	51
Chapter 104A - Degrees of Kinship	51
Chapter 104B - Hurricanes or Other Acts of Nature	51
Chapter 104C - Atomic Energy, Radioactivity and Ionizing Radiation [Repealed and Recodified.]	51
Chapter 104D - Southern States Energy Compact	51
Chapter 104E - North Carolina Radiation Protection Act	51
Chapter 104F - Southeast Interstate Low-Level Radioactive Waste Management Compact [Repealed]	51
Chapter 104G - North Carolina Low-Level Radioactive Waste Management Authority Act of 1987 [Repealed]	51
Chapter 105 - Taxation	51
Chapter 105 - Taxation (Continuation)	52
Chapter 105 - Taxation (Continuation)	53
Chapter 105 - Taxation (Continuation)	54
Chapter 105A - Setoff Debt Collection Act	55
Chapter 105B - Defaulted Student Loan Recovery Act	55
Chapter 106 - Agriculture	55
Chapter 106 - Agriculture (Continue)	56
Chapter 106 - Agriculture (Continue)	57
Chapter 107 - Agricultural Development Districts [Repealed.]	57
Chapter 108 - Social Services [Repealed and Recodified.]	57
Chapter 108A - Social Services	57
Chapter 108B - Community Action Programs	58
Chapter 108C Medicaid and Health Choice Provider Requirements.	58
Chapter 108D Medicaid Managed Care for Behavioral Health Services.	58
Chapter 109 - Bonds [Recodified.]	58

Chapter 110 - Child Welfare	58
Chapter 111 - Aid to the Blind	58
Chapter 112 - Confederate Homes and Pensions [Repealed.]	58
Chapter 113 - Conservation and Development	58
Chapter 113 - Conservation and Development (Continuation)	59
Chapter 113A - Pollution Control and Environment	59
Chapter 113A - Pollution Control and Environment (Continuation)	60
Chapter 113B - North Carolina Energy Policy Act of 1975	60
Chapter 114 - Department of Justice	60
Chapter 115 - Elementary and Secondary Education [Repealed.]	60
Chapter 115A - Community Colleges, Technical Institutes, and Industrial Education Centers [Repealed.]	60
Chapter 115B - Tuition and Fee Waivers	60
Chapter 115C - Elementary and Secondary Education	60
Chapter 115C - Elementary and Secondary Education (Continuation)	61
Chapter 115C - Elementary and Secondary Education (Continuation)	62
Chapter 115C - Elementary and Secondary Education (Continuation)	63
Chapter 115D - Community Colleges	63
Chapter 115E - Private Educational Facilities Finance Act [Recodified]	63
Chapter 116 - Higher Education	63
Chapter 116 - Higher Education (Continuation)	63
Chapter 116A - Escheats and Abandoned Property [Repealed.]	64
Chapter 116B - Escheats and Abandoned Property	64
Chapter 116C - Continuum of Education Programs	64
Chapter 116D - Higher Education Bonds	64
Chapter 117 - Electrification	64
Chapter 118 - Firemen's and Rescue Squad Workers' Relief and Pension Funds [Recodified.]	64
Chapter 118A - Firemen's Death Benefit Act [Repealed.]	64
Chapter 118B - Members of a Rescue Squad Death Benefit Act [Repealed.]	64
Chapter 119 - Gasoline and Oil Inspection and Regulation	64
Chapter 120 - General Assembly	65
Chapter 120 - General Assembly (Continuation)	66
Chapter 120 - General Assembly (Continuation)	67
Chapter 120C - Lobbying	67
Chapter 121 - Archives and History	67
Chapter 122 - Hospitals for the Mentally Disordered [Repealed.]	67
Chapter 122A - North Carolina Housing Finance Agency	67
Chapter 122B - North Carolina Agricultural Facilities	

Finance Act [Repealed.]	67
Chapter 122C - Mental Health, Developmental Disabilities, and Substance Abuse Act of 1985	67
Chapter 122C - Mental Health, Developmental Disabilities, and Substance Abuse Act of 1985 (Continuation)	68
Chapter 122D - North Carolina Agricultural Finance Act	68
Chapter 122E - North Carolina Housing Trust and Oil Overcharge Act	68
Chapter 123 - Impeachment	69
Chapter 123A - Industrial Development [Repealed.]	69
Chapter 124 - Internal Improvements	69
Chapter 125 - Libraries	69
Chapter 126 - State Personnel System	69
Chapter 127 - Militia [Repealed.]	69
Chapter 127A - Militia	69
Chapter 127B - Military Affairs	69
Chapter 127C - Advisory Commission on Military Affairs	69
Chapter 128 - Offices and Public Officers	69
Chapter 128 - Offices and Public Officers (Continuation)	70
Chapter 129 - Public Buildings and Grounds	70
Chapter 130 - Public Health [Repealed.]	70
Chapter 130A - Public Health	70
Chapter 130A - Public Health (Continuation)	71
Chapter 130A - Public Health (Continuation)	72
Chapter 130B - Hazardous Waste Management Commission [Repealed.]	72
Chapter 131 - Public Hospitals [Repealed.]	72
Chapter 131A - Health Care Facilities Finance Act	72
Chapter 131B - Licensing of Ambulatory Surgical Facilities [Repealed.]	72
Chapter 131C - Charitable Solicitation Licensure Act [Repealed.]	72
Chapter 131D - Inspection and Licensing of Facilities	72
Chapter 131E - Health Care Facilities and Services	72
Chapter 131E - Health Care Facilities and Services (Continuation)	73
Chapter 131F - Solicitation of Contributions	73
Chapter 132 - Public Records	73
Chapter 133 - Public Works	74
Chapter 134 - Youth Development [Recodified.]	74
Chapter 134A - Youth Services [Repealed.]	74
Chapter 135 - Retirement System for Teachers and State Employees; Social Security; Health Insurance Program for Children	74
Chapter 135 - Retirement System for Teachers and State Employees; Social Security; Health Insurance Program for Children	75

Chapter 136 - Transportation	75
Chapter 136 - Transportation (Continuation)	76
Chapter 137 - Rural Rehabilitation [Repealed.]	76
Chapter 138 - Salaries, Fees and Allowances	76
Chapter 138A - State Government Ethics Act	76
Chapter 139 - Soil and Water Conservation Districts	76
Chapter 140 - State Art Museum; Symphony and Art Societies	76
Chapter 140A - State Awards System	76
Chapter 141 - State Boundaries	76
Chapter 142 - State Debt	76
Chapter 143 - State Departments, Institutions, and Commissions	77
Chapter 143 - State Departments, Institutions, and Commissions (Continuation)	78
Chapter 143 - State Departments, Institutions, and Commissions (Continuation)	79
Chapter 143 - State Departments, Institutions, and Commissions (Continuation)	80
Chapter 143A - State Government Reorganization	80
Chapter 143B - Executive Organization Act of 1973	80
Chapter 143B - Executive Organization Act of 1973 (Continuation)	81
Chapter 143B - Executive Organization Act of 1973 (Continuation)	82
Chapter 143C - State Budget Act	83
Chapter 143D - The State Governmental Accountability and Internal Control Act	83
Chapter 144 - State Flag, Official Governmental Flags, Motto, and Colors	83
Chapter 145 - State Symbols and Other Official Adoptions.	83
Chapter 146 - State Lands	83
Chapter 147 - State Officers	83
Chapter 148 - State Prison System	84
Chapter 149 - State Song and Toast	84
Chapter 150 - Uniform Revocation of Licenses [Repealed.]	84
Chapter 150A - Administrative Procedure Act [Recodified.]	84
Chapter 150B - Administrative Procedure Act	84
Chapter 151 - Constables [Repealed.]	84
Chapter 152 - Coroners	84
Chapter 152A - County Medical Examiner [Repealed.]	84
Chapter 152A - County Medical Examiner [Repealed.] (Continuation)	85
Chapter 153 - Counties and County Commissioners [Repealed.]	85
Chapter 153A - Counties	85

Chapter 153B - Mountain Resources Planning Act	85
Chapter 153C - Uwharrie Regional Resources Act	85
Chapter 154 - County Surveyor [Repealed.]	85
Chapter 155 - County Treasurer [Repealed.]	85
Chapter 156 - Drainage	85
Chapter 156 – Drainage (Continuation)	86
Chapter 157 - Housing Authorities and Projects	86
Chapter 157A - Historic Properties Commissions [Transferred.]	86
Chapter 158 - Local Development	86
Chapter 159 - Local Government Finance	86
Chapter 159 - Local Government Finance (Continuation)	87
Chapter 159A - Pollution Abatement and Industrial Facilities Financing Act [Unconstitutional.]	87
Chapter 159B - Joint Municipal Electric Power and Energy Act	87
Chapter 159C - Industrial and Pollution Control Facilities Financing Act	87
Chapter 159D - The North Carolina Capital Facilities Financing Act	87
Chapter 159E - Registered Public Obligations Act	87
Chapter 159F - North Carolina Energy Development Authority [Repealed.]	87
Chapter 159G - Water Infrastructure	87
Chapter 159H - [Reserved.]	87
Chapter 159I - Solid Waste Management Loan Program and Local Government Special Obligation Bonds	87
Chapter 160 - Municipal Corporations [Repealed And Transferred.]	87
Chapter 160A - Cities and Towns	88
Chapter 160A - Cities and Towns (Continuation)	89
Chapter 160B - Consolidated City-County Act	89
Chapter 160C - Baseball Park Districts [Repealed.]	90
Chapter 161 - Register of Deeds	90
Chapter 162 - Sheriff	90
Chapter 162A - Water and Sewer Systems	90
Chapter 162B Continuity of Local Government in Emergency.	90
Chapter 163 Elections and Election Laws.	90
Chapter 163 Elections and Election Laws. (Continuation)	91
Chapter 164 Concerning the General Statutes of North Carolina.	92
Chapter 165 Veterans.	92
Chapter 166 Civil Preparedness Agencies [Repealed.]	92
Chapter 166A North Carolina Emergency Management Act.	92
Chapter 167 State Civil Air Patrol [Repealed.]	92
Chapter 168 Persons with Disabilities.	92
Chapter 168A Persons With Disabilities Protection Act.	92

§ 113A-88. North Carolina Trails Committee; composition; meetings and functions.

(a) Repealed by Session Laws 1973, c. 1262, s. 82.

(b) The Committee shall meet in various sections of the State not less than two times annually to advise the Department on all matters directly or indirectly pertaining to trails, their use, extent, location, and the other objectives and purposes of this Article.

(c) The Committee shall coordinate trail development among local governments, and shall assist local governments in the formation of their trail plans and advise the Department quarterly of its findings.

(d) The Secretary, with advice of the Committee, shall study trail needs and potentials, and make additions to the State Trails System as needed. He shall submit an annual report to the Governor and General Assembly on trail activities by the Department, including rights-of-way that have been established and on the program for implementing this Article. Each report shall include a short statement on the significance of the various trails to the System. The Secretary shall make such rules as to trail development, management, and use that are necessary for the proper implementation of this Article. (1973, c. 670, s. 1; c. 1262, s. 82; 1987, c. 827, s. 132.)

§ 113A-89. Location of trails.

The process of locating routes of designated trails to be added to the system shall be as follows:

For State scenic trails, the Secretary or a designee, after consulting with the Committee, shall recommend a route. For State recreation trails and for connecting or side trails, the Secretary or a designee, after consulting with the Committee, shall select the route. The Secretary may provide technical assistance to political subdivisions or private, nonprofit organizations that develop, construct, or maintain designated trails or other public trails that complement the State trails system. When a route shall traverse land within the jurisdiction of a governmental unit or political subdivision, the Department shall consult with such unit or such subdivision prior to its final determination of the location of the route. The selected route shall be compatible with preservation or enhancement of the environment it traverses. Reasonable effort shall be made to minimize any adverse effects upon adjacent landowners and users. Notice of the selected route shall be published by the Department in a newspaper of general circulation in the area in which the trail is located, together with appropriate maps and descriptions to be conspicuously posted at the appropriate courthouse. Such publication shall be prior to the designation of the trail by the Secretary. (1973, c. 670, s. 1; 1993, c. 184, s. 5.)

§ 113A-90. Scenic easements within right-of-way.

Within the boundaries of the right-of-way, the Secretary of the North Carolina Department of Administration may acquire, on behalf of the State of North Carolina, lands in fee title, or interest in land in the form of scenic easements, cooperative agreements, easements of surface ingress and egress running with the land, leases, or less than fee estates. Acquisition of land or of interest therein may be by gift, purchased with donated funds or funds appropriated by the governmental agencies for this purpose, proceeds from the sale of bonds or exchange. Any change in value of land resulting from the grant of an easement shall be taken into consideration in the assessment of the land for tax purposes. (1973, c. 670, s. 1.)

§ 113A-91. Trails within parks; conflict of laws.

Any component of the System that is or shall become a part of any State park, recreation area, wildlife management area, or similar area shall be subject to the provisions of this Article as well as any other laws under which the other areas are administered, and in the case of conflict between the provisions the more restrictive provisions shall apply. (1973, c. 670, s. 1.)

§ 113A-92. Uniform trail markers.

The Department, in consultation with the Committee, shall establish a uniform marker for trails contained in the System. An additional appropriate symbol characterizing specific trails may be included on the marker. The markers shall be placed at all access points, together with signs indicating the modes of locomotion that are prohibited for the trail, provided that where the trail constitutes a portion of a national scenic trail, use of the national scenic trail uniform marker shall be considered sufficient. The route of the trail and the boundaries of the right-of-way shall be adequately marked. (1973, c. 670, s. 1.)

§ 113A-92.1. Adopt-A-Trail Program.

The Department shall establish an Adopt-A-Trail Program to coordinate with the Trails Committee and local groups or persons on trail development and maintenance. Local involvement shall be encouraged, and interested groups are authorized to "adopt-a-trail" for such purposes as placing trail markers, trail building, trail blazing, litter control, resource protection, and any other activities related to the policies and purposes of this Article. (1987, c. 738, s. 153.)

§ 113A-93. Administrative policy.

The North Carolina Trails System shall be administered by the Department according to the policies and criteria set forth in this Article. The Department shall, in addition, have or designate the responsibility for maintaining the trails, building bridges, campsites, shelters, and related public-use facilities where required. (1973, c. 670, s. 1.)

§ 113A-94. Incorporation in National Trails System.

Nothing in this Article shall preclude a component of the State Trails System from becoming a part of the National Trails System. The Secretary shall coordinate the State Trails System with the National Trails System and is directed to encourage and assist any federal studies for inclusion of North Carolina trails in the National Trails System. The Department may enter into written cooperative agreements for joint federal-State administration of a North Carolina component of the National Trails System, provided such agreements for administration of land uses are not less restrictive than those set forth in this Article. (1973, c. 670, s. 1.)

§ 113A-95. Trail use liability.

(a) Any person, as an owner, lessee, occupant, or otherwise in control of land, who allows without compensation another person to use the land for designated trail or other public trail purposes or to construct, maintain, or cause to be constructed or maintained a designated trail or other public trail owes the person the same duty of care he owes a trespasser.

(b) Any person who without compensation has constructed, maintained, or caused to be constructed or maintained a designated trail or other public trail pursuant to a written agreement with any person who is an owner, lessee, occupant, or otherwise in control of land on which a trail is located shall owe a person using the trail the same duty of care owed a trespasser.

(c) Repealed by Session Laws 1993, c. 184, s. 6. (1987, c. 498; 1991, c. 38; 1993, c. 184, s. 6.)

§§ 113A-96 through 113A-99. Reserved for future codification purposes.

Article 7.

Coastal Area Management.

Part 1. Organization and Goals.

§ 113A-100. Short title.

This Article shall be known as the Coastal Area Management Act of 1974. (1973, c. 1284, s. 1; 1975, c. 452, s. 5; 1981, c. 932, s. 2.1.)

§ 113A-101. Cooperative State-local program.

This Article establishes a cooperative program of coastal area management between local and State governments. Local government shall have the initiative for planning. State government shall establish areas of environmental concern. With regard to planning, State government shall act primarily in a supportive standard-setting and review capacity, except where local governments do not elect to exercise their initiative. Enforcement shall be a concurrent State-local responsibility. (1973, c. 1284, s. 1; 1975, c. 452, s. 5; 1981, c. 932, s. 2.1.)

§ 113A-102. Legislative findings and goals.

(a)   Findings. - It is hereby determined and declared as a matter of legislative finding that among North Carolina's most valuable resources are its coastal lands and waters. The coastal area, and in particular the estuaries, are among the most biologically productive regions of this State and of the nation. Coastal and estuarine waters and marshlands provide almost ninety percent (90%) of the most productive sport fisheries on the east coast of the United States. North Carolina's coastal area has an extremely high recreational and esthetic value which should be preserved and enhanced.

In recent years the coastal area has been subjected to increasing pressures which are the result of the often-conflicting needs of a society expanding in industrial development, in population, and in the recreational aspirations of its citizens. Unless these pressures are controlled by coordinated management, the very features of the coast which make it economically, esthetically, and ecologically rich will be destroyed. The General Assembly therefore finds that an immediate and pressing need exists to establish a comprehensive plan for the protection, preservation, orderly development, and management of the coastal area of North Carolina.

In the implementation of the coastal area management plan, the public's opportunity to enjoy the physical, esthetic, cultural, and recreational qualities of the natural shorelines of the State shall be preserved to the greatest extent feasible; water resources shall be managed in order to preserve and enhance water quality and to provide optimum utilization of water resources; land resources shall be managed in order to guide growth and development and to minimize damage to the natural environment; and private property rights shall be preserved in accord with the Constitution of this State and of the United States.

(b)   Goals. - The goals of the coastal area management system to be created pursuant to this Article are as follows:

(1) To provide a management system capable of preserving and managing the natural ecological conditions of the estuarine system, the barrier dune system, and the beaches, so as to safeguard and perpetuate their natural productivity and their biological, economic and esthetic values;

(2) To insure that the development or preservation of the land and water resources of the coastal area proceeds in a manner consistent with the capability of the land and water for development, use, or preservation based on ecological considerations;

(3) To insure the orderly and balanced use and preservation of our coastal resources on behalf of the people of North Carolina and the nation;

(4) To establish policies, guidelines and standards for:

a. Protection, preservation, and conservation of natural resources including but not limited to water use, scenic vistas, and fish and wildlife; and management of transitional or intensely developed areas and areas especially suited to intensive use or development, as well as areas of significant natural value;

b. The economic development of the coastal area, including but not limited to construction, location and design of industries, port facilities, commercial establishments and other developments;

c. Recreation and tourist facilities and parklands;

d. Transportation and circulation patterns for the coastal area including major thoroughfares, transportation routes, navigation channels and harbors, and other public utilities and facilities;

e. Preservation and enhancement of the historic, cultural, and scientific aspects of the coastal area;

f. Protection of present common-law and statutory public rights in the lands and waters of the coastal area;

g. Any other purposes deemed necessary or appropriate to effectuate the policy of this Article. (1973, c. 1284, s. 1; 1975, c. 452, s. 5; 1981, c. 932, s. 2.1.)

§ 113A-103. Definitions.

As used in this Article:

(1) "Advisory Council" means the Coastal Resources Advisory Council created by G.S. 113A-105.

(1a) "Boat" means a vessel or watercraft of any type or size specifically designed to be self-propelled, whether by engine, sail, oar, or paddle or other means, which is used to travel from place to place by water.

(2) "Coastal area" means the counties that (in whole or in part) are adjacent to, adjoining, intersected by or bounded by the Atlantic Ocean (extending offshore to the limits of State jurisdiction, as may be identified by rule of the Commission for purposes of this Article, but in no event less than three geographical miles offshore) or any coastal sound. The Governor, in accordance with the standards set forth in this subdivision and in subdivision (3) of this section, shall designate the counties that constitute the "coastal area," as defined by this section, and his designation shall be final and conclusive. On or before May 1, 1974, the Governor shall file copies of a list of said coastal-area counties with the chairmen of the boards of commissioners of each county in the coastal area, with the mayors of each incorporated city within the coastal area (as so defined) having a population of 2,000 or more and of each incorporated city having a population of less than 2,000 whose corporate boundaries are contiguous with the Atlantic Ocean, and with the Secretary of State. By way of illustration, the counties designated as coastal-area counties under this subdivision as of July 1, 2012, are Beaufort, Bertie, Brunswick, Camden, Carteret, Chowan, Craven, Currituck, Dare, Gates, Hertford, Hyde, New Hanover, Onslow, Pamlico, Pasquotank, Pender, Perquimans, Tyrrell, and Washington. The coastal-area counties and cities shall transmit nominations to the Governor of members of the Coastal Resources Commission as provided in G.S. 113A-104(d).

(3) "Coastal sound" means Albemarle, Bogue, Core, Croatan, Currituck, Pamlico and Roanoke Sounds. For purposes of this Article, the inland limits of a sound on a tributary river shall be defined as the limits of seawater encroachment on said tributary river under normal conditions. "Normal conditions" shall be understood to include regularly occurring conditions of low stream flow and high tide, but shall not include unusual conditions such as those associated with hurricane and other storm tides. Unless otherwise determined by the Commission, the limits of seawater encroachment shall be considered to

be the confluence of a sound's tributary river with the river or creek entering it nearest to the farthest inland movement of oceanic salt water under normal conditions. For purposes of this Article, the aforementioned points of confluence with tributary rivers shall include the following:

a. On the Chowan River, its confluence with the Meherrin River;

b. On the Roanoke River, its confluence with the northeast branch of the Cashie River;

c. On the Tar River, its confluence with Tranters Creek;

d. On the Neuse River, its confluence with Swift Creek;

e. On the Trent River, its confluence with Ready Branch.

Provided, however, that no county shall be considered to be within the coastal area which: (i) is adjacent to, adjoining or bounded by any of the above points of confluence and lies entirely west of said point of confluence; or (ii) is not bounded by the Atlantic Ocean and lies entirely west of the westernmost of the above points of confluence.

(4)   "Commission" means the Coastal Resources Commission created by G.S. 113A-104.

(4a)   "Department" means the Department of Environment and Natural Resources.

(5)   a.   "Development" means any activity in a duly designated area of environmental concern (except as provided in paragraph b of this subdivision) involving, requiring, or consisting of the construction or enlargement of a structure; excavation; dredging; filling; dumping; removal of clay, silt, sand, gravel or minerals; bulkheading, driving of pilings; clearing or alteration of land as an adjunct of construction; alteration or removal of sand dunes; alteration of the shore, bank, or bottom of the Atlantic Ocean or any sound, bay, river, creek, stream, lake, or canal; or placement of a floating structure in an area of environmental concern identified in G.S. 113A-113(b)(2) or (b)(5).

b.   The following activities including the normal and incidental operations associated therewith shall not be deemed to be development under this section:

1. Work by a highway or road agency for the maintenance of an existing road, if the work is carried out on land within the boundaries of the existing right-of-way;

2. Work by any railroad company or by any utility and other persons engaged in the distribution and transmission of petroleum products, water, telephone or telegraph messages, or electricity for the purpose of inspecting, repairing, maintaining, or upgrading any existing substations, sewers, mains, pipes, cables, utility tunnels, lines, towers, poles, tracks, and the like on any of its existing railroad or utility property or rights-of-way, or the extension of any of the above distribution-related facilities to serve development approved pursuant to G.S. 113A-121 or 113A-122;

3. Work by any utility and other persons for the purpose of construction of facilities for the development, generation, and transmission of energy to the extent that such activities are regulated by other law or by present or future rules of the State Utilities Commission regulating the siting of such facilities (including environmental aspects of such siting), and work on facilities used directly in connection with the above facilities;

4. The use of any land for the purposes of planting, growing, or harvesting plants, crops, trees, or other agricultural or forestry products, including normal private road construction, raising livestock or poultry, or for other agricultural purposes except where excavation or filling affecting estuarine waters (as defined in G.S. 113-229) or navigable waters is involved;

5. Maintenance or repairs (excluding replacement) necessary to repair damage to structures caused by the elements or to prevent damage to imminently threatened structures by the creation of protective sand dunes.

6. The construction of any accessory building customarily incident to an existing structure if the work does not involve filling, excavation, or the alteration of any sand dune or beach;

7. Completion of any development, not otherwise in violation of law, for which a valid building or zoning permit was issued prior to ratification of this Article and which development was initiated prior to the ratification of this Article;

8. Completion of installation of any utilities or roads or related facilities not otherwise in violation of law, within a subdivision that was duly approved and

recorded prior to the ratification of this Article and which installation was initiated prior to the ratification of this Article;

9. Construction or installation of any development, not otherwise in violation of law, for which an application for a building or zoning permit was pending prior to the ratification of this Article and for which a loan commitment (evidenced by a notarized document signed by both parties) had been made prior to the ratification of this Article; provided, said building or zoning application is granted by July 1, 1974;

10. It is the intention of the General Assembly that if the provisions of any of the foregoing subparagraphs 1 to 10 of this paragraph are held invalid as a grant of an exclusive or separate emolument or privilege or as a denial of the equal protection of the laws, within the meaning of Article I, Secs. 19 and 32 of the North Carolina Constitution, the remainder of this Article shall be given effect without the invalid provision or provisions.

c. The Commission shall define by rule (and may revise from time to time) certain classes of minor maintenance and improvements which shall be exempted from the permit requirements of this Article, in addition to the exclusions set forth in paragraph b of this subdivision. In developing such rules the Commission shall consider, with regard to the class or classes of units to be exempted:

1. The size of the improved or scope of the maintenance work;

2. The location of the improvement or work in proximity to dunes, waters, marshlands, areas of high seismic activity, areas of unstable soils or geologic formations, and areas enumerated in G.S. 113A-113(b)(3); and

3. Whether or not dredging or filling is involved in the maintenance or improvement.

(5a) "Floating structure" means any structure, not a boat, supported by a means of floatation, designed to be used without a permanent foundation, which is used or intended for human habitation or commerce. A structure shall be considered a floating structure when it is inhabited or used for commercial purposes for more than thirty days in any one location. A boat may be considered a floating structure when its means of propulsion has been removed or rendered inoperative.

(6)   "Key facilities" include the site location and the location of major improvement and major access features of key facilities, and mean:

a.   Public facilities, as determined by the Commission, on nonfederal lands which tend to induce development and urbanization of more than local impact, including but not limited to:

1.   Any major airport designed to serve as a terminal for regularly scheduled air passenger service or one of State concern;

2.   Major interchanges between the interstate highway system and frontage-access streets or highways; major interchanges between other limited-access highways and frontage-access streets or highways;

3.   Major frontage-access streets and highways, both of State concern; and

4.   Major recreational lands and facilities;

b.   Major facilities on nonfederal lands for the development, generation, and transmission of energy.

(7)   "Lead regional organizations" means the regional planning agencies created by and representative of the local governments of a multi-county region, and designated as lead regional organizations by the Governor.

(8)   "Local government" means the governing body of any county or city which contains within its boundaries any lands or waters subject to this Article.

(9)   "Person" means any individual, citizen, partnership, corporation, association, organization, business trust, estate, trust, public or municipal corporation, or agency of the State or local government unit, or any other legal entity however designated.

(10)   Repealed by Session Laws 1987, c. 827, s. 133.

(11)   "Secretary" means the Secretary of Environment and Natural Resources, except where otherwise specified in this Article. (1973, c. 1284, s. 1; 1975, c. 452, s. 5; 1981, c. 913, s. 1; c. 932, s. 2.1; 1987, c. 827, s. 133; 1989, c. 727, s. 126; 1991 (Reg. Sess., 1992), c. 839, ss. 1, 4; 1995, c. 509, s. 58; 1997-443, s. 11A.119(a); 2012-202, s. 1.)

§ 113A-104. Coastal Resources Commission.

(a)   Established. - The General Assembly hereby establishes within the Department of Environment and Natural Resources a commission to be designated the Coastal Resources Commission.

(b)   Repealed by Session Laws 2013-360, s. 14.24(a), effective July 1, 2013.

(b1)   Composition. - The Coastal Resources Commission shall consist of 13 members as follows:

(1)   One appointed by the Governor who shall at the time of appointment be a coastal property owner or experienced in land development.

(2)   One appointed by the Governor who shall at the time of appointment be a coastal property owner or experienced in land development.

(3)   One appointed by the Governor who shall at the time of appointment be actively connected with or have experience in engineering in the coastal area or a marine-related science.

(4)   One appointed by the Governor who shall at the time of appointment be actively connected with or have experience in engineering in the coastal area or a marine-related science.

(5)   One appointed by the Governor who shall at the time of appointment be actively connected with or have experience in coastal-related business.

(6)   One appointed by the Governor who shall at the time of appointment be actively connected with or have experience in local government within the coastal area.

(7)   One appointed by the Governor who shall at the time of appointment be actively connected with or have experience in coastal agriculture.

(8)   One appointed by the Governor who shall at the time of appointment be actively connected with or have experience in commercial fishing.

(9)   One appointed by the Governor who shall at the time of appointment be actively connected with or have experience in coastal forestry.

(10)   One appointed by the General Assembly upon recommendation of the Speaker of the House of Representatives in accordance with G.S. 120-121 who shall at the time of appointment be actively connected with or have experience in sports fishing.

(11)   One appointed by the General Assembly upon recommendation of the Speaker of the House of Representatives in accordance with G.S. 120-121 who shall serve at large.

(12)   One appointed by the General Assembly upon recommendation of the President Pro Tempore of the Senate in accordance with G.S. 120-121 who shall at the time of appointment be actively connected with or have experience in wildlife.

(13)   One appointed by the General Assembly upon recommendation of the President Pro Tempore of the Senate in accordance with G.S. 120-121 who shall serve at large.

(c)   Appointment of Members. - As used in this section, the term "appointing authority" means the Governor in the case of members appointed by the Governor and means the General Assembly in the case of members appointed by the General Assembly. Appointments to the Commission shall be made to provide knowledge and experience in a diverse range of coastal interests. The members of the Commission shall serve and act on the Commission solely for the best interests of the public and public trust, and shall bring their particular knowledge and experience to the Commission for that end alone. Counties and cities in the coastal area may designate and transmit to the appointing authorities no later than May 1 of each even-numbered year qualified persons in the categories set out in subsection (b1) of this section corresponding to the Commission positions to be filled that year.

(c1)   The members of the Commission whose qualifications are described in subdivisions (3), (6), (7), (8), (9), (11), and (12) of subsection (b1) of this section shall be persons who do not derive any significant portion of their income from land development, construction, real estate sales, or lobbying and do not otherwise serve as agents for development-related business activities. The Governor shall require adequate disclosure of potential conflicts of interest by these members. The Governor, by executive order, shall promulgate criteria regarding conflicts of interest and disclosure thereof for determining the eligibility of persons under this subsection.

(c2)   All members of the Commission are covered persons for the purposes of Chapter 138A of the General Statutes, the State Government Ethics Act. As covered persons, members of the Commission shall comply with the applicable requirements of the State Government Ethics Act, including mandatory training, the public disclosure of economic interests, and ethical standards for covered persons. Members of the Commission shall comply with the provisions of the State Government Ethics Act to avoid conflicts of interest.

(d)   Repealed by Session Laws 2013-360, s. 14.24(a), effective July 1, 2013.

(e)   Repealed by Session Laws 2013-360, s. 14.24(a), effective July 1, 2013.

(f)   Office May Be Held Concurrently with Others. - Membership on the Coastal Resources Commission is hereby declared to be an office that may be held concurrently with other elective or appointive offices in addition to the maximum number of offices permitted to be held by one person under G.S. 128-1.1.

(g)   Terms. - The members shall serve staggered terms of office of four years. At the expiration of each member's term, the appointing authority shall reappoint or replace the member with a new member of like qualification as specified in subsection (b1) of this section.

(h)   Vacancies. - In the event of a vacancy arising otherwise than by expiration of term, the appointing authority shall appoint a successor of like qualification as specified in subsection (b1) of this section who shall then serve the remainder of his predecessor's term.

(i)   Officers. - The chairman shall be designated by the Governor from among the members of the Commission to serve as chairman at the pleasure of the Governor. The vice-chairman shall be elected by and from the members of the Commission and shall serve for a term of two years or until the expiration of the vice-chairman's regularly appointed term.

(j)   Compensation. - The members of the Commission shall receive per diem and necessary travel and subsistence expenses in accordance with the provisions of G.S. 138-5.

(k)   Repealed by Session Laws 2013-360, s. 14.24(a), effective July 1, 2013.

(l)   Attendance. - Regular attendance at Commission meetings is a duty of each member. The Commission shall develop procedures for declaring any seat on the Commission to be vacant upon failure by a member to perform this duty.

(m)   Quorum. - A majority of the Commission shall constitute a quorum. (1973, c. 1284, s. 1; 1975, c. 452, s. 5; 1977, c. 771, s. 4; c. 486, ss. 1-6; 1981, c. 932, s. 2.1; 1989, c. 505; c. 727, s. 218(64); 1997-443, s. 11A.119(a); 2013-360, s. 14.24(a).)

§ 113A-105. Coastal Resources Advisory Council.

(a)   Creation. - There is hereby created and established a council to be known as the Coastal Resources Advisory Council.

(b)   Membership and Terms. - The Coastal Resources Advisory Council shall consist of not more than 20 members appointed or designated by the Coastal Resources Commission. Counties and cities in the coastal area may nominate candidates for consideration by the Commission. The terms of all Council members serving on the Council on January 1, 2013, shall expire on July 31, 2013. A new Council shall be appointed in the manner provided by this subsection with terms beginning on August 1, 2013, and expiring on June 30, 2015. Members may be reappointed at the discretion of the Commission, provided that one-half of the membership at the beginning of any two-year term are residents of counties in the coastal area.

(c)   Functions and Duties. - The Advisory Council shall assist the Secretary and the Secretary of Administration in an advisory capacity:

(1)   On matters which may be submitted to it by either of them or by the Commission, including technical questions relating to the development of rules, and

(2)   On such other matters arising under this Article as the Council considers appropriate.

(d)   Multiple Offices. - Membership on the Coastal Resources Advisory Council is hereby declared to be an office that may be held concurrently with other elective or appointive offices (except the office of Commission member) in addition to the maximum number of offices permitted to be held by one person under G.S. 128-1.1.

(e) Chairman and Vice-Chairman. - A chairman and vice-chairman shall be elected annually by the Council.

(f) Compensation. - The members of the Advisory Council who are not State employees shall receive per diem and necessary travel and subsistence expenses in accordance with the provisions of G.S. 138-5. (1973, c. 1284, s. 1; 1975, c. 452, s. 5; 1977, c. 771, s. 4; 1981, c. 932, s. 2.1; 1983, c. 249, ss. 1, 2; 1989, c. 727, s. 127; c. 751, s. 8(14a); 1991 (Reg. Sess., 1992), c. 959, s. 26; 1995, c. 123, s. 4; c. 504, s. 7; 2013-360, s. 14.25.)

§ 113A-106. Scope of planning processes.

Planning processes covered by this Article include the development and adoption of State guidelines for the coastal area and the development and adoption of a land-use plan for each county within the coastal area, which plans shall serve as criteria for the issuance or denial of development permits under Part 4. (1973, c. 1284, s. 1; 1975, c. 452, s. 5; 1981, c. 932, s. 2.1.)

§ 113A-106.1. Adoption of Coastal Habitat Protection Plans.

The Commission shall approve Coastal Habitat Protection Plans as provided in G.S. 143B-279.8. (1997-400, s. 3.3.)

§ 113A-107. State guidelines for the coastal area.

(a) State guidelines for the coastal area shall consist of statements of objectives, policies, and standards to be followed in public and private use of land and water areas within the coastal area. Such guidelines shall be consistent with the goals of the coastal area management system as set forth in G.S. 113A-102. They shall give particular attention to the nature of development which shall be appropriate within the various types of areas of environmental concern that may be designated by the Commission under Part 3. Land and water areas addressed in the State guidelines may include underground areas and resources, and airspace above the land and water, as well as the surface of the land and surface waters. Such guidelines shall be used in the review of applications for permits issued pursuant to this Article and for review of and comment on proposed public, private and federal agency activities that are subject to review for consistency with State guidelines for the coastal area. Such comments shall be consistent with federal laws and regulations.

(b)   The Commission shall be responsible for the preparation, adoption, and amendment of the State guidelines. In exercising this function it shall be furnished such staff assistance as it requires by the Secretary of Environment and Natural Resources and the Secretary of the Department of Administration, together with such incidental assistance as may be requested of any other State department or agency.

(c)   The Commission shall mail proposed as well as adopted rules establishing guidelines for the coastal area to all cities, counties, and lead regional organizations within the area and to all State, private, federal, regional, and local agencies the Commission considers to have special expertise on the coastal area. A person who receives a proposed rule may send written comments on the proposed rule to the Commission within 30 days after receiving the proposed rule. The Commission shall consider any comments received in determining whether to adopt the proposed rule.

(d), (e) Repealed by Session Laws 1987, c. 827, s. 134.

(f)   The Commission shall review its rules establishing guidelines for the coastal area at least every five years to determine whether changes in the rules are needed. (1973, c. 1284, s. 1; 1975, c. 452, s. 5; 1975, 2nd Sess., c. 983, ss. 75, 76; 1977, c. 771, s. 4; 1981, c. 932, s. 2.1; 1987, c. 827, s. 134; 1989, c. 313; c. 727, s. 218(65); 1997-443, s. 11A.119(a).)

§ 113A-107.1. Sea-level policy.

(a)   The General Assembly does not intend to mandate the development of sea-level policy or the definition of rates of sea-level change for regulatory purposes.

(b) No rule, policy, or planning guideline that defines a rate of sea-level change for regulatory purposes shall be adopted except as provided by this section.

(c) Nothing in this section shall be construed to prohibit a county, municipality, or other local government entity from defining rates of sea-level change for regulatory purposes.

(d) All policies, rules, regulations, or any other product of the Commission or the Division related to rates of sea-level change shall be subject to the requirements of Chapter 150B of the General Statutes.

(e) The Commission shall be the only State agency authorized to define rates of sea-level change for regulatory purposes. If the Commission defines rates of sea-level change for regulatory purposes, it shall do so in conjunction with the Division of Coastal Management of the Department. The Commission and Division may collaborate with other State agencies, boards, and commissions; other public entities; and other institutions when defining rates of sea-level change. (2012-202, s. 2(a).)

§ 113A-108. Effect of State guidelines.

All local land-use plans adopted pursuant to this Article within the coastal area shall be consistent with the State guidelines. No permit shall be issued under Part 4 of this Article which is inconsistent with the State guidelines. Any State land policies governing the acquisition, use and disposition of land by State departments and agencies shall take account of and be consistent with the State guidelines adopted under this Article, insofar as lands within the coastal area are concerned. Any State land classification system which shall be promulgated shall take account of and be consistent with the State guidelines adopted under this Article, insofar as it applies to lands within the coastal area. (1973, c. 1284, s. 1; 1975, c. 452, s. 5; 1981, c. 932, s. 2.1.)

§ 113A-109. County letter of intent; timetable for preparation of land-use plan.

Within 120 days after July 1, 1974, each county within the coastal area shall submit to the Commission a written statement of its intent to develop a land-use plan under this Article or its intent not to develop such a plan. If any county states its intent not to develop a land-use plan or fails to submit a statement of intent within the required period, the Commission shall prepare and adopt a land-use plan for that county. If a county states its intent to develop a land-use plan, it shall complete the preparation and adoption of such plan within 480 days after adoption of the State guidelines. In the event of failure by any county to complete its required plan within this time, the Commission shall promptly prepare and adopt such a plan.

In any case where the Commission has adopted a land-use plan for a county that county may prepare its own land-use plan in accordance with the procedures of this Article, and upon approval of such plan by the Commission it shall supersede the Commission's plan on a date specified by the Commission. (1973, c. 1284, s. 1; 1975, c. 452, ss. 1, 5; 1981, c. 932, s. 2.1.)

§ 113A-110. Land-use plans.

(a)   A land-use plan for a county shall, for the purpose of this Article, consist of statements of objectives, policies, and standards to be followed in public and private use of land within the county, which shall be supplemented by maps showing the appropriate location of particular types of land or water use and their relationships to each other and to public facilities and by specific criteria for particular types of land or water use in particular areas. The plan shall give special attention to the protection and appropriate development of areas of environmental concern designated under Part 3. The plan shall be consistent with the goals of the coastal area management system as set forth in G.S. 113A-102 and with the State guidelines adopted by the Commission under G.S. 113A-107. The plan shall be adopted, and may be amended from time to time, in accordance with the procedures set forth in this section.

(b)   The body charged with preparation and adoption of a county's land-use plan (whether the county government or the Commission) may delegate some or all of its responsibilities to the lead regional organization for the region of which the county is a part. Any such delegation shall become effective upon the acceptance thereof by the lead regional organization. Any county proposing a delegation to the lead regional organization shall give written notice thereof to the Commission at least two weeks prior to the date on which such action is to be taken. Any city or county within the coastal area may also seek the assistance or advice of its lead regional organization in carrying out any planning activity under this Article.

(c) The body charged with preparation and adoption of a county's land-use plan (whether the county or the Commission or a unit delegated such responsibility) may either (i) delegate to a city within the county responsibility for preparing those portions of the land-use plan which affect land within the city's zoning jurisdiction or (ii) receive recommendations from the city concerning those portions of the land-use plan which affect land within the city's zoning jurisdiction, prior to finally adopting the plan or any amendments thereto or (iii) delegate responsibility to some cities and receive recommendations from other cities in the county. The body shall give written notice to the Commission of its election among these alternatives. On written application from a city to the Commission, the Commission shall require the body to delegate plan-making authority to that city for land within the city's zoning jurisdiction if the Commission finds that the city is currently enforcing its zoning ordinance, its subdivision regulations, and the State Building Code within such jurisdiction.

(d) The body charged with adoption of a land-use plan may either adopt it as a whole by a single resolution or adopt it in parts by successive resolutions; said parts may either correspond with major geographical sections or divisions of the county or with functional subdivisions of the subject matters of the plan. Amendments and extensions to the plan may be adopted in the same manner.

(e) Prior to adoption or subsequent amendment of any land-use plan, the body charged with its preparation and adoption (whether the county or the Commission or a unit delegated such responsibility) shall hold a public hearing at which public and private parties shall have the opportunity to present comments and recommendations. Notice of the hearing shall be given not less than 30 days before the date of the hearing and shall state the date, time, and place of the hearing; the subject of the hearing; the action which is proposed; and that copies of the proposed plan or amendment are available for public inspection at a designated office in the county courthouse during designated hours. Any such notice shall be published at least once in a newspaper of general circulation in the county.

(f) No land-use plan shall become finally effective until it has been approved by the Commission. The county or other unit adopting the plan shall transmit it, when adopted, to the Commission for review. The Commission shall afford interested persons an opportunity to present objections and comments regarding the plan, and shall review and consider each county land-use plan in light of such objections and comments, the State guidelines, the requirements of this Article, and any generally applicable standards of review adopted by rule of the Commission. Within 45 days after receipt of a county land-use plan the Commission shall either approve the plan or notify the county of the specific changes which must be made in order for it to be approved. Following such changes, the plan may be resubmitted in the same manner as the original plan.

(g) Copies of each county land-use plan which has been approved, and as it may have been amended from time to time, shall be maintained in a form available for public inspection by (i) the county, (ii) the Commission, and (iii) the lead regional organization of the region which includes the county. (1973, c. 1284, s. 1; 1975, c. 452, s. 5; 1981, c. 932, s. 2.1.)

§ 113A-111. Effect of land-use plan.

No permit shall be issued under Part 4 of this Article for development which is inconsistent with the approved land-use plan for the county in which it is proposed. No local ordinance or other local regulation shall be adopted which, within an area of environmental concern, is inconsistent with the land-use plan of the county or city in which it is effective; any existing local ordinances and regulations within areas of environmental concern shall be reviewed in light of the applicable local land-use plan and modified as may be necessary to make them consistent therewith. All local ordinances and other local regulations affecting a county within the coastal area, but not affecting an area of environmental concern, shall be reviewed by the Commission for consistency with the applicable county and city land-use plans and, if the Commission finds any such ordinance or regulation to be inconsistent with the applicable land-use plan, it shall transmit recommendations for modification to the adopting local government. (1973, c. 1284, s. 1; 1975, c. 452, s. 5; 1981, c. 932, s. 2.1.)

§ 113A-112. Planning grants.

The Secretary is authorized to make grants to local governmental units for the purpose of assisting in the development of local plans and management programs under this Article. The Secretary shall develop and administer generally applicable criteria under which local governments may qualify for such assistance. The Secretary may condition payment of a grant on the completion of the local plan or management program and may pay the grant in installments based on satisfactory completion of specific elements of the plan or program and on approval of the plan or program by the Commission. Of the funds appropriated to the Department to make grants under this section, the Department may carry forward to the next fiscal year funds in the amount necessary to pay grants awarded or extended in any fiscal year. (1973, c. 1284, s. 1; 1975, c. 452, s. 5; 1977, c. 771, s. 4; 1981, c. 932, s. 2.1; 1989, c. 727, s. 218(66); 1997-443, s. 11A.119(a); 2001-494, s. 6.)

Part 3. Areas of Environmental Concern.

§ 113A-113. Areas of environmental concern; in general.

(a) The Coastal Resources Commission shall by rule designate geographic areas of the coastal area as areas of environmental concern and specify the boundaries thereof, in the manner provided in this Part.

(b) The Commission may designate as areas of environmental concern any one or more of the following, singly or in combination:

(1) Coastal wetlands as defined in G.S. 113-229(n)(3) and contiguous areas necessary to protect those wetlands;

(2) Estuarine waters, that is, all the water of the Atlantic Ocean within the boundary of North Carolina and all the waters of the bays, sounds, rivers, and tributaries thereto seaward of the dividing line between coastal fishing waters and inland fishing waters, as set forth in the most recent official published agreement adopted by the Wildlife Resources Commission and the Department of Environment and Natural Resources;

(3) Renewable resource areas where uncontrolled or incompatible development which results in the loss or reduction of continued long-range productivity could jeopardize future water, food or fiber requirements of more than local concern, which may include:

a. Watersheds or aquifers that are present sources of public water supply, as identified by the Department or the Environmental Management Commission, or that are classified for water-supply use pursuant to G.S. 143-214.1;

b. Capacity use areas that have been declared by the Environmental Management Commission pursuant to G.S. 143-215.13(c) and areas wherein said Environmental Management Commission (pursuant to G.S. 143-215.3(d) or 143-215.3(a)(8)) has determined that a generalized condition of water depletion or water or air pollution exists;

c. Prime forestry land (sites capable of producing 85 cubic feet per acre-year, or more, of marketable timber), as identified by the Department.

(4) Fragile or historic areas, and other areas containing environmental or natural resources of more than local significance, where uncontrolled or incompatible development could result in major or irreversible damage to important historic, cultural, scientific or scenic values or natural systems, which may include:

a. Existing national or State parks or forests, wilderness areas, the State Nature and Historic Preserve, or public recreation areas; existing sites that have been acquired for any of the same, as identified by the Secretary; and proposed sites for any of the same, as identified by the Secretary, provided that the proposed site has been formally designated for acquisition by the governmental agency having jurisdiction;

b. Present sections of the natural and scenic rivers system;

c. Stream segments that have been classified for scientific or research uses by the Environmental Management Commission, or that are proposed to be so classified in a proceeding that is pending before said Environmental Management Commission pursuant to G.S. 143-214.1 at the time of the designation of the area of environmental concern;

d. Existing wildlife refuges, preserves or management areas, and proposed sites for the same, as identified by the Wildlife Resources Commission, provided that the proposed site has been formally designated for acquisition (as hereinafter defined) or for inclusion in a cooperative agreement by the governmental agency having jurisdiction;

e. Complex natural areas surrounded by modified landscapes that do not drastically alter the landscape, such as virgin forest stands within a commercially managed forest, or bogs in an urban complex;

f. Areas that sustain remnant species or aberrations in the landscape produced by natural forces, such as rare and endangered botanical or animal species;

g. Areas containing unique geological formations, as identified by the State Geologist; and

h. Historic places that are listed, or have been approved for listing by the North Carolina Historical Commission, in the National Register of Historic Places pursuant to the National Historic Preservation Act of 1966; historical, archaeological, and other places and properties owned, managed or assisted by the State of North Carolina pursuant to Chapter 121; and properties or areas that are or may be designated by the Secretary of the Interior as registered natural landmarks or as national historic landmarks;

(5) Areas such as waterways and lands under or flowed by tidal waters or navigable waters, to which the public may have rights of access or public trust rights, and areas which the State of North Carolina may be authorized to preserve, conserve, or protect under Article XIV, Sec. 5 of the North Carolina Constitution;

(6) Natural-hazard areas where uncontrolled or incompatible development could unreasonably endanger life or property, and other areas especially vulnerable to erosion, flooding, or other adverse effects of sand, wind and water, which may include:

a. Sand dunes along the Outer Banks;

b. Ocean and estuarine beaches and the shoreline of estuarine and public trust waters;

c. Floodways and floodplains;

d. Areas where geologic and soil conditions are such that there is a substantial possibility of excessive erosion or seismic activity, as identified by the State Geologist;

e. Areas with a significant potential for air inversions, as identified by the Environmental Management Commission.

(7) Areas which are or may be impacted by key facilities.

(8) Outstanding Resource Waters as designated by the Environmental Management Commission and such contiguous land as the Coastal Resources Commission reasonably deems necessary for the purpose of maintaining the exceptional water quality and outstanding resource values identified in the designation.

(9) Primary Nursery Areas as designated by the Marine Fisheries Commission and such contiguous land as the Coastal Resources Commission reasonably deems necessary to protect the resource values identified in the designation including, but not limited to, those values contributing to the continued productivity of estuarine and marine fisheries and thereby promoting the public health, safety and welfare.

(c) In those instances where subsection (b) of this section refers to locations identified by a specified agency, said agency is hereby authorized to make the indicated identification from time to time and is directed to transmit the identification to the Commission; provided, however, that no designation of an area of environmental concern based solely on an agency identification of a proposed location may remain effective for longer than three years unless, in the case of paragraphs (4)a and d of subsection (b) of this section, the proposed site has been at least seventy-five percent (75%) acquired. Within the meaning of this section, "formal designation for acquisition" means designation in a formal resolution adopted by the governing body of the agency having jurisdiction (or by its chief executive, if it has no governing body), together with a direction in said resolution that the initial step in the land acquisition process be taken (as by filing an application with the Department of Administration to acquire property pursuant to G.S. 146-23).

(d) Additional grounds for designation of areas of environmental concern are prohibited unless enacted into law by an act of the General Assembly. (1973, c. 476, s. 128; c. 1262, ss. 23, 86; c. 1284, s. 1; 1975, c. 452, s. 5; 1977, c. 771, s. 4; 1981, c. 932, s. 2.1; 1983, c. 518, s. 1; 1989, c. 217, s. 1; c. 727, s. 128; 1997-443, s. 11A.119(a).)

§ 113A-114. Repealed by Session Laws 1983, c. 518, s. 2, effective June 13, 1983.

§ 113A-115. Designation of areas of environmental concern.

(a) Prior to adopting any rule permanently designating any area of environmental concern the Secretary and the Commission shall hold a public hearing in each county in which lands to be affected are located, at which public and private parties shall have the opportunity to present comments and views. Hearings required by this section are in addition to the hearing required by Article 2A of Chapter 150B of the General Statutes. The following provisions shall apply for all such hearings:

(1) Notice of any such hearing shall be given not less than 30 days before the date of such hearing and shall state the date, time and place of the hearing, the subject of the hearing, and the action to be taken. The notice shall specify that a copy of the description of the area or areas of environmental concern proposed by the Secretary is available for public inspection at the county courthouse of each county affected.

(2) Any such notice shall be published at least once in one newspaper of general circulation in the county or counties affected at least 30 days before the date on which the public hearing is scheduled to begin.

(3) Any person who desires to be heard at such public hearing shall give notice thereof in writing to the Secretary on or before the first date set for the hearing. The Secretary is authorized to set reasonable time limits for the oral presentation of views by any one person at any such hearing. The Secretary shall permit anyone who so desires to file a written argument or other statement with him in relation to any proposed plan any time within 30 days following the conclusion of any public hearing or within such additional time as he may allow by notice given as prescribed in this section.

(4) Upon completion of the hearing and consideration of submitted evidence and arguments with respect to any proposed action pursuant to this section, the Commission shall adopt its final action with respect thereto and shall file a duly certified copy thereof with the Attorney General and with the board of commissioners of each county affected thereby.

(b) In addition to the notice required by G.S. 113A-115(a)(2) notice shall be given to any interested State agency and to any citizen or group that has filed a request to be notified of a public hearing to be held under this section.

(c) The Commission shall review the designated areas of environmental concern at least biennially. New areas may be designated and designated areas may be deleted, in accordance with the same procedures as apply to the original designations of areas under this section. Areas shall not be deleted unless it is found that the conditions upon which the original designation was based shall have been found to be substantially altered. (1973, c. 1284, s. 1; 1975, c. 452, s. 5; 1975, 2nd Sess., c. 983, s. 78; 1981, c. 932, s. 2.1; 1987, c. 827, s. 135; 2000-189, s. 11.)

§ 113A-115.1. Limitations on erosion control structures.

(a) As used in this section:

(1) "Erosion control structure" means a breakwater, bulkhead, groin, jetty, revetment, seawall, or any similar structure.

(1a) "Estuarine shoreline" means all shorelines that are not ocean shorelines that border estuarine waters as defined in G.S. 113A-113(b)(2).

(2) "Ocean shoreline" means the Atlantic Ocean, the oceanfront beaches, and frontal dunes. The term "ocean shoreline" includes an ocean inlet and lands adjacent to an ocean inlet but does not include that portion of any inlet and lands adjacent to the inlet that exhibits characteristics of estuarine shorelines.

(3) "Terminal groin" means one or more structures constructed at the terminus of an island or on the side of an inlet, with a main stem generally perpendicular to the beach shoreline, that is primarily intended to protect the terminus of the island from shoreline erosion and inlet migration. A "terminal groin" shall be pre-filled with beach quality sand and allow sand moving in the littoral zone to flow past the structure. A "terminal groin" may include other design features, such as a number of smaller supporting structures, that are consistent with sound engineering practices and as recommended by a professional engineer licensed to practice pursuant to Chapter 89C of the General Statutes. A "terminal groin" is not a jetty.

(b) No person shall construct a permanent erosion control structure in an ocean shoreline. The Commission shall not permit the construction of a temporary erosion control structure that consists of anything other than sandbags in an ocean shoreline. This subsection shall not apply to any of the following:

(1)   Any permanent erosion control structure that is approved pursuant to an exception set out in a rule adopted by the Commission prior to July 1, 2003.

(2)   Any permanent erosion control structure that was originally constructed prior to July 1, 1974, and that has since been in continuous use to protect an inlet that is maintained for navigation.

(3)   Any terminal groin permitted pursuant to this section.

(b1)   This section shall not be construed to limit the authority of the Commission to adopt rules to designate or protect areas of environmental concern, to govern the use of sandbags, or to govern the use of erosion control structures in estuarine shorelines.

(c)   The Commission may renew a permit for an erosion control structure issued pursuant to a variance granted by the Commission prior to July 1, 1995. The Commission may authorize the replacement of a permanent erosion control structure that was permitted by the Commission pursuant to a variance granted by the Commission prior to July 1, 1995, if the Commission finds that: (i) the structure will not be enlarged beyond the dimensions set out in the original permit; (ii) there is no practical alternative to replacing the structure that will provide the same or similar benefits; and (iii) the replacement structure will comply with all applicable laws and with all rules, other than the rule or rules with respect to which the Commission granted the variance, that are in effect at the time the structure is replaced.

(d)   Any rule that prohibits permanent erosion control structures shall not apply to terminal groins permitted pursuant to this section.

(e)   In addition to the requirements of Part 4 of Article 7 of Chapter 113A of the General Statutes, an applicant for a permit for the construction of a terminal groin shall submit all of the following to the Commission:

(1)   Information to demonstrate that structures or infrastructure are threatened by erosion.

(2)   An environmental impact statement that satisfies the requirements of G.S. 113A-4. An environmental impact statement prepared pursuant to the

National Environmental Policy Act (NEPA), 42 U.S.C. § 4321, et seq., for the construction of the terminal groin shall satisfy the requirements of this subdivision.

(3)   A list of property owners and local governments that may be affected by the construction of the proposed terminal groin and its accompanying beach fill project and proof that the property owners and local governments have been notified of the application for construction of the terminal groin and its accompanying beach fill project.

(4)   A plan for the construction and maintenance of the terminal groin and its accompanying beach fill project prepared by a professional engineer licensed to practice pursuant to Chapter 89C of the General Statutes.

(5)   A plan for the management of the inlet and the estuarine and ocean shorelines immediately adjacent to and under the influence of the inlet. The inlet management plan monitoring and mitigation requirements must be reasonable and not impose requirements whose costs outweigh the benefits. The inlet management plan is not required to address sea level rise. The inlet management plan shall do all of the following relative to the terminal groin and its accompanying beach fill project:

a.   Describe the post-construction activities that the applicant will undertake to monitor the impacts on coastal resources.

b.   Define the baseline for assessing any adverse impacts and the thresholds for when the adverse impacts must be mitigated.

c.   Provide for mitigation measures to be implemented if adverse impacts reach the thresholds defined in the plan.

d.   Provide for modification or removal of the terminal groin if the adverse impacts cannot be mitigated.

(6)   Proof of financial assurance verified by the Commission or the Secretary of Environment and Natural Resources in the form of a bond, insurance policy, escrow account, guaranty, local government taxing or assessment authority, a property owner association's approved assessment, or other financial instrument or combination of financial instruments that is adequate to cover the cost of implementing all of the following components of the inlet management plan:

a. Long-term maintenance and monitoring of the terminal groin.

b. Implementation of mitigation measures.

c. Modification or removal of the terminal groin.

d. Repealed by Session Laws 2013-384, s. 3(a), effective August 23, 2013, and applicable to permit applications submitted on or after that date.

(f) The Commission shall issue a permit for the construction of a terminal groin if the Commission finds no grounds for denying the permit under G.S. 113A-120 and the Commission finds all of the following:

(1) The applicant has complied with all of the requirements of subsection (e) of this section.

(2) Repealed by Session Laws 2013-384, s. 3(a), effective August 23, 2013, and applicable to permit applications submitted on or after that date.

(3) The terminal groin will be accompanied by a concurrent beach fill project to prefill the groin.

(4) Construction and maintenance of the terminal groin will not result in significant adverse impacts to private property or to the public recreational beach. In making this finding, the Commission shall take into account the potential benefits of the project, including protection of the terminus of the island from shoreline erosion and inlet migration, beaches, protective dunes, wildlife habitats, roads, homes, and infrastructure, and mitigation measures, including the accompanying beach fill project, that will be incorporated into the project design and construction and the inlet management plan.

(5) The inlet management plan is adequate for purposes of monitoring the impacts of the proposed terminal groin and mitigating any adverse impacts identified as a result of the monitoring.

(6) Except to the extent expressly modified by this section, the project complies with State guidelines for coastal development adopted by the Commission pursuant to G.S. 113A-107.

(g) The Commission may issue no more than four permits for the construction of a terminal groin pursuant to this section.

(h) A local government may not use funds generated from any of the following financing mechanisms for any activity related to the terminal groin or its accompanying beach fill project:

(1) Special obligation bonds issued pursuant to Chapter 159I of the General Statutes.

(2) Nonvoted general obligation bonds issued pursuant to G.S. 159-48(b)(4).

(3) Financing contracts entered into under G.S. 160A-20 or G.S. 159-148.

(i) No later than September 1 of each year, the Coastal Resources Commission shall report to the Environmental Review Commission on the implementation of this section. The report shall provide a detailed description of each proposed and permitted terminal groin and its accompanying beach fill project, including the information required to be submitted pursuant to subsection (e) of this section. For each permitted terminal groin and its accompanying beach fill project, the report shall also provide all of the following:

(1) The findings of the Commission required pursuant to subsection (f) of this section.

(2) The status of construction and maintenance of the terminal groin and its accompanying beach fill project, including the status of the implementation of the plan for construction and maintenance and the inlet management plan.

(3) A description and assessment of the benefits of the terminal groin and its accompanying beach fill project, if any.

(4) A description and assessment of the adverse impacts of the terminal groin and its accompanying beach fill project, if any, including a description and assessment of any mitigation measures implemented to address adverse impacts. (2003-427, s. 3; 2004-195, s. 1.2; 2004-203, s. 43; 2011-387, s. 1; 2012-201, s. 2(a); 2013-384, s. 3(a).)

Part 4. Permit Letting and Enforcement.

§ 113A-116. Local government letter of intent.

Within two years after July 1, 1974, each county and city within the coastal area shall submit to the Commission a written statement of its intent to act, or not to act, as a permit-letting agency under G.S. 113A-121. If any city or county states its intent not to act as a permit-letting agency or fails to submit a statement of intent within the required period, the Secretary shall issue permits therein under G.S. 113A-121; provided that a county may submit a letter of intent to issue permits in any city within said county that disclaims its intent to issue permits or fails to submit a letter of intent. Provided, however, should any city or county fail to become a permit-letting agency for any reason, but shall later express its desire to do so, it shall be permitted by the Coastal Resources Commission to qualify as such an agency by following the procedure herein set forth for qualification in the first instance. (1973, c. 1284, s. 1; 1975, c. 452, s. 2; 1977, c. 771, s. 4; 1989, c. 727, s. 129.)

§ 113A-117. Implementation and enforcement programs.

(a)   The Secretary shall develop and present to the Commission for consideration and to all cities and counties and lead regional organizations within the coastal area for comment a set of criteria for local implementation and enforcement programs. In the preparation of such criteria, the Secretary shall emphasize the necessity for the expeditious processing of permit applications. Said criteria may contain recommendations and guidelines as to the procedures to be followed in developing local implementation and enforcement programs, the scope and coverage of said programs, minimum standards to be prescribed in said programs, staffing of permit-letting agencies, permit-letting procedures, and priorities of regional or statewide concern. Within 20 months after July 1, 1974, the Commission shall adopt and transmit said criteria (with any revisions) to each coastal-area county and city that has filed an applicable letter of intent, for its guidance.

(b)   The governing body of each city in the coastal area that filed an affirmative letter of intent shall adopt an implementation and enforcement plan with respect to its zoning area within 36 months after July 1, 1974. The board of commissioners of each coastal-area county that filed an affirmative letter of intent shall adopt an implementation plan with respect to portions of the county outside city zoning areas within 36 months after July 1, 1974, provided, however, that a county implementation and enforcement plan may also cover city jurisdictions for those cities within the counties that have not filed affirmative letters of intent pursuant to G.S. 113A-116. Prior to adopting the implementation and enforcement program the local governing body shall hold a public hearing at which public and private parties shall have the opportunity to present comments and views. Notice of the hearing shall be given not less than 15 days before the date of the hearing, and shall state the date, time and place of the hearing, the subject of the hearing, and the action which is to be taken. The notice shall state that copies of the proposed implementation and enforcement program are available for public inspection at the county courthouse. Any such notice shall be published at least once in one newspaper of general circulation in the county at least 15 days before the date on which the public hearing is scheduled to begin.

(c) Each coastal-area county and city shall transmit its implementation and enforcement program when adopted to the Commission for review. The Commission shall afford interested persons an opportunity to present objections and comments regarding the program, and shall review and consider each local implementation and enforcement program submitted in light of such objections and comments, the Commission's criteria and any general standards of review applicable throughout the coastal area as may be adopted by the Commission. Within 45 days after receipt of a local implementation and enforcement program the Commission shall either approve the program or notify the county or city of the specific changes that must be made in order for it to be approved. Following such changes, the program may be resubmitted in the same manner as the original program.

(d) If the Commission determines that any local government is failing to administer or enforce an approved implementation and enforcement program, it shall notify the local government in writing and shall specify the deficiencies of administration and enforcement. If the local government has not taken corrective action within 90 days of receipt of notification from the Commission, the Commission shall assume enforcement of the program until such time as the local government indicates its willingness and ability to resume administration and enforcement of the program. (1973, c. 1284, s. 1; 1975, c. 452, s. 3; 1977, c. 771, s. 4; 1989, c. 727, s. 130.)

§ 113A-118. Permit required.

(a) After the date designated by the Secretary pursuant to G.S. 113A-125, every person before undertaking any development in any area of environmental concern shall obtain (in addition to any other required State or local permit) a permit pursuant to the provisions of this Part.

(b)   Under the expedited procedure provided for by G.S. 113A-121, the permit shall be obtained from the appropriate city or county for any minor development; provided, that if the city or county has not developed an approved implementation and enforcement program, the permit shall be obtained from the Secretary.

(c)   Permits shall be obtained from the Commission or its duly authorized agent.

(d)   Within the meaning of this Part:

(1)   A "major development" is any development which requires permission, licensing, approval, certification or authorization in any form from the Environmental Management Commission, the Department of Environment and Natural Resources, the Department of Administration, the North Carolina Mining and Energy Commission, the North Carolina Pesticides Board, the North Carolina Sedimentation Control Board, or any federal agency or authority; or which occupies a land or water area in excess of 20 acres; or which contemplates drilling for or excavating natural resources on land or under water; or which occupies on a single parcel a structure or structures in excess of a ground area of 60,000 square feet.

(2)   A "minor development" is any development other than a "major development."

(e)   If, within the meaning of G.S. 113A-103(5)b3, the siting of any utility facility for the development, generation or transmission of energy is subject to regulation under this Article rather than by the State Utilities Commission or by other law, permits for such facilities shall be obtained from the Coastal Resources Commission rather than from the appropriate city or county.

(f)   The Secretary may issue special emergency permits under this Article. These permits may only be issued in those extraordinary situations in which life or structural property is in imminent danger as a result of storms, sudden failure of man-made structures, or similar occurrence. These permits may carry any conditions necessary to protect the public interest, consistent with the emergency situation and the impact of the proposed development. If an application for an emergency permit includes work beyond that necessary to reduce imminent dangers to life or property, the emergency permit shall be limited to that development reasonably necessary to reduce the imminent danger; all further development shall be considered under ordinary permit procedures. This emergency permit authority of the Secretary shall extend to all development in areas of environmental concern, whether major or minor development, and the mandatory notice provisions of G.S. 113A-119(b) shall not apply to these emergency permits. To the extent feasible, these emergency permits shall be coordinated with any emergency permits required under G.S. 113-229(e1). The fees associated with any permit issued pursuant to this subsection or rules adopted pursuant to this subsection shall be waived. (1973, c. 476, s. 128; c. 1282, ss. 23, 33; c. 1284, s. 1; 1975, c. 452, s. 5; 1977, c. 771, s. 4; 1979, c. 253, s. 5; 1981, c. 932, s. 2.1; 1983, c. 173; c. 518, s. 3; 1987, c. 827, s. 136; 1989, c. 727, s. 131; 1997-443, s. 11A.119(a); 2007-485, s. 5; 2012-143, s. 1(d).)

§ 113A-118.1. General permits.

(a) The Commission may, by rule, designate certain classes of major and minor development for which a general or blanket permit may be issued. In developing these rules, the Commission shall consider:

(1) The size of the development;

(2) The impact of the development on areas of environmental concern;

(3) How often the class of development is carried out;

(4) The need for onsite oversight of the development; and

(5) The need for public review and comment on individual development projects.

(b) General permits may be issued by the Commission. Individual developments carried out under the provisions of general permits shall not be subject to the mandatory notice provisions of G.S. 113A-119.

(c) The Commission may impose reasonable notice provisions and other appropriate conditions and safeguards on any general permit it issues.

(d) The variance, appeals, and enforcement provisions of this Article shall apply to any individual development projects undertaken under a general permit.

(e) The Commission shall allow the use of riprap in the construction of groins in estuarine and public trust waters on the same basis as the Commission allows the use of wood. (1983, c. 171; c. 442, s. 1; 1987, c. 827, s. 137; 2002-126, s. 29.2(f).)

§ 113A-118.2. Development in Primary Nursery Areas and Outstanding Resource Waters areas of environmental concern.

Public notice, opportunity for public comment, and agency review shall be required for all development within the Primary Nursery Areas or Outstanding Resource Waters areas of environmental concern. Provided, however, that the Coastal Resources Commission may by rule exempt or issue general permits for minor maintenance and improvement projects as defined in G.S. 113A-103(5)c. and for single-family residential development pursuant to use standards or conditions adopted by the Coastal Resources Commission. (1989, c. 217, s. 2.)

§ 113A-119. Permit applications generally.

(a) Any person required to obtain a permit under this Part shall file with the Secretary and (in the case of a permit sought from a city or county) with the designated local official an application for a permit in accordance with the form and content designated by the Secretary and approved by the Commission. The applicant must submit with the application a check or money order payable to the Department or the city or county, as the case may be, constituting a fee set by the Commission pursuant to G.S. 113A-119.1.

(b) Upon receipt of any application, a significant modification to an application for a major permit, or an application to modify substantially a previously issued major permit, the Secretary shall issue public notice of the proposed development (i) by mailing a copy of the application or modification, or a brief description thereof together with a statement indicating where a detailed copy of the proposed development may be inspected, to any citizen or group which has filed a request to be notified of the proposed development, and to any interested State agency; (ii) by posting or causing to be posted a notice at the location of the proposed development stating that an application, a modification of an application for a major permit, or an application to modify a previously issued major permit for development has been made, where the application or modification may be inspected, and the time period for comments; and (iii) with the exception of minor permit applications, by publishing notice of the application or modification at least once in one newspaper of general circulation in the county or counties wherein the development would be located at least 20 days before final action on a major permit or before the beginning of the hearing on a permit under G.S. 113A-122. The notice shall set out that any comments on the development should be submitted to the Secretary by a specified date, not less than 15 days from the date of the newspaper publication of the notice or 15 days after mailing of the mailed notice, whichever is later.

(c)   Within the meaning of this Part, the "designated local official" is the official who has been designated by the local governing body to receive and consider permit applications under this Part. (1973, c. 1284, s. 1; 1975, c. 452, s. 5; 1977, c. 771, s. 4; 1981, c. 932, s. 2.1; 1983, c. 307; 1985, c. 372; 1989, c. 53; c. 727, s. 132; 1989 (Reg. Sess., 1990), c. 987, s. 1; 2013-413, s. 30.)

§ 113A-119.1. Permit fees.

(a)   The Commission shall have the power to establish a graduated fee schedule for the processing of applications for permits, renewals of permits, modifications of permits, or transfers of permits issued pursuant to this Article. In determining the fee schedule, the Commission shall consider the administrative and personnel costs incurred by the Department for processing the applications, related compliance activities, and the complexity of the development sought to be undertaken for which a permit is required under this Article. The fee to be charged for processing an application may not exceed four hundred dollars ($400.00). The total funds collected from fees authorized by the Commission pursuant to this section in any fiscal year shall not exceed thirty-three and one-third percent (33 1/3%) of the total personnel and administrative costs incurred by the Department for permit processing and compliance programs within the Division of Coastal Area Management.

(b)   Fees collected under this section shall be applied to the costs of administering this Article.

(c) Repealed by Session Laws 1991 (Regular Session, 1992), c. 1039, s. 4. (1989 (Reg. Sess., 1990), c. 987, s. 2; 1991 (Reg. Sess., 1992), c. 1039, s. 4.)

§ 113A-119.2. Review of offshore fossil fuel facilities.

(a) In addition to the definitions set out in G.S. 113A-103, as used in this section, the following definitions shall apply:

(1) "Coastal fishing waters" has the same meaning as in G.S. 113-129.

(2) "Discharge" has the same meaning as in G.S. 143-215.77.

(3) "Offshore fossil fuel facility" means those facilities for the exploration, development, or production of oil or natural gas which, because of their size, magnitude, or scope of impacts, have the potential to affect any land or water use or natural resource of the coastal area. For purposes of this definition, offshore fossil fuel facilities shall include, but are not limited to:

a. Structures, including drill ships and floating platforms and structures relocated from other states or countries, located in coastal fishing waters.

b. Any equipment associated with a structure described in sub-subdivision a. of this subdivision, including, but not limited to, pipelines and vessels that are used to carry, transport, or transfer oil, natural gas, liquid natural gas, liquid propane gas, or synthetic gas.

c. Onshore support or staging facilities associated with a structure described in sub-subdivision a. of this subdivision.

(4) "Oil" has the same meaning as in G.S. 143-215.77.

(b) In addition to any other information necessary to determine consistency with State guidelines adopted pursuant to G.S. 113A-107, the following information is required for the review of an offshore fossil fuel facility located in coastal fishing waters:

(1) All information required to be included in an Exploration Plan required pursuant to Subpart B of Part 250 of 30 C.F.R. (July 1, 2009 edition).

(2) All information required to be included in an Oil-Spill Response Plan required pursuant to Subpart B of Part 254 of 30 C.F.R. (July 1, 2009 edition).

(3) An assessment of alternatives to the proposed offshore fossil fuel facility that would minimize the likelihood of an unauthorized discharge.

(4) An assessment of the potential for an unauthorized discharge to cause temporary or permanent violations of the federal and State water quality standards, including the antidegradation policy adopted pursuant to section 303(d) of the federal Clean Water Act (33 U.S.C. § 1313(d)).

(5) Any other information that the Commission determines necessary for consistency review. (2010-179, s. 2.)

§ 113A-120. Grant or denial of permits.

(a) The responsible official or body shall deny an application for a permit upon finding:

(1) In the case of coastal wetlands, that the development would contravene an order that has been or could be issued pursuant to G.S. 113-230.

(2) In the case of estuarine waters, that a permit for the development would be denied pursuant to G.S. 113-229(e).

(3) In the case of a renewable resource area, that the development will result in loss or significant reduction of continued long-range productivity that would jeopardize one or more of the water, food or fiber requirements of more than local concern identified in subdivisions a through c of G.S. 113A-113(b)(3).

(4) In the case of a fragile or historic area, or other area containing environmental or natural resources of more than local significance, that the development will result in major or irreversible damage to one or more of the historic, cultural, scientific, environmental or scenic values or natural systems identified in subdivisions a through h of G.S. 113A-113(b)(4).

(5) In the case of areas covered by G.S. 113A-113(b)(5), that the development will jeopardize the public rights or interests specified in said subdivision.

(6) In the case of natural hazard areas, that the development would occur in one or more of the areas identified in subdivisions a through e of G.S. 113A-113(b)(6) in such a manner as to unreasonably endanger life or property.

(7) In the case of areas which are or may be impacted by key facilities, that the development is inconsistent with the State guidelines or the local land-use plans, or would contravene any of the provisions of subdivisions (1) to (6) of this subsection.

(8) In any case, that the development is inconsistent with the State guidelines or the local land-use plans.

(9) In any case, that considering engineering requirements and all economic costs there is a practicable alternative that would accomplish the overall project purposes with less adverse impact on the public resources.

(10) In any case, that the proposed development would contribute to cumulative effects that would be inconsistent with the guidelines set forth in subdivisions (1) through (9) of this subsection. Cumulative effects are impacts attributable to the collective effects of a number of projects and include the effects of additional projects similar to the requested permit in areas available for development in the vicinity.

(b) In the absence of such findings, a permit shall be granted. The permit may be conditioned upon the applicant's amending his proposal to take whatever measures or agreeing to carry out whatever terms of operation or use of the development that are reasonably necessary to protect the public interest with respect to the factors enumerated in subsection (a) of this section.

(b1) In addition to those factors set out in subsection (a) of this section, and notwithstanding the provisions of subsection (b) of this section, the responsible official or body may deny an application for a permit upon finding that an applicant, or any parent or subsidiary corporation if the applicant is a corporation:

(1) Is conducting or has conducted any activity causing significant environmental damage for which a major development permit is required under this Article without having previously obtained such permit or has received a notice of violation with respect to any activity governed by this Article and has not complied with the notice within the time specified in the notice;

(2) Has failed to pay a civil penalty assessed pursuant to this Article, a local ordinance adopted pursuant to this Article, or Article 17 of Chapter 113 of the General Statutes which is due and for which no appeal is pending;

(3) Has been convicted of a misdemeanor pursuant to G.S. 113A-126, G.S. 113-229(k), or any criminal provision of a local ordinance adopted pursuant to this Article; or

(4) Has failed to substantially comply with State rules or local ordinances and regulations adopted pursuant to this Article or with other federal and state laws, regulations, and rules for the protection of the environment.

(b2) For purposes of subsection (b1) of this section, an applicant's record may be considered for only the two years prior to the application date.

(c) Repealed by Session Laws 1989, c. 676, s. 7. (1973, c. 1284, s. 1; 1975, c. 452, s. 5; 1981, c. 932, s. 2.1; 1983, c. 518, ss. 4, 5; 1987, c. 827, s. 138; 1989, c. 51; c. 676, s. 7; 1997-337, s. 2; 1997-456, s. 55.2B; 1997-496, s. 2; 2000-172, s. 2.1.)

§ 113A-120.1. Variances.

(a) Any person may petition the Commission for a variance granting permission to use the person's land in a manner otherwise prohibited by rules or standards prescribed by the Commission, or orders issued by the Commission, pursuant to this Article. To qualify for a variance, the petitioner must show all of the following:

(1) Unnecessary hardships would result from strict application of the rules, standards, or orders.

(2) The hardships result from conditions that are peculiar to the property, such as the location, size, or topography of the property.

(3) The hardships did not result from actions taken by the petitioner.

(4) The requested variance is consistent with the spirit, purpose, and intent of the rules, standards, or orders; will secure public safety and welfare; and will preserve substantial justice.

(b) The Commission may impose reasonable and appropriate conditions and safeguards upon any variance it grants. (1989, c. 676, s. 8; 2002-68, s. 1.)

§ 113A-120.2. Expired.

§ 113A-121. Permits for minor developments under expedited procedures.

(a) Applications for permits for minor developments shall be expeditiously processed so as to enable their promptest feasible disposition.

(b) In cities and counties that have developed approved implementation and enforcement programs, applications for permits for minor developments shall be considered and determined by the designated local official of the city or county as the case may be. In cities and counties that have not developed approved implementation and enforcement programs, such applications shall be considered and determined by the Secretary. Minor development projects proposed to be undertaken by a local government within its own permit-letting jurisdiction shall be considered and determined by the Secretary.

(c) Failure of the Secretary or the designated local official (as the case may be) to approve or deny an application for a minor permit within 25 days from receipt of application shall be treated as approval of the application, except that the Secretary or the designated local official (as the case may be) may extend the deadline by not more than an additional 25 days in exceptional cases. No waiver of the foregoing time limitation (or of the time limitation established in G.S. 113A-122(c)) shall be required of any applicant.

(d) Repealed by Session Laws 1981, c. 913, s. 2. (1973, c. 1284, s. 1; 1977, c. 771, s. 4; 1981, c. 913, s. 2; 1983, c. 172, s. 1; c. 399; 1989, c.727, s. 133.)

§ 113A-121.1. Administrative review of permit decisions.

(a) An applicant for a minor or major development permit who is dissatisfied with the decision on his application may file a petition for a contested case hearing under G.S. 150B-23 within 20 days after the decision is made. When a local official makes a decision to grant or deny a minor development permit and the Secretary is dissatisfied with the decision, the Secretary may file a petition for a contested case within 20 days after the decision is made.

(b) A person other than a permit applicant or the Secretary who is dissatisfied with a decision to deny or grant a minor or major development permit may file a petition for a contested case hearing only if the Commission determines that a hearing is appropriate. A request for a determination of the appropriateness of a contested case hearing shall be made in writing and received by the Commission within 20 days after the disputed permit decision is made. A determination of the appropriateness of a contested case shall be made within 15 days after a request for a determination is received and shall be based on whether the person seeking to commence a contested case:

(1) Has alleged that the decision is contrary to a statute or rule;

(2) Is directly affected by the decision; and

(3) Has alleged facts or made legal arguments that demonstrate that the request for the hearing is not frivolous.

If the Commission determines a contested case is appropriate, the petition for a contested case shall be filed within 20 days after the Commission makes its determination. A determination that a person may not commence a contested case is a final agency decision and is subject to judicial review under Article 4 of Chapter 150B of the General Statutes. If, on judicial review, the court determines that the Commission erred in determining that a contested case would not be appropriate, the court shall remand the matter for a contested case hearing under G.S. 150B-23 and final decision on the permit pursuant to G.S. 113A-122. Decisions in such cases shall be rendered pursuant to those rules, regulations, and other applicable laws in effect at the time of the commencement of the contested case.

(c) A permit is suspended from the time a person seeks administrative review of the decision concerning the permit until the Commission determines that the person seeking the review cannot commence a contested case or the Commission makes a final decision in a contested case, as appropriate, and no action may be taken during that time that would be unlawful in the absence of a permit. (1981, c. 913, s. 3; 1983, c. 400, ss. 1, 2; 1987, c. 827, s. 139; 1995, c. 409, s. 1; 2011-398, s. 37.)

§ 113A-122. Procedures for hearings on permit decisions.

(a)   Repealed by Session Laws 1987, c. 827, s. 140.

(b)   The following provisions shall be applicable in connection with hearings pursuant to this section:

(1), (2) Repealed by Session Laws 1987, c. 827, s. 140.

(3)   A full and complete record of all proceedings at any hearing under this section shall be taken by a reporter appointed by the Commission or by other method approved by the Attorney General. Any party to a proceeding shall be entitled to a copy of such record upon the payment of the reasonable cost thereof as determined by the Commission.

(4)   to (6) Repealed by Session Laws 1987, c. 827, s. 140.

(7)   The burden of proof at any hearing on a decision granting a permit shall be upon the person who requested the hearing.

(8), (9) Repealed by Session Laws 1987, c. 827, s. 140.

(10)   The Commission shall grant or deny the permit in accordance with the provisions of G.S. 113A-120. All such orders and decisions of the Commission shall set forth separately the Commission's findings of fact and conclusions of law and shall, wherever necessary, cite the appropriate provision of law or other source of authority on which any action or decision of the Commission is based.

(11)   The Commission shall have the authority to adopt a seal which shall be the seal of said Commission and which shall be judicially noticed by the courts of the State. Any document, proceeding, order, decree, special order, rule, rule of procedure or any other official act or records of the Commission or its minutes may be certified by the Executive Director under his hand and the seal of the Commission and when so certified shall be received in evidence in all actions or proceedings in the courts of the State without further proof of the identity of the same if such records are competent, relevant and material in any such action to proceedings. The Commission shall have the right to take official notice of all studies, reports, statistical data or any other official reports or records of the federal government or of any sister state and all such records, reports and data may be placed in evidence by the Commission or by any other person or interested party where material, relevant and competent.

(c) Failure of the Commission to approve or deny an application for a permit pursuant to this section within 75 days from receipt of application shall be treated as approval of the application, except the Commission may extend the deadline by not more than an additional 75 days in exceptional cases.

Failure of the Commission to dispose of an appeal pursuant to this section within 90 days from notice of appeal shall be treated as approval of the action appealed from, except that the Commission may extend the deadline by not more than an additional 90 days if necessary to properly consider the appeal.

(d) All notices which are required to be given by the Secretary or Commission or by any party to a proceeding under this section shall be given by registered or certified mail to all persons entitled thereto. The date of receipt or refusal for such registered or certified mail shall be the date when such notice is deemed to have been given. Notice by the Commission may be given to any person upon whom a summons may be served in accordance with the provisions of law covering civil actions in the superior courts of this State. The Commission may prescribe the form and content of any particular notice. (1973, c. 1284, s. 1; 1979, c. 253, s. 6; 1981, c. 913, ss. 4-6; 1983, c. 172, s. 2; 1987, c. 827, s. 140.)

§ 113A-123. Judicial review.

(a) Any person directly affected by any final decision or order of the Commission under this Part may appeal such decision or order to the superior court of the county where the land or any part thereof is located, pursuant to the provisions of Chapter 150B of the General Statutes. Pending final disposition of any appeal, no action shall be taken which would be unlawful in the absence of a permit issued under this Part.

(b) Any person having a recorded interest or interest by operation of law in or registered claim to land within an area of environmental concern affected by any final decision or order of the Commission under this Part may, within 90 days after receiving notice thereof, petition the superior court to determine whether the petitioner is the owner of the land in question, or an interest, therein, and in case he is adjudged the owner of the subject land, or an interest therein, the court shall determine whether such order so restricts the use of his property as to deprive him of the practical uses thereof, being not otherwise authorized by law, and is therefore an unreasonable exercise of the police power because the order constitutes the equivalent of taking without compensation. The burden of proof shall be on petitioner as to ownership and the burden of proof shall be on the Commission to prove that the order is not an unreasonable exercise of the police power, as aforesaid. Either party shall be entitled to a jury trial on all issues of fact, and the court shall enter a judgment in accordance with the issues, as to whether the Commission order shall apply to the land of the petitioner. The Secretary shall cause a copy of such finding to be recorded forthwith in the register of deeds office in the county where the land is located. The method provided in this subsection for the determination of the issue of whether such order constitutes a taking without compensation shall be exclusive and such issue shall not be determined in any other proceeding. Any action authorized by this subsection shall be calendared for trial at the next civil session of superior court after the summons and complaint have been served for 30 days, regardless of whether issues were joined more than 10 days before the session. It is the duty of the presiding judge to expedite the trial of these actions and to give them a preemptory setting over all others, civil or criminal. From any decision of the superior court either party may appeal to the court of appeals as a matter of right.

(c) After a finding has been entered that such order shall not apply to certain land as provided in the preceding subsection, the Department of Administration, upon the request of the Commission and upon finding that sufficient funds are available therefor, and with the consent of the Governor and Council of State may take the fee or any lesser interest in such land in the name of the State by eminent domain under the provisions of Chapter 146 of the General Statutes and hold the same for the purposes set forth in this Article. (1973, c. 1284, s. 1; c. 1331, s. 3; 1977, c. 771, s. 4; 1987, c. 827, s. 1; 1989, c.727, s. 134.)

§ 113A-124. Additional powers and duties.

(a) The Secretary shall have the following additional powers and duties under this Article:

(1) To conduct or cause to be conducted, investigations of proposed developments in areas of environmental concern in order to obtain sufficient evidence to enable a balanced judgment to be rendered concerning the issuance of permits to build such developments.

(2) To cooperate with the Secretary of the Department of Administration in drafting State guidelines for the coastal area.

(3) To keep a list of interested persons who wish to be notified of proposed developments and proposed rules designating areas of environmental concern and to so notify these persons of such proposed developments by regular mail. A reasonable registration fee to defray the cost of handling and mailing notices may be charged to any person who so registers with the Commission.

(4) To propose rules to implement this Article for consideration by the Commission.

(5) To delegate such of his powers as he may deem appropriate to one or more qualified employees of the Department or to any local government, provided that the provisions of any such delegation of power shall be set forth in departmental rules.

(6) To delegate the power to conduct a hearing, on his behalf, to any member of the Commission or to any qualified employee of the Department. Any person to whom a delegation of power is made to conduct a hearing shall report his recommendations with the record of the hearing to the Secretary for decision or action.

(b) In order to carry out the provisions of this Article the secretaries of Administration and of Environment and Natural Resources may employ such clerical, technical and professional personnel, and consultants with such qualifications as the Commission may prescribe, in accordance with the State personnel rules and budgetary laws, and are hereby authorized to pay such personnel from any funds made available to them through grants, appropriations, or any other sources. In addition, the said secretaries may contract with any local governmental unit or lead regional organization to carry out the planning provisions of this Article.

(c) The Commission shall have the following additional powers and duties under this Article:

(1) To recommend to the Secretary the acceptance of donations, gifts, grants, contributions and appropriations from any public or private source to use in carrying out the provisions of this Article.

(2) To recommend to the Secretary of Administration the acquisition by purchase, gift, condemnation, or otherwise, lands or any interest in any lands within the coastal area.

(3) To hold such public hearings as the Commission deems appropriate.

(4) To delegate the power to conduct a hearing, on behalf of the Commission, to any member of the Commission or to any qualified employee of the Department. Any person to whom a delegation of power is made to conduct a hearing shall report his recommendations with the evidence and the record of the hearing to the Commission for decision or action.

(5) Repealed by Session Laws 1987, c. 827, s. 141.

(6) To delegate the power to determine whether a contested case hearing is appropriate in accordance with G.S. 113A-121.1(b).

(7) To delegate the power to grant or deny requests for declaratory rulings under G.S. 150B-4 in accordance with standards adopted by the Commission.

(8) To adopt rules to implement this Article.

(d) The Attorney General shall act as attorney for the Commission and shall initiate actions in the name of, and at the request of, the Commission, and shall represent the Commission in the hearing of any appeal from or other review of any order of the Commission. (1973, c. 1284, s. 1; 1975, c. 452, s. 5; 1977, c. 771, s. 4; 1981, c. 932, s. 2.1; 1987, c. 827, ss. 125, 141; 1989, c. 727, s. 135; 1991 (Reg. Sess., 1992), c. 839, s. 2; 1997-443, s. 11A.119(a).)

§ 113A-125. Transitional provisions.

(a) Existing regulatory permits shall continue to be administered within the coastal area by the agencies presently responsible for their administration until a date (not later than 44 months after July 1, 1974), to be designated by the Secretary of Natural and Economic Resources as the permit changeover date. Said designation shall be effective from and after its filing with the Secretary of State.

(b) From and after the "permit changeover date," all existing regulatory permits within the coastal area shall be administered in coordination and consultation with (but not subject to the veto of) the Commission. No such existing permit within the coastal area shall be issued, modified, renewed or terminated except after consultation with the Commission. The provisions of this subsection concerning consultation and coordination shall not be interpreted to authorize or require the extension of any deadline established by this Article or any other law for completion of any permit, licensing, certification or other regulatory proceedings.

(c) Within the meaning of this section, "existing regulatory permits" include dredge and fill permits issued pursuant to G.S. 113-229; sand dune permits issued pursuant to G.S. 104B-4; air pollution control and water pollution control permits, special orders or certificates issued pursuant to G.S. 143-215.1 and 143-215.2, or any other permits, licenses, authorizations, approvals or certificates issued by the Board of Water and Air Resources pursuant to Chapter 143; capacity use area permits issued pursuant to G.S. 143-215.15; final approval of dams pursuant to G.S. 143-215.30; floodway permits issued pursuant to G.S. 143-215.54; water diversion authorizations issued pursuant to G.S. 143-354(c); oil refinery permits issued pursuant to G.S. 143-215.99; mining operating permits issued pursuant to G.S. 74-51; permissions for construction of wells issued pursuant to G.S. 87-88; and rules concerning pesticide application within the coastal area issued pursuant to G.S. 143-458; approvals by the Department of Health and Human Services of plans for water supply, drainage or sewerage, pursuant to G.S. 130-161.1 and 130-161.2; standards and approvals for solid waste disposal sites and facilities, adopted by the Department of Health and Human Services pursuant to Chapter 130, Article 13B; permits relating to sanitation of shellfish, crustacea or scallops issued pursuant to Chapter 130, Articles 14A or 14B; permits, approvals, authorizations and rules issued by the Department of Health and Human Services pursuant to Articles 23 or 24 of Chapter 130 with reference to mosquito control programs or districts; any permits, licenses, authorizations, rules, approvals or certificates issued by the Department of Health and Human Services relating to septic tanks or water wells; oil or gas well rules and orders issued for the protection of environmental values or resources pursuant to G.S. 113-391; a certificate of public convenience and necessity issued by the State Utilities Commission pursuant to Chapter 62 for any public utility plant or system, other than a carrier of persons or property; permits, licenses, leases, options, authorization or approvals relating to the use of State forestlands, State parks or other state-owned land issued by the State Department of Administration, the State Department of Natural and Economic Resources or any other State department, agency or institution; any approvals of erosion and sedimentation control plans that may be issued by the North Carolina Sedimentation Control Commission pursuant to G.S. 113A-60 or 113A-61; and any permits, licenses, authorizations, rules, approvals or certificates issued by any State agency pursuant to any environmental protection legislation not specified in this subsection that may be enacted prior to the permit changeover date.

(d)   The Commission shall conduct continuing studies addressed to developing a better coordinated and more unified system of environmental and land-use permits in the coastal area, and shall report its recommendations thereon from time to time to the General Assembly. (1973, c. 1284, s. 1; 1975, c. 452, ss. 4, 5; 1979, c. 299; 1981, c. 932, s. 2.1; 1987, c. 827, ss. 125, 142; 1997-443, s. 11A.122; 2002-165, s. 2.16.)

§ 113A-126. Injunctive relief and penalties.

(a)   Upon violation of any of the provisions of this Article or of any rule or order adopted under the authority of this Article the Secretary may, either before or after the institution of proceedings for the collection of any penalty imposed by this Article for such violation, institute a civil action in the General Court of Justice in the name of the State upon the relation of the Secretary for injunctive relief to restrain the violation and for a preliminary and permanent mandatory injunction to restore the resources consistent with this Article and rules of the Commission. If the court finds that a violation is threatened or has occurred, the court shall, at a minimum, order the relief necessary to prevent the threatened violation or to abate the violation consistent with this Article and rules of the Commission. Neither the institution of the action nor any of the proceedings thereon shall relieve any party to such proceedings from any penalty prescribed by this Article for any violation of same.

(b)   Upon violation of any of the provisions of this Article relating to permits for minor developments issued by a local government, or of any rule or order adopted under the authority of this Article relating to such permits, the designated local official may, either before or after the institution of proceedings for the collection of any penalty imposed by this Article for such violation, institute a civil action in the General Court of Justice in the name of the affected local government upon the relation of the designated local official for injunctive relief to restrain the violation and for a preliminary and permanent mandatory injunction to restore the resources consistent with this Article and rules of the

Commission. If the court finds that a violation is threatened or has occurred, the court shall, at a minimum, order the relief necessary to prevent the threatened violation or to abate the violation consistent with this Article and rules of the Commission. Neither the institution of the action nor any of the proceedings thereon shall relieve any party to such proceedings from any penalty prescribed by this Article for any violation of same.

(c) Any person who shall be adjudged to have knowingly or willfully violated any provision of this Article, or any rule or order adopted pursuant to this Article, shall be guilty of a Class 2 misdemeanor. In addition, if any person continues to violate or further violates, any such provision, rule or order after written notice from the Secretary or (in the case of a permit for a minor development issued by a local government) written notice from the designated local official, the court may determine that each day during which the violation continues or is repeated constitutes a separate violation subject to the foregoing penalties.

(d) (1) A civil penalty of not more than one thousand dollars ($1,000) for a minor development violation and ten thousand dollars ($10,000) for a major development violation may be assessed by the Commission against any person who:

a. Is required but fails to apply for or to secure a permit required by G.S. 113A-118, or who violates or fails to act in accordance with the terms, conditions, or requirements of such permit.

b. Fails to file, submit, or make available, as the case may be, any documents, data or reports required by the Commission pursuant to this Article.

c. Refuses access to the Commission or its duly designated representative, who has sufficiently identified himself by displaying official credentials, to any premises, not including any occupied dwelling house or curtilage, for the purpose of conducting any investigations provided for in this Article.

d. Violates a rule of the Commission implementing this Article.

(2) For each willful action or failure to act for which a penalty may be assessed under this subsection, the Commission may consider each day the action or inaction continues after notice is given of the violation as a separate violation; a separate penalty may be assessed for each such separate violation.

(3) The Commission shall notify a person who is assessed a penalty or investigative costs by registered or certified mail. The notice shall state the reasons for the penalty. A person may contest the assessment of a penalty or investigative costs by filing a petition for a contested case under G.S. 150B-23 within 20 days after receiving the notice of assessment. If a person fails to pay any civil penalty or investigative cost assessed under this subsection, the Commission shall refer the matter to the Attorney General for collection. An action to collect a penalty must be filed within three years after the date the final decision was served on the violator.

(4) In determining the amount of the civil penalty, the Commission shall consider the following factors:

a. The degree and extent of harm, including, but not limited to, harm to the natural resources of the State, to the public health, or to private property resulting from the violation;

b. The duration and gravity of the violation;

c. The effect on water quality, coastal resources, or public trust uses;

d. The cost of rectifying the damage;

e. The amount of money saved by noncompliance;

f. Whether the violation was committed willfully or intentionally;

g. The prior record of the violator in complying or failing to comply with programs over which the Commission has regulatory authority; and

h. The cost to the State of the enforcement procedures.

(4a) The Commission may also assess a person who is assessed a civil penalty under this subsection the reasonable costs of any investigation, inspection, or monitoring that results in the assessment of the civil penalty. For a minor development violation, the amount of an assessment of investigative costs shall not exceed one-half of the amount of the civil penalty assessed or one thousand dollars ($1,000), whichever is less. For a major development violation, the amount of an assessment of investigative costs shall not exceed one-half of the amount of the civil penalty assessed or two thousand five hundred dollars ($2,500), whichever is less.

(5) The clear proceeds of penalties assessed pursuant to this subsection shall be remitted to the Civil Penalty and Forfeiture Fund in accordance with G.S. 115C-457.2. (1973, c. 1284, s. 1; 1975, c. 452, s. 5; 1977, c. 771, s. 4; 1981, c. 932, s. 2.1; 1983, c. 485, ss. 1-3; c. 518, s. 6; 1987, c. 827, ss. 11, 143; 1991, c. 725, s. 6; 1991 (Reg. Sess., 1992), c. 839, s. 3; c. 890, s. 8; 1993, c. 539, s. 874; 1994, Ex. Sess., c. 24, s. 14(c); 1998-215, s. 53(a); 2006-229, s. 1; 2011-398, s. 38.)

§ 113A-127. Coordination with the federal government.

All State agencies shall keep informed of federal and interstate agency plans, activities, and procedures within their area of expertise that affect the coastal area. Where federal or interstate agency plans, activities or procedures conflict with State policies, all reasonable steps shall be taken by the State to preserve the integrity of its policies. (1973, c. 1284, s. 1; 1975, c. 452, s. 5; 1981, c. 932, s. 2.1.)

§ 113A-128. Protection of landowners' rights.

Nothing in this Article authorizes any governmental agency to adopt a rule or issue any order that constitutes a taking of property in violation of the Constitution of this State or of the United States. (1973, c. 1284, s. 1; 1987, c. 827, s. 144.)

§ 113A-129: Reserved for future codification purposes.

Part 5. Coastal Reserves.

§ 113A-129.1. Legislative Findings and Purposes.

(a) Findings. - It is hereby determined and declared as a matter of legislative finding that the coastal area of North Carolina contains a number of important undeveloped natural areas. These areas are vital to continued fishery and wildlife protection, water quality maintenance and improvement, preservation of unique and important coastal natural areas, aesthetic enjoyment, and public trust rights such as hunting, fishing, navigation, and recreation. Such land and water areas are necessary for the preservation of estuarine areas of the State, constitute important research facilities, and provide public access to waters of the State.

(b) Purposes. - Important public purposes will be served by the preservation of certain of these areas in an undeveloped state. Such areas would thereafter be available for research, education, and other consistent public uses. These areas would also continue to contribute perpetually to the natural productivity and biological, economic, and aesthetic values of North Carolina's coastal area. (1989, c. 344, s. 1.)

§ 113A-129.2. Coastal Reserve Program.

(a) There is hereby created a North Carolina Coastal Reserve System for the purpose of acquiring, improving, and maintaining undeveloped coastal land and water areas in a natural state.

(b) This system shall be established and administered by the Department of Environment and Natural Resources. In so doing the Department shall consult with and seek the ongoing advice of the Coastal Resources Commission. The Department may by rule define the areas to be included in this system and set standards for its use.

(c) This system shall be established within the coastal area as defined by G.S. 113A-103(2).

(d) All acquisitions or dispositions of property for lands within this system shall be in accordance with the provisions of Chapter 146 of the General Statutes.

(e) All lands and waters within the system shall be used primarily for research and education. Other public uses, such as hunting, fishing, navigation, and recreation, shall be allowed to the extent consistent with these primary uses. Improvements and alterations to the lands shall be limited to those consistent with these uses. (1989, c. 344, s. 1; c. 727, s. 218(58); 1997-443, s. 11A.119(a).)

§ 113A-129.3. Coordination.

(a) To the extent feasible, this system shall be carried out in coordination with the National Estuarine Reserve Research System established by 16 U.S.C. § 1461.

(b) To the extent feasible, lands and waters within this system shall be dedicated as components of the "State Nature and Historic Preserve" as provided in Article XIV, Section 5, of the Constitution and as nature reserves pursuant to G.S. 113A-164.1 to G.S. 113A-164.11. (1989, c. 344, s. 1, c. 770, s. 47.)

§§ 113A-130 through 113A-134. Reserved for future codification purposes.

Part 6. Public Beach and Coastal Waterfront Access Program.

§ 113A-134.1. Legislative findings.

(a) The General Assembly finds that there are many privately owned lots or tracts of land in close proximity to the Atlantic Ocean and the coastal waters in North Carolina that have been and will be adversely affected by hazards such as erosion, flooding, and storm damage. The sand dunes on many of these lots provide valuable protective functions for public and private property and serve as an integral part of the beach sand supply system. Placement of permanent substantial structures on these lots will lead to increased risks of loss of life and property, increased public costs, and potential eventual encroachment of structures onto the beach.

(b) The public has traditionally fully enjoyed the State's beaches and coastal waters and public access to and use of the beaches and coastal waters. The beaches provide a recreational resource of great importance to North Carolina and its citizens and this makes a significant contribution to the economic well-being of the State. The General Assembly finds that the beaches and coastal waters are resources of statewide significance and have been customarily freely used and enjoyed by people throughout the State. Public access to beaches and coastal waters in North Carolina is, however, becoming severely limited in some areas. Also, the lack of public parking is increasingly making the use of existing public access difficult or impractical in some areas. The public interest would best be served by providing increased access to beaches and coastal waters and by making available additional public parking facilities. There is therefore, a pressing need in North Carolina to establish a comprehensive program for the identification, acquisition, improvement, and maintenance of public accessways to the beaches and coastal waters. (1981, c. 925, s. 1; 1983, c. 751, s. 13; 1989, c. 344; s. 2; 1995, c. 183, s. 2.)

§ 113A-134.2. Creation of program; administration; purpose; definitions.

(a) There is created the Public Beach and Coastal Waterfront Access Program, to be administered by the Commission and the Department, for the purpose of acquiring, improving, and maintaining property along the Atlantic Ocean and coastal waterways to which the public has rights-of-access or public trust rights as provided in this Part.

(b) As used in this Part:

(1) "Public trust resources" has the same meaning as in G.S. 113-131(e).

(2) "Public trust rights" has the same meaning as in G.S. 1-45.1. (1981, c. 925, s. 1; 1983, c. 757, s. 13; 1989, c. 344, s. 2; c. 727, s. 136; c. 751, s. 13; 1995, c. 183, s. 3.)

§ 113A-134.3. Standards for public access program.

(a) The Commission, with the support of the Department, shall establish and carry out a program to assure the acquisition, improvement, and maintenance of a system of public access to coastal beaches and public trust waters. This public access program shall include standards to be adopted by the Commission for the acquisition of property and the use and maintenance of the property. The standards shall be written to assure that land acquisition funds shall only be used to purchase interests in property that will be of benefit to the general public. Priority shall be given to acquisition of lands that due to adverse effects of natural hazards, such as past and potential erosion, flooding, and storm damage, are unsuitable for the placement of permanent structures, including lands for which a permit for improvements has been denied under rules adopted pursuant to State law. The program shall be designed to provide and maintain reasonable public access and necessary parking, within the limitations of the resources available, to all coastal beaches and public trust waters where access is compatible with the natural resources involved and where reasonable access is not available.

(b) To the maximum extent possible, this program shall be coordinated with State and local beach and coastal water management and recreational programs and shall be carried out in cooperation with local governments. Prior to the purchase of any interests in property, the Secretary or his designee shall make a written finding of the public purpose to be served by the acquisition. Once property is purchased, the Department may allow property, without charge, to be controlled and operated by the county or municipality in which the property is located, subject to an agreement requiring that the local government use and maintain the property for its intended public purpose.

(c) Subject to any restrictions imposed by law, any funds appropriated or otherwise made available to the Public Beach and Coastal Waterfront Access Program may be used to meet matching requirements for federal or other funds. The Department shall make every effort to obtain funds from sources other than the General Fund to implement this program. Funds may be used to acquire or develop land for pedestrian access including parking and to make grants to local governments to accomplish the purposes of this Part. All acquisitions or dispositions of property made pursuant to this Part shall be in accordance with the provisions of Chapter 146 of the General Statutes. All grants to local governments pursuant to this Part for land acquisitions shall be made on the condition that the local government agrees to transfer title to any real property acquired with the grant funds to the State if the local government uses the property for a purpose other than beach or coastal waters access. (1981, c. 925, s. 1; 1983, c. 334; c. 757, s. 13; 1987, c. 827, s. 145; 1989, c. 344, s. 2; c. 727, s. 137; c. 751, s. 13; 1995, c. 183, s. 4.)

§§ 113A-134.4 through 113A-134.9. Reserved for future codification purposes.

Article 7B.

Bogue Inlet Access Program.

§ 113A-134.10: Repealed by Session Laws 1991, c. 365.

Article 7C.

Beach Management Plan.

§ 113A-134.11. Department to compile and evaluate information.

The Department of Environment and Natural Resources shall compile and evaluate information on the current conditions and erosion rates of beaches, on coastal geology, and on storm and erosion hazards for use in developing a State plan and strategy for beach management and restoration. The Department of Environment and Natural Resources shall make this information available to local governments for use in land-use planning. (2000-67, s. 13.9(b).)

§ 113A-134.12. Multiyear beach management and restoration strategy and plan.

(a) The Department of Environment and Natural Resources shall develop a multiyear beach management and restoration strategy and plan that does all of the following:

(1) Utilizes the data and expertise available in the Divisions of Water Resources, Coastal Management, and Energy, Mineral, and Land Resources.

(2) Identifies the erosion rate at each beach community and estimates the degree of vulnerability to storm and hurricane damage.

(3) Uses the best available geological and geographical information to determine the need for and probable effectiveness of beach nourishment.

(4) Provides for coordination with the U.S. Army Corps of Engineers, the North Carolina Department of Transportation, the North Carolina Division of

Emergency Management, and other State and federal agencies concerned with beach management issues.

(5) Provides a status report on all U.S. Army Corps of Engineers' beach protection projects in the planning, construction, or operational stages.

(6) Makes maximum feasible use of suitable sand dredged from navigation channels for beach nourishment to avoid the loss of this resource and to reduce equipment mobilization costs.

(7) Promotes inlet sand bypassing where needed to replicate the natural flow of sand interrupted by inlets.

(8) Provides for geological and environmental assessments to locate suitable materials for beach nourishment.

(9) Considers the regional context of beach communities to determine the most cost-effective approach to beach nourishment.

(10) Provides for and requires adequate public beach access, including handicapped access.

(11) Recommends priorities for State funding for beach nourishment projects, based on the amount of erosion occurring, the potential damage to property and to the economy, the benefits for recreation and tourism, the adequacy of public access, the availability of local government matching funds, the status of project planning, the adequacy of project engineering, the cost-effectiveness of the project, and the environmental impacts.

(12) Includes recommendations on obtaining the maximum available federal financial assistance for beach nourishment.

(13) Is subject to a public hearing to receive citizen input.

(b) Each plan shall be as complete as resources and available information allow. The Department of Environment and Natural Resources shall revise the plan every two years and shall submit the revised plan to the General Assembly no later than March 1 of each odd-numbered year. The Department may issue a supplement to the plan in even-numbered years if significant new information becomes available. (2000-67, s. 13.9(c), (d); 2012-143, s. 1(f).)

Article 8.

North Carolina Land Conservancy Corporation.

§§ 113A-135 through 113A-149: Repealed by Session Laws 1983 (Regular Session 1984), c. 995, s. 4.

Article 9.

Land Policy Act.

§ 113A-150. Short title.

This Article shall be known as the Land Policy Act of 1974. (1973, c. 1306, s. 1.)

§ 113A-151. Findings, intent and purpose.

(a)   Findings. - The General Assembly hereby finds that:

(1)   The land of North Carolina is a resource basic to the welfare of her people.

(2)   A lack of coordination of governmental action; a lack of clearly stated, sound, and widely understood guidelines for planning; and a lack of systematic collection, classification, and utilization of information regarding the land resource have led to inconsistencies in policy and inadequacies in planning for the present and future uses of the land resource.

(3)   Governmental agencies responsible for controlling land use and private and public users of the land resource are often unable to independently develop guidelines for land-use practices which provide adequate and meaningful provision for future demands on the land resource, while allowing current needs to be met.

(4)   Systematic and sound decisions as to the location and nature of major public investments in key facilities cannot be made without a comprehensive State policy regarding the land resource.

(5) Those affected by State land-use policy and decisions must be given an opportunity for full participation in the policy-and decision-making process. Such a process must allow for the final implementation of policy by local governments. The State should take whatever steps necessary to encourage and assist local governments in meeting their obligation to control current uses and plan for future uses of the land resource.

(b) Intent and Purpose. - The General Assembly declares that it is the intent of this Article to undertake the continuing development and implementation of a State land-use policy, incorporating environmental, esthetic, economic, social, and other factors so as to promote the public interest, to preserve and enhance environmental quality, to protect areas of natural beauty and historic sites, to encourage beneficial economic development, and to protect and promote the public health, safety, and welfare. Such policy shall serve as a guide for decision-making in State and federally assisted programs which affect land use, and shall provide a framework for the development of land-use policies and programs by local governments. It is the purpose of this Article to:

(1) Promote patterns of land use which are in accord with a State land-use policy which encourages the wise and balanced use of the State's resources;

(2) Establish a State policy to give local governments guidance and assistance in the establishment and implementation of local land planning and management programs so as to effectively meet their responsibilities for economically and environmentally sound land-use management;

(3) Establish a State land-use policy which seeks to provide essential public services equitably to all persons within the State and to assure that citizens shall have, consistent with sound principles of land resource use, maximum freedom and opportunity to live and conduct their activities in locations of their personal choice;

(4) Condition the distribution of certain federal and State funds on meeting reasonable and flexible State requirements for basic land planning; such conditions to include a clear statement of the State's authority and responsibility for review of planning and management by local governments;

(5) Develop and maintain coordination of all State programs having a land-use impact, including joint planning and management of State lands with adjacent nonstate lands, so as to ensure consistency with the purposes of this Article;

(6) Promote the development of systematic methods for the exchange of land-use, environmental, economic, and social information among all levels of government, and among agencies at all levels of government. (1973, c. 1306, s. 1.)

§ 113A-152. Definitions.

Unless the context otherwise requires, the following terms as used in this Article are defined as follows:

(1) "Areas of environmental concern" means: those areas of this State where uncontrolled development, unregulated use, or other man-related activities could result in major or irreversible damage to important environmental, historic, cultural, scientific or scenic values, or natural systems or processes which are of more than local significance, or could unreasonably endanger life or property as a result of natural hazards, or could result in loss of continued long-range productivity in renewable resource areas.

(2) "Principal officer" means the duly appointed or elected public official in responsible charge of a principal department of State government.

(3) "Key facilities" means public facilities which tend to induce development and urbanization of more than local impact and includes, but is not limited to, major facilities for the development, generation, and transmission of energy, for communication, and for transportation.

(4) "Local government" means any county, incorporated village, town, or city, or any combination of counties, incorporated villages, towns, and cities, acting through a joint program pursuant to the provisions of this Article.

(5) "New communities and large-scale developments" means private development which, because of its magnitude or the magnitude of its effect on the surrounding environment, is likely to present issues of more than local significance.

(6) "Project of regional impact" means land use, public development, and private development on government or nongovernmental lands for which there is a demonstrable impact affecting the interests of constituents of more than one local unit of government.

(7) "Region" or "regional" means or refers to one or more of the official planning regions established pursuant to the laws of this State. (1973, c. 1306, s. 1.)

§ 113A-153. North Carolina Land Policy Council.

(a), (b) Repealed by Session Laws 1981, c. 881, s. 3.

(c) Duties. -

(1) To assemble and analyze significant existing laws, policies and programs in State and local government as they pertain to or have substantial effect upon the use, management, development or conservation of all lands and waters, public and private, within the State of North Carolina.

(2) To define and cause to be prepared and periodically revised, a system of information and data concerning the land resources of the entire State, including, but not limited to, esthetic, economic, ecological, demographic, geologic, and physical conditions, both current and projected, as well as a continuing inventory of governmental and private needs and priorities for the use of land resources. All State agencies and units of local government including the register of deeds of each county shall make all pertinent data in their custody available to the Land Policy Council.

(3) To consider, and to consult with the federal government and relevant states on, the interstate aspects of land-use issues of more than intrastate concern.

(4) To prepare, and revise on a continuing basis, an inventory of public and private institutional and financial resources available for land-use planning and management within the State and of State and local programs, projects, and activities which have a regional impact of more than local concern.

(5) To establish a method for identifying new community and large-scale development and land-use projects with regional impact.

(6) To prepare, in consultation with concerned State agencies and other recognized authorities, principles and guidelines for the systematic identification of areas of environmental concern.

(7)   To provide technical assistance and training programs for State and local agency personnel concerned with the development and implementation of State and local land-use programs.

(8)   To establish a method for coordinating all State and local agency programs and services which significantly affect land use.

(9)   To prepare, in conjunction with the Advisory Committee on Land Policy as described in G.S. 113A-154, and following procedures established by this Article, a State land policy as defined in G.S. 113A-155.

(10)   To prepare, in conjunction with the Advisory Committee on Land Policy as described in G.S. 113A-154, and after consultation with the duly constituted and authorized planning agencies of local governments, and following procedures established by this Article, a State land policy and State land classification system as defined further in this Article.

(11)   To prepare and recommend to the General Assembly a system of valuation of property for tax purposes related to the range of public services available or to be made available to properties designated in each of the several land classifications.

(d)   Hearings. - The Council shall conduct such public hearings as it shall determine to be necessary or appropriate to the development of the State land policy and the State land classification system, provided only that there be no fewer than six such hearings held, two in each of the three major physiographic regions of the State. The Council shall give adequate public notice of each hearing at least 30 calendar days prior to the date of the hearing and shall consider all relevant statements and matters presented at hearings.

The Council shall designate the place and time of hearing and may adopt appropriate rules of procedure governing the conduct of the hearing, including the presentation of oral and written statements, and the form, content and method of giving notice of hearing.

(e)   Acceptance and Administration of Federal or Private Funds. - The Department of Environment and Natural Resources shall have power and authority to accept, receive and administer, on behalf of the Council, any funds, gifts, devises, or other financial assistance given, granted or provided by legislative appropriation, or under any federal act or acts or from any federal agency, or from foundations or private sources, and to comply with all conditions and requirements necessary for the receipt, acceptance and use of said funds to the extent not inconsistent with the laws of this State and the rules thereunder pertaining to land-use planning and management. The Council shall have authority to formulate plans and projects for the approval of all funding agencies and institutions and to enter into such contracts and agreements as may be necessary for such purposes or to enter into joint agreements with any other agency or division of government for such purposes and to furnish such information as may be requested for any project or program related to or conducted pursuant to such plans and contracts. Such funds received by the Council pursuant to this provision shall be deposited in the State treasury to the account of the Council and shall remain in such account until used by the Council. (1973, c. 1306, s. 1; 1977, c. 771, ss. 4, 15; 1979, c. 44, s. 1; 1981, c. 47, s. 1; c. 881, s. 3; 1987, c. 827, s. 146; 1989, c. 727, s. 218(67); 1997-443, s. 11A.119(a); 2011-284, s. 75.)

§ 113A-154. Repealed by Session Laws 1981, c. 881, s. 3.

§ 113A-155. State land policy.

(a) Content. - The State land policy of North Carolina shall consist of the following:

(1) Consistent, comprehensive, and coordinated principles, guidelines, and methods for the transaction of all matters and affairs by any agency of State or local government dealing with, or related to, the acquisition, ownership, use, management, and disposition, in part or whole, of title or interests in state-owned and other public lands;

(2) A compilation of all appropriate State laws, appellate court decisions, and current administrative practices, policies and principles, as established by precedent or administrative order, when accepted and recognized as such by the Land Policy Council; and

(3) Principles, guidelines and methods regarding specific land-use and management problems identified by the Land Policy Council, which shall include, but not be limited to, the following:

a. Specific policies and principles for early acquisition of a reserve of lands to form a resource base from which needs for parklands, recreation sites, water reservoirs, key facilities, and other public needs may be met.

b. Specific policies and principles for the location, coordination, consolidation and joint use of utility rights-of-way, of whatever sort, whether above, below, or on the surface of the ground.

c. Specific policies regarding large-scale and special public projects and assemblage of land therefor.

d. Specific policies for determination and certification of areas of environmental concern.

e. Specific policies regarding new communities and large-scale developments on nongovernment lands.

f. Specific policies regarding projects of regional impact.

g. Other similar and related policies and directives as may be necessary to carry out the purpose of this Article.

(b) Effect. - Such policies, principles, directives and methods, when not inconsistent or in conflict with existing law or rules, shall guide and determine the administrative procedures, findings, decisions and objectives of all agencies of State and local government with regard to acquisition, management, and disposition of public lands and interests therein and the regulation of private lands involved in or affected by areas of environmental concern, new communities, large-scale developments and projects of regional impact.

(c) Repealed by Session Laws 1987, c. 827, s. 147. (1973, c. 1306, s. 1; 1987, c. 827, s. 147.)

§ 113A-156. State land classification system.

(a) Purpose. - Within two years following July 1, 1974, the North Carolina Land Policy Council shall develop a State land classification system, which shall include comprehensive guidelines and policies and a method for the classification of all lands in the State for the purposes of:

(1) Providing to State and local governmental agencies a system for achieving the stated purposes of this Article.

(2) Promoting the orderly growth and development of the State in a manner consistent with the wise use and conservation of the land resources.

(3) Assuring that the use and development of land in areas of environmental concern within the State is not inconsistent with the State land policy.

(4) Assuring that the use of land for key facilities, new communities, and large-scale developments, or in areas which are or may be impacted by key facilities, new communities, and large-scale developments, is not inconsistent with the State land policy.

(b) Criteria for Classification. - The Council shall develop and adopt as a part of the classification system no fewer than four nor more than eight classifications which recognize all lands as a basic social and natural resource and which provide for the full range of private and public purposes in the use and conservation of the land resource. Emphasis shall be given to a harmonious relationship among the use potentials of the land, the physical and fiscal feasibility of providing necessary public services, and other facilities and social services. Areas of environmental concern, key facilities, projects of regional impact, new communities, and large-scale developments shall be recognized and made a part of the land classification system in order to further the stated purposes of this Article.

(c) Basis for Land Classification. - Full consideration shall be given, but shall not be limited to, the following aspects and characteristics of the lands of the State:

(1) Topographic features such as land elevations and gradients.

(2) Surface and underground waters, natural or artificial.

(3) Geological, chemical, mineral and physical characteristics of the land.

(4) The existing or potential utility of lands and sites having intrinsic historic, ecological, recreational, scenic or esthetic values or virtues.

(5)   The availability or potential availability of public services, including key facilities, health, education, and other community facilities and social services.

(6)   Areas of environmental concern, existing or potential key facilities, projects of regional impact, new communities, and large-scale development.

(d)   Content. - The State land classification system shall include, but specifically is not limited to, the following:

(1)   Concise and explicit descriptions of each of the classification categories.

(2)   Guidelines and procedures for the preparation of official land-use plans by the land-planning agencies of local government, including a procedure for review by an appropriate State agency for sufficiency and consistency with the provisions of this Article, and a procedure for assembling local plans into regional plans.

(3)   Rules and procedures for land reclassification together with an appellate procedure for property owners and other affected individuals, including officers of any level of government.

(e)   Repealed by Session Laws 1987, c. 827, s. 148. (1973, c. 1306, s. 1; 1987, c. 827, s. 148.)

§ 113A-157. Repealed by Session Laws 1981, c. 881, s. 3.

§ 113A-158. Protection of rights.

Nothing in this Article authorizes any governmental agency to adopt a rule or issue any order that constitutes a taking of property in violation of the Constitution of this State or of the United States, without payment of full compensation. (1973, c. 1306, s. 5; 1987, c. 827, s. 144.)

§ 113A-159. Interpretation.

It is the intention of the General Assembly that this Article be interpreted consistently with, and administered in coordination with, the Coastal Area Management Act of 1974. (1973, c. 1306, s. 6.)

§§ 113A-160 through 113A-164. Reserved for future codification purposes.

Article 9A.

Nature Preserves Act.

§ 113A-164.1. Short title.

This Article shall be known as the Nature Preserves Act. (1985, c. 216, s. 1.)

§ 113A-164.2. Declaration of policy and purpose.

(a) The continued population growth and land development in North Carolina have made it necessary and desirable that areas of natural significance be identified and preserved before they are destroyed. These natural areas are irreplaceable as laboratories for scientific research, as reservoirs of natural materials for uses that may not now be known, as habitats for plant and animal species and biotic communities, as living museums where people may observe natural biotic and environmental systems and the interdependence of all forms of life, and as reminders of the vital dependence of the health of the human community on the health of the other natural communities.

(b) It is important to the people of North Carolina that they retain the opportunity to maintain contact with these natural communities and environmental systems of the earth and to benefit from the scientific, aesthetic, cultural, and spiritual values they possess. The purpose of this Article is to establish and maintain a State Registry of Natural Heritage Areas and to prescribe methods by which nature preserves may be dedicated for the benefit of present and future citizens of the State. (1985, c. 216, s. 1.)

§ 113A-164.3. Definitions.

As used in this Article, unless the context requires otherwise:

(1) "Articles of dedication" means the writing by which any estate, interest, or right in a natural area is formally dedicated as a nature preserve as authorized in G.S. 113A-164.6.

(2) "Dedicate" means to transfer to the State an estate, interest, or right in a natural area in any manner authorized in G.S. 113A-164.6.

(3) "Natural area" means an area of land, water, or both land and water, whether publicly or privately owned, that (i) retains or has reestablished its natural character, (ii) provides habitat for rare or endangered species of plants or animals, (iii) or has biotic, geological, scenic, or paleontological features of scientific or educational value.

(4) "Nature preserve" means a natural area that has been dedicated pursuant to G.S. 113A-164.6.

(5) "Owner" means any individual, corporation, partnership, trust, or association, and all governmental units except the State, its departments, agencies or institutions.

(6) "Registration" means an agreement between the Secretary and the owner of a natural area to protect and manage the natural area for its specified natural heritage resource values.

(7) "Secretary" means the Secretary of Environment and Natural Resources. (1985, c. 216, s. 1; 1989, c. 727, s. 218(68); 1989 (Reg. Sess., 1990), c. 1004, s. 19(b); 1997-443, s. 11A.119(a).)

§ 113A-164.4. Powers and duties of the Secretary.

The Secretary shall:

(1) Establish by rule the criteria for selection, registration, and dedication of natural areas and nature preserves.

(2) Cooperate or contract with any federal, State, or local government agency, private conservation organization, or person in carrying out the purposes of this Article.

(3) Maintain a Natural Heritage Program to provide assistance in the selection and nomination for registration or dedication of natural areas. The Program shall include classification of natural heritage resources, an inventory of their locations, and a data bank for that information. The Program shall cooperate with the Department of Agriculture and Consumer Services in the selection and nomination of areas that contain habitats for endangered and rare plant species, and shall cooperate with the Wildlife Resources Commission in the selection and nomination of areas that contain habitats for endangered and rare animal species. Information from the natural heritage data bank may be made available to public agencies and private persons for environmental assessment and land management purposes. Use of the inventory data for any purpose inconsistent with the Natural Heritage Program may not be authorized. The Program shall include other functions as may be assigned for registration, dedication, and protection of natural areas and nature preserves.

(4) Prepare a Natural Heritage Plan that shall govern the Natural Heritage Program in the creation of a system of registered and dedicated natural areas.

(5) Publish and disseminate information pertaining to natural areas and nature preserves within the State.

(6) Appoint advisory committees composed of representatives of federal, State, and local governmental agencies, scientific and academic institutions, conservation organizations, and private business, to advise him on the identification, selection, registration, dedication, and protection of natural areas and nature preserves.

(7) Submit to the Governor and the General Assembly a biennial report on or before February 15, 1987, and on or before February 15 of subsequent odd-numbered years describing the activities of the past biennium and plans for the coming biennium, and detailing specific recommendations for action that the Secretary deems necessary for the improvement of the Program. (1985, c. 216, s. 1; 1987, c. 827, s. 152; 1997-261, s. 82.)

§ 113A-164.5. Registration of natural areas.

(a) The Secretary shall maintain a State Registry of voluntarily protected natural areas to be called the North Carolina Registry of Natural Heritage Areas. Registration of natural areas shall be accomplished through voluntary agreement between the owner of the natural area and the Secretary. State-owned lands may be registered by agreement with the agency to which the land is allocated. Registration agreements may be terminated by either party at any time, and termination removes the area from the Registry.

(b) A natural area shall be registered when an agreement to protect and manage the natural area for its specified natural heritage resource value has been signed by the owner and the Secretary. The owner of a registered natural area shall be given a certificate signifying the inclusion of the area in the Registry. (1985, c. 216, s. 1.)

§ 113A-164.6. Dedication of nature preserves.

(a) The State may accept the dedication of nature preserves on lands deemed by the Secretary to qualify as outstanding natural areas. Nature preserves may be dedicated by voluntary act of the owner. The owner of a qualified natural area may transfer fee simple title or other interest in land to the State. Nature preserves may be acquired by gift, grant, or purchase. Dedication of a preserve shall become effective only upon acceptance of the articles of dedication by the State. Articles of dedication shall be recorded in the office of the register of deeds in the county or counties in which the natural area is located.

(b) Articles of dedication may:

(1) Contain restrictions and other provisions relating to management, use, development, transfer, and public access, and may contain any other restrictions and provisions as may be necessary or advisable to further the purposes of this Article;

(2) Define, consistently with the purposes of this Article, the respective rights and duties of the owner and of the State and provide procedures to be followed in case of violation of the restrictions;

(3) Recognize and create reversionary rights, transfers upon conditions or with limitations, and gifts over; and

(4) Vary in provisions from one nature preserve to another in accordance with differences in the characteristics and conditions of the several areas.

(c) Subject to the approval of the Governor and Council of State, the State may enter into amendments of any articles of dedication upon finding that the amendment will not permit an impairment, disturbance, use, or development of the area inconsistent with the purposes of this Article. If the fee simple estate in the nature preserve is not held by the State under this Article, no amendment may be made without the written consent of the owner of the other interests therein. (1985, c. 216, s. 1.)

§ 113A-164.7. Nature preserves held in trust.

Lands dedicated for nature preserves pursuant to this Article are held in trust by the State for those uses and purposes expressed in this Article for the benefit of the people of North Carolina. These lands shall be managed and protected according to regulations adopted by the Secretary. Lands dedicated as a nature preserve pursuant to G.S. 113A-164.6 may not be used for any purpose inconsistent with the provisions of this Article, or disposed of, by the State without a finding by the Governor and Council of State that the other use or disposition is in the best interest of the State. (1985, c. 216, s. 1.)

§ 113A-164.8. Dedication of state-owned lands to nature preserves; procedures.

Subject to the approval of the Governor and Council of State, state-owned lands may be dedicated as a nature preserve. State-owned lands shall be dedicated by allocation pursuant to the provisions of G.S. 143-341(4)g. Lands dedicated pursuant to this section may be removed from dedication upon the approval of the Governor and Council of State. (1985, c. 216, s. 1.)

§ 113A-164.9. Dedication of preserves by local governmental units.

All local units of government may dedicate lands as nature preserves by transfer of fee simple title or other interest in land to the State. (1985, c. 216, s. 1.)

§ 113A-164.10. Acquisition of land by State.

All acquisitions or dispositions of an interest in land by the State pursuant to this Article shall be subject to the provisions of Chapter 146 of the General Statutes. (1985, c. 216, s. 1.)

§ 113A-164.11. Assessment of land subject to permanent dedication agreement.

For purposes of taxation, privately owned land subject to a nature preserve dedication agreement shall be assessed on the basis of the true value of the land less any reduction in value caused by the agreement. (1985, c. 216, s. 1.)

Article 10.

Control of Outdoor Advertising near the Blue Ridge Parkway.

§ 113A-165. Advertisements prohibited within 1,000 feet of centerline; exceptions.

No advertisement or advertising structure shall be erected, constructed, installed, maintained or operated within 1,000 feet of the centerline of the Blue Ridge Parkway, except the following:

(1) Sign displays or devices which advertise sale, lease, rental, or development of the property on which it is located.

(2) On-premises Signs. - For the purpose of this Article, those signs, displays or devices which carry only advertisements strictly related to the lawful use of the property on which it is located including signs, displays or devices which identify the business transacted, services rendered, goods sold or produced on the property, name of the business, [and] name of the person, firm or corporation occupying or owning the property. The size of signs advertising the major business activity is not regulated hereunder. Signs which advertise brand-name products or service sold or offered for sale on the property shall not be displayed as on-premise[s] signs unless such signs are on or attached to the building in which such products are sold. All such signs permitted under this

subsection shall be located not more than 150 feet from the building in which such business activity is carried on.

(3)   Historic markers erected by duly constituted and authorized public authorities.

(4)   Highway markers and signs erected or caused to be erected by the Board of Transportation or other authorized authorities in accordance with the law.

(5)   Directional and official signs or notices erected and maintained by public officers or agencies pursuant to and in accordance with lawful authorization for the purpose of carrying out the official duty or responsibility.

(6)   Signs located within a 1,000-foot radius of intersections created by the crossing of the centerline of the Blue Ridge Parkway with the centerlines of components of the National System of Interstate and Defense Highways, Federal Aid Primary Highway System, or the North Carolina System of Primary Highways, not, however, inconsistent with other provisions of the General Statutes. (1973, c. 507, s. 5; 1975, c. 385.)

§ 113A-166. Rules.

The Secretary of Environment and Natural Resources may adopt rules needed to implement this Article. (1975, c. 385; 1977, c. 771, s. 4; 1987, c. 827, s. 149; 1989, c. 727, s. 218(69); 1989 (Reg. Sess., 1990), c. 1004, s. 19(b); 1997-443, s. 11A.119(a).)

§ 113A-167. Existing billboards.

Any billboard in existence upon May 26, 1975, and which does not conform to the requirements of this Article may be maintained for the life of such advertisement or advertising structure, provided that: The Department of Environment and Natural Resources is authorized to acquire by purchase, gift or condemnation all outdoor advertising and all property rights pertaining thereto existing on May 26, 1975, which are nonconforming.

(1) In any acquisition, purchase or condemnation, just compensation to the owner of the outdoor advertising where the owner of the outdoor advertising does not own the fee shall be limited to the fair market value at the time of the taking of the outdoor advertising owner's interest in the real property on which the outdoor advertising is located and such value shall include the value of the outdoor advertising.

(2) In any acquisition, purchase or condemnation, just compensation to the owner of the fee or other interest in the real property upon which the outdoor advertising is located where said owner does not own the outdoor advertising located thereon shall be limited to the difference in the fair market value of the entire tract immediately before and immediately after the taking by the Commission of the right to erect and maintain such outdoor advertising thereon, and in arriving at the fair market value after the taking, any special or general benefits accruing to the property by reason of the acquisition shall be taken into consideration.

(3) In any acquisition, purchase or condemnation, just compensation to the owner of the fee in the real property upon which the outdoor advertising is located where said owner also owns the outdoor advertising located thereon shall be limited to the fair market value of the outdoor advertising plus the difference in the fair market value of the entire tract immediately before and immediately after the taking by the Department of Environment and Natural Resources of the right to erect and maintain such outdoor advertising thereon and in arriving at the fair market value after the taking, any special or general benefits accruing to the property by reason of the acquisition shall be taken into consideration. (1975, c. 385; 1977, c. 771, s. 4; 1989, c. 727, s. 218(70); 1997-443, s. 11A.119(a).)

§ 113A-168. Removal, etc., of unlawful advertising.

Any outdoor advertising erected or established after May 26, 1975, in violation of the provisions of this Article shall be unlawful and shall constitute a nuisance. The Department of Environment and Natural Resources shall give 30 days' notice by certified mail to the owner of the nonconforming outdoor advertising structure, if such owner is known or can by reasonable diligence be ascertained, to move the outdoor advertising structure or to make it conform to the provisions of this Article and rules and regulations promulgated by the Department of Environment and Natural Resources hereunder. The Department or its agents shall have the right to remove or contract to have removed the nonconforming outdoor advertising at the expense of the said owner if the said owner fails to act within 30 days after receipt of such notice. The Department or its agents or contractor and his employees may enter upon private property for the purpose of removing outdoor advertising prohibited by this Article or its implementing rules without civil or criminal liability. (1975, c. 385; 1977, c. 771, s. 4; 1987, c. 827, s. 150; 1989, c. 727, s. 138; 1997-443, s. 11A.119(a).)

§ 113A-169. Condemnation procedure.

For the purposes of this Article, the Department of Environment and Natural Resources shall use the procedure for condemnation of property as provided for by Article 9 of Chapter 136 of the General Statutes. (1975, c. 385; 1977, c. 771, s. 4; 1989, c. 727, s. 218(71); 1997-443, s. 11A.119(a).)

§ 113A-170. Violation a misdemeanor; injunctive relief.

Any person, firm, corporation or association placing or erecting outdoor advertising structure or junkyard along the Blue Ridge Parkway in violation of this Article or a rule adopted under this Article shall be guilty of a Class 1 misdemeanor. In addition thereto, the Department of Environment and Natural Resources may seek injunctive relief in the superior court of the county in which the said nonconforming outdoor advertising is located and require the outdoor advertising to conform to the provisions of this Article or a rule adopted under this Article, or require the removal of the said nonconforming outdoor advertising. (1975, c. 385; 1977, c. 771, s. 4; 1987, c. 827, s. 151; 1989, c. 727, s. 218(72); 1993, c. 539, s. 875; 1994, Ex. Sess., c. 24, s. 14(c); 1997-443, s. 11A.119(a).)

§§ 113A-171 through 113A-175. Reserved for future codification purposes.

Article 11.

Forest Development Act.

§§ 113A-176 through 113A-183: Recodified as Article 83 of Chapter 106, G.S. 106-1010 through G.S. 106-1018, by Session Laws 2011-145, s. 13.25(gg), effective July 1, 2011.

§ 113A-184: Reserved for future codification purposes.

§ 113A-185: Reserved for future codification purposes.

§ 113A-186: Reserved for future codification purposes.

§ 113A-187: Reserved for future codification purposes.

§ 113A-188: Reserved for future codification purposes.

Article 12.

Primary Forest Product Assessment Act.

§§ 113A-189 through 113A-196: Recodified as Article 84 of Chapter 106, G.S. 106-1025 through G.S. 106-1032, by Session Laws 2011-145, s. 13.25(ii), effective July 1, 2011.

§ 113A-197: Reserved for future codification purposes.

§ 113A-198: Reserved for future codification purposes.

§ 113A-199: Reserved for future codification purposes.

§ 113A-200: Reserved for future codification purposes.

§ 113A-201: Reserved for future codification purposes.

Article 13.

Toxic Substances Task Force and Incident Response Procedures.

§§ 113A-202 through 113A-204. Repealed by Session Laws 1979, 2nd Session, c. 1310, s. 3.

Article 14.

Mountain Ridge Protection.

§ 113A-205. Short title.

This Article shall be known as the Mountain Ridge Protection Act of 1983. (1983, c. 676, s. 1.)

§ 113A-206. Definitions.

Within the meaning of this Article:

(1)   The word "person" includes any individual, partnership, firm, association, joint venture, public or private corporation, trust, estate, commission, board, public or private institution, utility, cooperative, interstate body, the State of North Carolina and its agencies and political subdivisions, or other legal entity.

(2)   A person, as defined in this section, doing business or maintaining an office within a county is a resident of the county.

(3)   "Tall buildings or structures" include any building, structure or unit within a multiunit building with a vertical height of more than 40 feet measured from the top of the foundation of said building, structure or unit and the uppermost point of said building, structure or unit; provided, however, that where such foundation measured from the natural finished grade of the crest or the natural finished grade of the high side of the slope of a ridge exceeds 3 feet, then such measurement in excess of 3 feet shall be included in the 40-foot limitation described herein; provided, further, that no such building, structure or unit shall protrude at its uppermost point above the crest of the ridge by more than 35 feet. "Tall buildings or structures" do not include:

a. Water, radio, telephone or television towers or any equipment for the transmission of electricity or communications or both.

b. Structures of a relatively slender nature and minor vertical projections of a parent building, including chimneys, flagpoles, flues, spires, steeples, belfries, cupolas, antennas, poles, wires, or windmills.

c. Buildings and structures designated as National Historic Sites on the National Archives Registry.

(4) "Construction" includes reconstruction, alteration, or expansion.

(5) "Ridge" means the elongated crest or series of crests at the apex or uppermost point of intersection between two opposite slopes or sides of a mountain, and includes all land within 100 feet below the elevation of any portion of such line or surface along the crest.

(6) "Protected mountain ridges" are all mountain ridges whose elevation is 3,000 feet and whose elevation is 500 or more feet above the elevation of an adjacent valley floor; provided, however, that a county, or a city with a population of fifty thousand (50,000) or more, may elect to eliminate the requirement for an elevation of 3,000 feet, and such election shall apply both to an ordinance adopted under G.S. 113A-208 and the prohibition against construction under G.S. 113A-209; provided, further, that such ordinance shall be adopted pursuant to the procedures of G.S. 113A-208.

(7) "Crest" means the uppermost line of a mountain or chain of mountains from which the land falls away on at least two sides to a lower elevation or elevations. (1983, c. 676, s. 1; 1985, c. 713, s. 1.)

§ 113A-207. Legislative findings.

The construction of tall or major buildings and structures on the ridges and higher elevations of North Carolina's mountains in an inappropriate or badly designed manner can cause unusual problems and hazards to the residents of and to visitors to the mountains. Supplying water to, and disposing of the sewage from, buildings at high elevations with significant numbers of residents may infringe on the ground water rights and endanger the health of those persons living at lower elevations. Providing fire protection may be difficult given the lack of water supply and pressure and the possibility that fire will be fanned by high winds. Extremes of weather can endanger buildings, structures, vehicles, and persons. Tall or major buildings and structures located on ridges are a hazard to air navigation and persons on the ground and detract from the natural beauty of the mountains. (1983, c. 676, s. 1.)

§ 113A-208. Regulation of mountain ridge construction by counties and cities.

(a) Any county or city may adopt, effective not later than January 1, 1984, and may enforce an ordinance that regulates the construction of tall buildings or structures on protected mountain ridges by any person. The ordinance may provide for the issuance of permits to construct tall buildings on protected mountain ridges, the conditioning of such permits, and the denial of permits for such construction. Any ordinance adopted hereunder shall be based upon studies of the mountain ridges within the county, a statement of objectives to be sought by the ordinance, and plans for achieving these objectives. Any such county ordinance shall apply countywide except as otherwise provided in G.S. 160A-360, and any such city ordinance shall apply citywide, to construction of tall buildings on protected mountain ridges within the city or county, as the case may be.

A city with a population of 50,000 or more may adopt, prior to January 1, 1986, an ordinance eliminating the requirement for an elevation of 3,000 feet, as permitted by G.S. 113A-206(6).

(b) Under the ordinance, permits shall be denied if a permit application (and shall be revoked if a project) fails to provide for:

(1) Sewering that meets the requirements of a public wastewater disposal system that it discharges into, or that is part of a separate system that meets applicable State and federal standards;

(2) A water supply system that is adequate for fire protection, drinking water and other projected system needs; that meets the requirements of any public water supply system that it interconnects with; and that meets any applicable State standards, requirements and approvals;

(3) Compliance with applicable State and local sedimentation control regulations and requirements; and

(4) Adequate consideration to protecting the natural beauty of the mountains, as determined by the local governing body.

(c) Permits may be conditioned to insure proper operation, to avoid or mitigate any of the problems or hazards recited in the findings of G.S. 113A-207, to protect natural areas or the public health, and to prevent badly designed, unsafe or inappropriate construction.

(d) An ordinance adopted under the authority of this section applies to all protected mountain ridges as defined in G.S. 113A-206. A county or city may apply the ordinance to other mountain ridges within its jurisdiction if it finds that this application is reasonably necessary to protect against some or all of the hazards or problems set forth in G.S. 113A-207. Additionally, a city with a population of 50,000 or more may apply the ordinance to other mountain ridges within its extraterritorial planning jurisdiction if it finds that this application is reasonably necessary to protect against some or all of the hazards or problems set forth in G.S. 113A-207.

(e) Determinations by the county or city governing board of heights or elevations under this Article shall be conclusive in the absence of fraud. Any county or city that adopts a ridge ordinance under the authority of this section or other authority shall send a copy of the ordinance to the Secretary of Environment and Natural Resources.

(f) Any county or city that adopts an ordinance pursuant to this section must hold a public hearing before adopting the ordinance upon the question of adopting the ordinance or of allowing the construction of tall buildings on protected mountain ridges to be governed by G.S. 113A-209. The public hearing required by this section shall be held upon at least 10 days' notice in a newspaper of general circulation in the unit adopting the ordinance. Testimony at the hearing shall be recorded and any and all exhibits shall be preserved within the custody of the governing body. The testimony and evidence shall be made available for inspection and scrutiny by any person.

(g) Any resident of a county or city that adopted an ordinance pursuant to this section, or of an adjoining county, may bring a civil action against the ordinance-adopting unit, contesting the ordinance as not meeting the requirements of this section. If the ordinance is found not to meet all of the requirements of this section, the county or city shall be enjoined from enforcing the ordinance and the provisions of G.S. 113A-209 shall apply. Nothing in this Article authorizes the State of North Carolina or any of its agencies to bring a civil action to contest an ordinance, or for a violation of this Article or of an ordinance adopted pursuant to this Article. (1983, c. 676, s. 1; 1985, c. 713, ss. 2, 4; 1989, c. 727, s. 218(78); 1997-443, s. 11A.119(a).)

§ 113A-209. Certain buildings prohibited.

(a) This section applies beginning January 1, 1984, in any county or city that has failed to adopt a ridge protection ordinance pursuant to G.S. 113A-208 by January 1, 1984.

(b) No county or city may authorize the construction of, and no person may construct, a tall building or structure on any protected mountain ridge.

(c) No county or city may authorize the providing of the following utility services to any building or structure constructed in violation of subsection (b) of this section: electricity, telephone, gas, water, sewer, or septic system. (1983, c. 676, s. 1.)

§ 113A-210. Application to existing buildings.

General Statutes 113A-208 and 113A-209 apply to buildings that existed upon the effective date of this Article as follows:

(1) No reconstruction, alteration or expansion may aggravate or intensify a violation by an existing building or structure that did not comply (a) with G.S. 113A-209 upon its effective date, or (b) with an ordinance adopted under G.S. 113A-208 upon its effective date.

(2) No reconstruction, alteration or expansion may cause or create a violation by an existing building or structure that did comply (a) with G.S. 113A-209 upon its effective date, or (b) with an ordinance adopted under G.S. 113A-208 upon its effective date. (1983, c. 676, s. 1.)

§ 113A-211. Enforcement and penalties.

(a) Violations of this Article shall be subject to the same criminal sanctions, civil penalties and equitable remedies as violations of county ordinances under G.S. 153A-123.

(b) Any person injured by a violation of this Article or any person who resides in the county in which the violation occurred may bring a civil action against the person alleged to be in violation. The action may seek:

(1) Injunctive relief; or

(2) An order enforcing the provision violated; or

(3) Damages caused by the violation; or

(4) Both damages and injunctive relief; or

(5) Both damages and an enforcement order; or

(6) Both an enforcement order and injunctive relief.

If actual damages as found by the court or jury in suits brought under this subsection are five hundred dollars ($500.00) or less, the plaintiff shall be awarded double the amount of actual damages; if the amount of actual damages as found by the court or jury is greater than five hundred dollars ($500.00), the plaintiff shall receive damages in the amount so found. Injunctive relief or an enforcement order under this subsection may be based upon a threatened injury, an actual injury, or both.

Civil actions under this subsection shall be brought in the General Court of Justice of the county in which the alleged violation occurred. The court, in issuing any final order in any action brought pursuant to this section may award costs of litigation, including reasonable attorney and expert-witness fees, to any party, whenever it determines that such an award is appropriate. The court may, if a temporary restraining order or preliminary injunction is sought, require the filing of a bond or equivalent security, the amount of such bond or security to be determined by the court. Nothing in this section shall restrict any right which any person or class of persons may have under the common law or under any statute to seek injunctive or other relief.

(c) Within the meaning of this section, violations of this Article include violations of local ordinances adopted pursuant to G.S. 113A-208. (1983, c. 676, s. 1.)

§ 113A-212. Assistance to counties and cities under ridge law.

(a) The Secretary of Environment and Natural Resources shall provide assistance upon request to the counties and cities in carrying out their functions pursuant to this Article, such as by providing model studies, plans, and ordinances for their consideration.

(b) The Secretary of Environment and Natural Resources shall identify the protected mountain ridge crests in each county by showing them on a map or drawing, describing them in a document, or any combination thereof. Such maps, drawings, or documents shall identify the protected mountain ridges as defined in G.S. 113A-206 and such other mountain ridges as any county may request, and shall specify those protected mountain ridges that serve as all or part of the boundary line between two counties. By November 1, 1983, the map, drawing, or document tentatively identifying the protected mountain ridge crests of each county shall be filed with the board of county commissioners and with the city governing body of each city that requests it. By January 1, 1984, the map, drawing, or document identifying the protected mountain ridge crests shall be permanently filed by the Secretary with the register of deeds in the county where the land lies, and made available for inspection at the Secretary's office in Raleigh. Copies of the maps, drawings, or documents certified by the register of deeds, shall be admitted in evidence in all courts and shall have the same force and effect as would the original.

(b1) By January 1, 1986, a map, drawing, or document tentatively identifying the protected mountain ridge crests of each city with a population of fifty thousand (50,000) or more that has eliminated the requirement for a minimum elevation of 3,000 feet, shall be filed by the Secretary of Environment and Natural Resources with the board of county commissioners and with the city governing body. By March 1, 1986, the map, drawing, or document identifying the protected mountain ridge crests in the city with a population of fifty thousand (50,000) or more shall be permanently filed by the Secretary with the register of deeds in the county where the land within that city with a population of fifty thousand (50,000) or more lies, and shall be made available for inspection at the Secretary's office in Raleigh. Copies of the maps, drawings, or documents certified by the register of deeds shall be admitted in evidence in all courts and shall have the same force and effect as would the original.

(c)   Determinations by the Secretary of elevations under this section shall be conclusive in the absence of fraud. (1983, c. 676, s. 1; 1985, c. 713, s. 3; 1989, c. 727, s. 218(79); 1997-443, s. 11A.119(a).)

§ 113A-213. Article is supplemental.

This Article provides a supplemental source of authority in addition to other present or future legislation and shall not be construed as prescribing an exclusive procedure or as granting exclusive powers. (1983, c. 676, s. 1.)

§ 113A-214. Choosing coverage or removal from coverage of this Article.

(a)   This Article shall apply in all counties and cities unless and until the jurisdiction adopts an ordinance exempting itself from the coverage of this Article.

This exemption shall only be effective after a binding referendum, in which all registered voters in the jurisdiction are eligible to vote, which shall be held on or before May 8, 1984. The binding referendum shall be held either as a result of a resolution passed by the governing body of the jurisdiction or as a result of an initiative petition signed by fifteen percent (15%) of the registered voters in the jurisdiction and filed with the Board of Elections of that county not later than 60 days before the election is to be held. At that referendum, each qualified voter desiring to vote shall be provided a ballot on which shall be printed the following:

[] FOR coverage under the Mountain Ridge Protection Act of 1983.

[] AGAINST coverage under the Mountain Ridge Protection Act of 1983.

(b)   If a jurisdiction removes itself from the coverage of this Article, by means of a binding referendum, as provided for in subsection (a) of this section, then it shall have until May 13, 1986 to place itself again under the coverage of this Article by means of an ordinance passed after a similar binding referendum.

Once a jurisdiction opts out and then opts back under the Article, it may not take any further action to again remove itself from the coverage of the Article.

(c) If a county has chosen the permit procedure authorized by G.S. 113A-208, and then opts out of and either the county or any city in the county opts back under the coverage of this Article, then that jurisdiction may choose the permit procedure even after January 1, 1984.

(d) When a county removes itself from the coverage of this Article all cities within the county shall be removed from the coverage of this Article. Provided, however, a city in a county that has removed itself from coverage may, under the procedure set forth in subsection (b) of this section, place itself again under the coverage of this Article.

(e) When a protected mountain ridge is any part of the boundary between two jurisdictions then that part of the ridge shall be covered by this Article unless both jurisdictions remove themselves from the coverage of this Article. (1983, c. 676, s. 1.)

§§ 113A-215 through 113A-219. Reserved for future codification purposes.

Article 15.

Aquatic Weed Control.

§ 113A-220. Short title.

This Article shall be known as the Aquatic Weed Control Act of 1991. (1991, c. 132.)

§ 113A-221. Definitions.

Unless a different meaning is required by the context, the following definitions shall apply throughout this Article:

(1)   "Department" means the Department of Environment and Natural Resources.

(2)   "Secretary" means the Secretary of Environment and Natural Resources or his designee.

(3)   "Noxious aquatic weed" means any plant organism so designated under this Article.

(4)   "Waters of the State" means any surface body or accumulation of water, whether publicly or privately owned and whether naturally occurring or artificially created, which is contained within, flows through, or borders upon any part of this State. (1991, c. 132, s. 1; 1997-443, s. 11A.119(a).)

§ 113A-222. Designation of noxious aquatic weeds.

(a)   The Secretary, after consultation with the Director of the North Carolina Agricultural Extension Service, the Wildlife Resources Commission, and the Marine Fisheries Commission, and with the concurrence of the Commissioner of Agriculture, may designate as a noxious aquatic weed any plant organism which:

(1)   Grows in or is closely associated with the aquatic environment, whether floating, emersed, submersed, or ditch-bank species, and including terrestrial phases of any such plant organism;

(2)   Exhibits characteristics of obstructive nature and either massive productivity or choking density; and

(3)   Is or may become a threat to public health or safety or to existing or new beneficial uses of the waters of the State.

(b)   A plant organism may be designated as being a noxious aquatic weed either throughout the State or within specified areas within the State.

(c)   The Secretary shall designate a plant organism as a noxious aquatic weed by rules adopted pursuant to Chapter 150B of the General Statutes.

(d) The Secretary may modify or withdraw any designation of a plant organism as a noxious aquatic weed made previously under this section. Any modification or withdrawal of such designation shall be made following the procedures for designation set out in this section. (1991, c. 132.)

§ 113A-223. Powers and duties of the Secretary.

(a) The Secretary shall direct the control, eradication, and regulation of noxious aquatic weeds so as to protect and preserve human health, safety, and the beneficial uses of the waters of the State and to prevent injury to property and beneficial plant and animal life. The Secretary shall have the power to:

(1) Conduct research and planning related to the control of noxious aquatic weeds;

(2) Coordinate activities of all public bodies, authorities, agencies, and units of local government in the control and eradication of noxious aquatic weeds;

(3) Delegate to any public body, authority, agency, or unit of local government any power or duty under this Article, except that the Secretary may not delegate the designation of noxious aquatic weeds;

(4) Accept donations, grants, and services from both public and private sources;

(5) Enter into contracts or agreements, including cost-sharing agreements, with public or private agencies for research and development of methods of control of noxious aquatic weeds or for the performance of noxious aquatic weed control activities;

(6) Construct, acquire, operate, and maintain facilities and equipment necessary for the control of noxious aquatic weeds; and

(7) Enter upon private property for purposes of conducting investigations and engaging in aquatic weed control activities.

(b) The Secretary may control, remove, or destroy any noxious aquatic weed located in the waters of the State or in areas adjacent to such waters wherever such weeds threaten to invade such waters. The Secretary may employ any appropriate control technology which is consistent with federal and State law, regulations, and rules. Control technologies may include, but are not limited to drawdown of waters, application of chemicals to shoreline and surface waters, mechanical controls, physical removal from transport mechanisms, quarantine of transport mechanisms, and biological controls. Any biological control technology may be implemented only after the environmental review provisions of the State Environmental Policy Act have been satisfied.

(c) In determining the appropriate strategies and technologies, the Secretary shall consider their relative short-term and long-term cost-efficiency and effectiveness, consistent with a margin of safety adequate to protect public health and the resources of the State.

(d) All activities carried out by the Secretary, his designees, and others authorized to perform any function under this Article shall be consistent with all applicable federal and State law, regulations, and rules. (1991, c. 132.)

§ 113A-224. Powers of the Commissioner of Agriculture.

(a) The Commissioner of Agriculture may regulate the importation, sale, use, culture, collection, transportation, and distribution of a noxious aquatic weed as a plant pest under Article 36 of Chapter 106 of the General Statutes.

(b) This Article shall not be construed to limit any power of the Commissioner of Agriculture, the Department of Agriculture and Consumer Services, or the Board of Agriculture under any other provision of law. (1991, c. 132, s. 1; 1997-261, s. 109.)

§ 113A-225. Responsibilities of other State agencies.

All State agencies shall cooperate with the Secretary to assist in the implementation of this Article. (1991, c. 132.)

§ 113A-226. Enforcement.

(a) Any person who violates this Article or any rule adopted pursuant to this Article shall be guilty of a Class 2 misdemeanor for each offense.

(b) Whenever there exists reasonable cause to believe that any person has violated this Article or rules adopted pursuant to this Article, the Secretary may request the Attorney General to institute a civil action for injunctive relief to restrain the violation. The Attorney General may institute such action in the name of the State upon relation of the Department in the superior court of the county in which the violation occurred. Upon a determination by the court that the alleged violation of the provisions of this Article or of rules adopted pursuant to this Article has occurred or is threatened, the court shall grant the relief necessary to prevent or abate the violation or threatened violation. Neither the institution of the action, nor any of the proceedings thereon shall relieve any party to such proceedings from any penalty otherwise prescribed for violations of this Article. (1991, c. 132, c. 761, s. 20; 1993, c. 539, s. 877; 1994, Ex. Sess., c. 24, s. 14(c).)

§ 113A-227. Adoption of rules.

The Secretary may adopt rules necessary to implement the provisions of this Article pursuant to Chapter 150B of the General Statutes. (1991, c. 132.)

§ 113A-228. Reserved for future codification purposes.

§ 113A-229. Reserved for future codification purposes.

Article 16.

Conservation Easements Program.

§ 113A-230. Legislative findings; intent.

The General Assembly finds that a statewide network of protected natural areas, riparian buffers, and greenways can best be accomplished through a conservation easements program. The General Assembly further finds that other public conservation and use programs, such as natural area protection, beach access, trail systems, historic landscape protection, and agricultural preservation, can benefit from increased conservation tools. In this Article, the General Assembly therefore intends to extend the ability of the Department of Environment and Natural Resources to achieve these purposes and to strengthen the capability of private nonprofit land trusts to participate in land and water conservation. (1997-226, s. 6; 1997-443, s. 11A.119(b).)

§ 113A-231. Program to accomplish conservation purposes.

The Department of Environment and Natural Resources shall develop a nonregulatory program that uses conservation tax credits as a prominent tool to accomplish conservation purposes, including the maintenance of ecological systems. As a part of this program, the Department shall exercise its powers to protect real property and interests in real property: donated for tax credit under G.S. 105-130.34 or G.S. 105-151.12; conserved with the use of other financial incentives; or, conserved through nonregulatory programs. The Department shall call upon the Attorney General for legal assistance in developing and implementing the program. (1997-226, s. 6; 1997-443, s. 11A.119(b); 2002-155, s. 1.)

§ 113A-232. Conservation Grant Fund.

(a) Fund Created. - The Conservation Grant Fund is created within the Department of Environment and Natural Resources. The Fund shall be administered by the Department. The purpose of the Fund is to stimulate the use of conservation easements and conservation tax credits, to improve the capacity of private nonprofit land trust organizations to successfully accomplish conservation projects, to better equip real estate related professionals to pursue opportunities for conservation, to increase landowner participation in land and water conservation, and to provide an opportunity to leverage private and other public monies for conservation easements.

(b) Fund Sources. - The Conservation Grant Fund shall consist of any monies appropriated to it by the General Assembly and any monies received from public or private sources. Unexpended monies in the Fund that were appropriated from the General Fund by the General Assembly shall revert at the end of the fiscal year unless the General Assembly otherwise provides. Unexpended monies in the Fund from other sources shall not revert and shall remain available for expenditure in accordance with this Article.

(c) Property Eligibility. - In order for real property or an interest in real property to be the subject of a grant under this Article, the real property or interest in real property must possess or have a high potential to possess ecological value, must be reasonably restorable, and must qualify for tax credits under G.S. 105-130.34 or G.S. 105-151.12.

(c1) Grant Eligibility. - State conservation land management agencies, local government conservation land management agencies, and private nonprofit land trust organizations are eligible to receive grants from the Conservation Grant Fund. Private nonprofit land trust organizations must be qualified pursuant to G.S. 105-130.34 and G.S. 105-151.12 and must be certified under section 501(c)(3) of the Internal Revenue Code.

(d) Use of Revenue. - Revenue in the Conservation Grant Fund may be used only for the following purposes:

(1) The administrative costs of the Department in administering the Fund.

(2) Conservation grants made in accordance with this Article.

(3) To establish an endowment account, the interest from which will be used for a purpose described in G.S. 113A-233(a). (1997-226, s. 6; 1997-443, s. 11A.119(b); 2002-155, s. 2; 2003-340, s. 1.4.)

§ 113A-233. Uses of a grant from the Conservation Grant Fund.

(a) Allowable Uses. - A grant from the Conservation Grant Fund may be used only to pay for one or more of the following costs:

(1) Reimbursement for total or partial transaction costs for a donation of real property or an interest in real property from an individual or corporation satisfying either of the following:

a. Insufficient financial ability to pay all costs or insufficient taxable income to allow these costs to be included in the donated value.

b. Insufficient tax burdens to allow these costs to be offset by the value of tax credits under G.S. 105-130.34 or G.S. 105-151.12 or by charitable deductions.

(2) Management support, including initial baseline inventory and planning.

(3) Monitoring compliance with conservation easements, the related use of riparian buffers, natural areas, and greenways, and the presence of ecological integrity.

(4) Education on conservation, including information materials intended for landowners and education for staff and volunteers.

(5) Stewardship of land.

(6) Transaction costs for recipients, including legal expenses, closing and title costs, and unusual direct costs, such as overnight travel.

(7) Administrative costs for short-term growth or for building capacity.

(b) Prohibition. - The Fund shall not be used to pay the purchase price of real property or an interest in real property. (1997-226, s. 6; 2002-155, s. 3.)

§ 113A-234. Administration of grants.

(a) Grant Procedures and Criteria. - The Secretary of Environment and Natural Resources shall establish the procedures and criteria for awarding grants from the Conservation Grant Fund. The criteria shall focus grants on those areas, approaches, and techniques that are likely to provide the optimum positive effect on environmental protection. The Secretary shall make the final decision on the award of grants and shall announce the award publicly in a timely manner.

(b) Grant Administration. - The Secretary may administer the grants under this Article or may contract for selected activities under this Article. If administrative services are contracted, the Department shall establish guidance and criteria for its operation and contract with a statewide nonprofit land trust service organization. (1997-226, s. 6; 1997-443, s. 11A.119(b); 2002-155, s. 4.)

§ 113A-235. Conservation easements.

(a) Acquisition and Protection of Conservation Easements. - Ecological systems and appropriate public use of these systems may be protected through conservation easements, including conservation agreements under Article 4 of Chapter 121 of the General Statutes, the Conservation and Historic Preservation Agreements Act, and conservation easements under the Conservation Reserve Enhancement Program. The Department of Environment and Natural Resources shall work cooperatively with State and local agencies and qualified nonprofit organizations to monitor compliance with conservation easements and conservation agreements and to ensure the continued viability of the protected ecosystems. Soil and water conservation districts established under Chapter 139 of the General Statutes may acquire easements under the Conservation Reserve Enhancement Program by purchase or gift.

(b) Conveyance of Conservation Lands. - The Department may convey real property or an interest in real property that has been acquired for conservation in perpetuity to a federal agency, State agency, a local government, or a private nonprofit conservation organization in accordance with State law governing the conveyance of real property. The grantee of real property or an interest in real property shall manage and maintain the real property or interest in real property for the purposes set out in subsection (a) of this section. When conveying real property or an interest in real property under this subsection, the Department shall retain a possibility of reverter, a right of entry, or other appropriate property interest to ensure that the real property or interest in real property will continue to be managed and maintained in a manner that protects ecological systems and the appropriate public use of these systems.

(c) Report. - The Department shall report on the implementation of this Article to the Environmental Review Commission no later than 1 October of each year. The Department shall maintain an inventory of all conservation easements held by the Department. The inventory shall be included in the report required by this subsection. (1997-226, s. 6; 1997-443, s. 11A.119(b); 1999-329, s. 6.3; 2002-155, s. 5; 2004-195, s. 2.2.)

§§ 113A-236 through 113A-239. Reserved for future codification purposes.

Article 17.

Conservation, Farmland, And Open Space Protection And Coordination.

§ 113A-240. Intent.

(a) It is the intent of the General Assembly to continue to support and accelerate the State's programs of land conservation and protection, to find means to assure and increase funding for these programs, to support the long-term management of conservation lands acquired by the State, and to improve the coordination, efficiency, and implementation of the various State and local land protection programs operating in North Carolina.

(b) It is the further intent of the General Assembly that the State's lands should be protected in a manner that minimizes any adverse impacts on the ability of local governments to carry out their broad mandates. (2000-23, s. 2.)

§ 113A-241. State to Preserve One Million Acres; Annual Report.

(a) The State of North Carolina shall encourage, facilitate, plan, coordinate, and support appropriate federal, State, local, and private land protection efforts so that an additional one million acres of farmland, open space, and conservation lands in the State are permanently protected by December 31, 2009. These lands shall be protected by acquisition in fee simple or by acquisition of perpetual conservation easements by public conservation organizations or by private entities that are organized to receive and administer lands for conservation purposes.

(b) The Secretary of Environment and Natural Resources shall lead the effort to add one million acres to the State's protected lands and shall plan and coordinate with other public and private organizations and entities that are receiving and administering lands for conservation purposes.

(c)   The Secretary of Environment and Natural Resources shall report to the Governor and the Environmental Review Commission on or before 1 October of each year on the State's progress towards attaining the goal established in this section. (2000-23, ss. 2, 3; 2001-452, s. 2.2; 2004-195, s. 2.3.)

§§ 113A-242 through 113A-250. Reserved for future codification purposes.

Article 18.

Clean Water Management Trust Fund.

§ 113A-251. Purpose.

The General Assembly recognizes that a critical need exists in this State to clean up pollution in the State's surface waters and to protect, preserve, and conserve those waters that are not yet polluted. The task of cleaning up polluted waters and protecting and enhancing the State's water resources is multifaceted and requires different approaches, including innovative pilot projects, that take into account the problems, the type of pollution, the geographical area, and the recognition that the hydrological and ecological values of each resource sought to be upgraded, conserved, and protected are unique.

It is the intent of the General Assembly that moneys from the Fund created under this Article shall be used to help finance projects that specifically address water pollution problems and focus on upgrading surface waters, eliminating pollution, and protecting, preserving, and conserving unpolluted surface waters, including enhancement or development of drinking water supplies. It is the further intent of the General Assembly that moneys from the Fund also be used to build a network of riparian buffers and greenways for environmental, educational, and recreational benefits. It is lastly the intent of the General Assembly that moneys from the Fund also be used to preserve lands that could be used for water supply reservoirs. While the purpose of this Article is to focus on the cleanup and prevention of pollution of the State's surface waters, the establishment of a network of riparian buffers and greenways, and the preservation of property for establishing clean water supplies, the General Assembly believes that the results of these efforts will also be beneficial to wildlife and marine fisheries habitats. (1996, 2nd Ex. Sess., c. 18, s. 27.6(a); 2003-340, s. 1.3; 2007-549, s. 1; 2011-374, s. 2.1.)

§ 113A-252. Definitions.

The following definitions apply in this Article:

(1) Council. - The advisory council for the Clean Water Management Trust Fund.

(2) Economically distressed local government unit. - An economically distressed county, as defined in G.S. 143B-437.01, or a local government unit located in that county.

(3) Fund. - The Clean Water Management Trust Fund created pursuant to this Article.

(4) Land. - Real property and any interest in, easement in, or restriction on real property.

(4a) Local government unit. - Defined in G.S. 159G-20.

(4b) Stormwater quality project. - Defined in G.S. 159G-20.

(5) Trustees. - The trustees of the Clean Water Management Trust Fund.

(6) Wastewater collection system. - Defined in G.S. 159G-20.

(7) Wastewater treatment works. - Defined in G.S. 159G-20. (1996, 2nd Ex. Sess., c. 18, s. 27.6(a); 2003-340, s. 1.3; 2005-454, s. 4; 2006-252, s. 2.13.)

§ 113A-253. Clean Water Management Trust Fund.

(a) Fund Established. - The Clean Water Management Trust Fund is established as a special revenue fund to be administered by the Department of

Environment and Natural Resources. The Fund receives revenue from the following sources and may receive revenue from other sources:

(1) Annual appropriations.

(2) Special registration plates under G.S. 20-81.12.

(3) Other special registration plates under G.S. 20-79.7.

(b) Fund Earnings, Assets, and Balances. - The State Treasurer shall hold the Fund separate and apart from all other moneys, funds, and accounts. Investment earnings credited to the assets of the Fund shall become part of the Fund. Any balance remaining in the Fund at the end of any fiscal year shall be carried forward in the Fund for the next succeeding fiscal year. Payments from the Fund shall be made on the warrant of the Chair of the Board of Trustees.

(c) Fund Purposes. - Moneys from the Fund are appropriated annually to finance projects to clean up or prevent surface water pollution and for land preservation in accordance with this Article. Revenue in the Fund may be used for any of the following purposes:

(1) To acquire land for riparian buffers for the purposes of providing environmental protection for surface waters and urban drinking water supplies and establishing a network of riparian greenways for environmental, educational, and recreational uses.

(2) To acquire conservation easements or other interests in real property for the purpose of protecting and conserving surface waters and enhancing drinking water supplies, including the development of water supply reservoirs.

(3) To coordinate with other public programs involved with lands adjoining water bodies to gain the most public benefit while protecting and improving water quality.

(4) To restore previously degraded lands to reestablish their ability to protect water quality.

(5) through (7) Repealed by Session Laws 2013-360, s. 14.3(d), effective August 1, 2013.

(8) To facilitate planning that targets reductions in surface water pollution.

(8a) To finance innovative efforts, including pilot projects, to improve stormwater management, to reduce pollutants entering the State's waterways, to improve water quality, and to research alternative solutions to the State's water quality problems.

(8b) To provide buffers around military bases or for State matching funds for the Readiness and Environmental Protection Initiative, a federal funding initiative that provides funds for military buffers.

(8c) To acquire land that represents the ecological diversity of North Carolina, including natural features such as riverine, montane, coastal, and geologic systems and other natural areas to ensure their preservation and conservation for recreational, scientific, educational, cultural, and aesthetic purposes.

(8d) To acquire land that contributes to the development of a balanced State program of historic properties.

(8e) To authorize expenditures from the Fund not to exceed seven hundred fifty thousand dollars ($750,000) to pay for the inventory of natural areas conducted under the Natural Heritage Program established pursuant to the Nature Preserves Act, Article 9A of Chapter 113A of the General Statutes, and to pay for conservation and protection planning and for informational programs for owners of natural areas, as defined in G.S. 113A-164.3.

(9) To fund operating expenses of the Board of Trustees and its staff.

(d) Limit on Operating and Administrative Expenses. - For the fiscal year beginning July 1, 2013, the limit on operating and administrative expenses of the Board of Trustees and its staff is one million two hundred fifty thousand dollars ($1,250,000). For fiscal years beginning on or after July 1, 2014, the limit on operating and administrative expenses of the Board of Trustees and its staff is the amount for the preceding year, adjusted to include any change in the distribution of statewide salary and benefits reserves. (1996, 2nd Ex. Sess., c. 18, s. 27.6(a); 2001-424, s. 32.17; 2003-340, s. 1.3; 2004-179, s. 4.4; 2005-454, s. 5; 2007-549, s. 2; 2011-145, s. 13.26(b); 2011-374, s. 2.2; 2013-360, s. 14.3(d).)

§ 113A-253.1: Repealed by Session Laws 2011-145, s. 13.26(a), effective July 1, 2011.

§ 113A-253.2. North Carolina Conservation Easement Endowment Fund.

(a) The North Carolina Conservation Easement Endowment Fund is established as a special fund in the Office of the State Treasurer. The principal of the Endowment Fund shall consist of a portion of grant funds transferred by the Trustees to the Endowment Fund from the Clean Water Management Trust Fund for stewardship activities related to projects for conservation easements funded from the Clean Water Management Trust Fund. The principal of the Endowment Fund may also consist of any proceeds of any gifts, grants, or contributions to the State that are specifically designated for inclusion in the Endowment Fund and any investment income that is not used in accordance with subsection (b) of this section. The State Treasurer shall hold the Endowment Fund separate and apart from all other moneys, funds, and accounts. The State Treasurer shall invest the assets of the Endowment Fund in accordance with the provisions of G.S. 147-69.2 and G.S. 147-69.3. The State Treasurer shall disburse the endowment investment income only upon the written direction of the Chair of the Board of Trustees. No expenditure or disbursement shall be made from the principal of the Endowment Fund.

(b) The Trustees may authorize the disbursement of the endowment investment income only for activities related to stewardship of conservation easements owned by the State. (2008-107, s. 12.9(a).)

§ 113A-254. Grant requirements.

(a) Eligible Applicants. - Any of the following are eligible to apply for a grant from the Fund for the purpose of protecting and enhancing water quality:

(1) A State agency.

(2) A local government unit.

(3) A nonprofit corporation whose primary purpose is the conservation, preservation, and restoration of our State's environmental and natural resources.

(a1) Criteria. - The criteria developed by the Trustees under G.S. 113A-256 apply to grants made under this Article. The common criteria for water projects set in G.S. 159G-23 and the criteria set out in this section also apply to wastewater collection system projects, wastewater treatment works projects, and stormwater quality projects. An application for a wastewater collection system project or a wastewater treatment works project that serves an economically distressed local government unit has priority.

(b) Matching Requirement. - The Board of Trustees shall establish matching requirements for grants awarded under this Article. This requirement may be satisfied by the donation of land to a public or private nonprofit conservation organization as approved by the Board of Trustees. The Board of Trustees may also waive the requirement to match a grant pursuant to guidelines adopted by the Board of Trustees.

(c) Restriction. - No grant shall be awarded under this article to satisfy compensatory mitigation requirements under 33 USC § 1344 or G.S. 143-214.11.

(d) Wastewater Limits. - A wastewater collection system project or a wastewater treatment works project is eligible for a grant under this Article only if it is a high-unit-cost project, as defined in G.S. 159G-20. A planning grant or a technical assistance grant for a regional wastewater collection system or a regional wastewater treatment works is not subject to the high-unit-cost threshold. A grant made under this Article for a wastewater collection system project or a wastewater treatment works project is subject to the cost limits and recipient limits set in G.S. 159G-36 for a grant awarded from the Wastewater Reserve.

(e) Stormwater Limits. - The amount of a grant awarded under this Article for a stormwater quality project may not exceed the construction costs of the project. The total amount of grants awarded under this Article to the same recipient for stormwater quality projects for a fiscal year may not exceed the limit set in G.S. 159G-36(c)(1) for grants to the same recipient from the Wastewater Reserve.

(f) Withdrawal. - An award of a grant under this Article is withdrawn if the grant recipient fails to enter into a construction contract for the project within one year after the date of the award, unless the Trustees find that the applicant has good cause for the failure. If the Trustees find good cause for a recipient's failure, the Trustees must set a date by which the recipient must take action or forfeit the grant. (1996, 2nd Ex. Sess., c. 18, s. 27.6(a); 2003-340, s. 1.3; 2005-454, s. 6; 2006-178, s. 1; 2007-185, s. 1.)

§ 113A-255. Clean Water Management Trust Fund: Board of Trustees established; membership qualifications; vacancies; meetings and meeting facilities.

(a)   Board of Trustees Established. - There is established the Clean Water Management Trust Fund Board of Trustees. The Clean Water Management Trust Fund Board of Trustees shall be administratively located within the Department of Environment and Natural Resources.

(b)   Membership. - The Clean Water Management Trust Fund Board of Trustees shall be composed of nine members appointed to three-year terms as follows:

(1)   One member appointed by the Governor to a term that expires on July 1 of years that precede by one year those years that are evenly divisible by three.

(2)   One member appointed by the Governor to a term that expires on July 1 of years that follow by one year those years that are evenly divisible by three.

(3)   One member appointed by the Governor to a term that expires on July 1 of years that are evenly divisible by three.

(4)   One member appointed by the General Assembly upon the recommendation of the President Pro Tempore of the Senate to a term that expires on July 1 of years that precede by one year those years that are evenly divisible by three.

(5)   One member appointed by the General Assembly upon the recommendation of the President Pro Tempore of the Senate to a term that expires on July 1 of years that follow by one year those years that are evenly divisible by three.

(6)   One member appointed by the General Assembly upon the recommendation of the President Pro Tempore of the Senate to a term that expires on July 1 of years that are evenly divisible by three.

(7) One member appointed by the General Assembly upon the recommendation of the Speaker of the House of Representatives to a term that expires on July 1 of years that precede by one year those years that are evenly divisible by three.

(8) One member appointed by the General Assembly upon the recommendation of the Speaker of the House of Representatives to a term that expires on July 1 of years that follow by one year those years that are evenly divisible by three.

(9) One member appointed by the General Assembly upon the recommendation of the Speaker of the House of Representatives to a term that expires on July 1 of years that are evenly divisible by three.

(b1) Qualifications. - The office of Trustee is declared to be an office that may be held concurrently with any other executive or appointive office, under the authority of Article VI, Section 9, of the North Carolina Constitution. When appointing members of the Authority, the Governor, the President Pro Tempore of the Senate, and the Speaker of the House of Representatives shall give consideration to adequate representation from the various regions of the State and shall give consideration to the appointment of members who are knowledgeable in any of the following areas:

(1) Acquisition and management of natural areas.

(2) Conservation and restoration of water quality.

(3) Wildlife and fisheries habitats and resources.

(4) Environmental management.

(b2) Limitation on Length of Service. - No member of the Board of Trustees shall serve more than two consecutive three-year terms or a total of 10 years.

(c) Chair. - The Governor shall appoint one member to serve as Chair of the Board of Trustees.

(d) Vacancies. - An appointment to fill a vacancy on the Board of Trustees created by the resignation, removal, disability, or death of a member shall be for the balance of the unexpired term. Vacancies in appointments made by the General Assembly shall be filled as provided in G.S. 120-122.

(e) Frequency of Meetings. - The Board of Trustees shall meet at least twice each year and may hold special meetings at the call of the Chair or a majority of the members.

(e1) Quorum. - A majority of the membership of the Board of Trustees constitutes a quorum for the transaction of business.

(f) Per Diem and Expenses. - Each member of the Board of Trustees shall receive per diem and necessary travel and subsistence expenses in accordance with the provisions of G.S. 120-3.1, 138-5, and 138-6, as applicable. Per diem, subsistence, and travel expenses of the Trustees shall be paid from the Fund.

(g) Repealed by Session Laws 2013-360, s. 14.3(e), effective August 1, 2013. (1996, 2nd Ex. Sess., c. 18, s. 27.6(a); 1997-443, s. 11A.119(a); 2001-474, s. 10; 2003-340, s. 1.3; 2003-422, s. 1; 2006-178, s. 2; 2013-360, s. 14.3(e).)

§ 113A-256. Clean Water Management Trust Fund Board of Trustees: powers and duties.

(a) Allocate Grant Funds. - The Trustees shall allocate moneys from the Fund as grants. A grant may be awarded only for a project or activity that satisfies the criteria and furthers the purposes of this Article.

(b) Develop Grant Criteria. - The Trustees shall develop criteria for awarding grants under this Article. The criteria developed shall include consideration of the following:

(1) The significant enhancement and conservation of water quality in the State.

(2) The objectives of the basinwide management plans for the State's river basins and watersheds.

(3) The promotion of regional integrated ecological networks insofar as they affect water quality.

(4) The specific areas targeted as being environmentally sensitive.

(5) The geographic distribution of funds as appropriate.

(6) The preservation of water resources with significant recreational or economic value and uses.

(7) The development of a network of riparian buffer-greenways bordering and connecting the State's waterways that will serve environmental, educational, and recreational uses.

(8) Water supply availability and the public's need for resources adequate to meet demand for essential water uses. Criteria developed pursuant to this subdivision may include consideration of the likelihood of a proposed water supply project ultimately being permitted and built.

(9) The protection or preservation of land with outstanding natural or cultural heritage values.

(10) The protection or preservation of land that contains a relatively undisturbed and outstanding example of a native North Carolina ecological community that is now uncommon; contains a major river or tributary, watershed, wetland, significant littoral, estuarine, or aquatic site, or important geologic feature; or represents a type of landscape, natural feature, or natural area that is not currently in the State's inventory of parks and natural areas.

(11) The protection or preservation of a site or structure that is of such historical significance as to be essential to the development of a balanced State program of historic properties.

(c) Develop Additional Guidelines. - The Trustees may develop guidelines in addition to the grant criteria consistent with and as necessary to implement this Article.

(d) Acquisition of Land. - The Trustees may acquire land by purchase, negotiation, gift, or devise. Any acquisition of land by the Trustees must be reviewed and approved by the Council of State and the deed for the land subject to approval of the Attorney General before the acquisition can become effective. In determining whether to acquire land as permitted by this Article, the Trustees shall consider whether the acquisition furthers the purposes of this Article and may also consider recommendations from the Council. Nothing in this section shall allow the Trustees to acquire land under the right of eminent domain.

(e)   Exchange of Land. - The Trustees may exchange any land they acquire in carrying out the powers conferred on the Trustees by this Article.

(f)   Land Management. - The Trustees may designate managers or managing agencies of the lands acquired under this Article.

(g)   Repealed by Session Laws 2013-414, s. 58(b), effective January 1, 2014.

(h)   Rule-making Authority. - The Trustees may adopt rules to implement this Article. Chapter 150B of the General Statutes applies to the adoption of rules by the Trustees.

(i)   Repealed by Session Laws 1999-237, s. 15.11, effective July 1, 1999.

(j)   Repealed by Session Laws 2013-360, s. 14.3(f), effective August 1, 2013. (1996, 2nd Ex. Sess., c. 18, s. 27.6(a), (c); 1999-237, s. 15.11; 2003-340, s. 1.3; 2004-179, s. 4.5; 2011-374, s. 2.4; 2013-360, s. 14.3(f); 2013-414, s. 58(b).)

§ 113A-257. Clean Water Management Trust Fund: reporting requirement.

The Chair of the Board of Trustees shall report each year by 1 December to the Joint Legislative Commission on Governmental Operations, the Environmental Review Commission, the Subcommittees on Natural and Economic Resources of the House of Representatives and Senate Appropriations Committees, and the Fiscal Research Division of the General Assembly regarding the implementation of this Article. The report shall include a list of the projects awarded grants from the Fund for the previous 12-month period. The list shall include for each project a description of the project, the amount of the grant awarded for the project, and the total cost of the project. (1997-443, s. 7.10; 2002-148, s. 3; 2003-340, s. 1.3.)

§ 113A-258. Clean Water Management Trust Fund: Executive Director and staff.

The Secretary of Environment and Natural Resources shall select and appoint a competent person in accordance with this section as Executive Director of the Clean Water Management Trust Fund Board of Trustees. The Executive Director shall be charged with the supervision of all activities under the jurisdiction of the Trustees and shall serve as the chief administrative officer of the Trustees. Subject to the approval of the Secretary of Environment and Natural Resources, the Executive Director may employ such clerical and other assistants as may be deemed necessary.

The person selected as Executive Director shall have had training and experience in conservation, protection, and management of surface water resources. The salary of the Executive Director shall be fixed by the Secretary of Environment and Natural Resources, and the Executive Director shall be allowed travel and subsistence expenses in accordance with G.S. 138-6. The Executive Director's salary and expenses shall be paid from the Fund. The term of office of the Executive Director shall be at the pleasure of the Secretary of Environment and Natural Resources.

These employees shall be exempt from the North Carolina Human Resources Act, as provided in G.S. 126-5(c1). (1996, 2nd Ex. Sess., c. 18, s. 27.6(a); 2001-424, s. 32.16(b); 2003-340, s. 1.3; 2013-360, s. 14.3(g); 2013-382, s. 9.1(c).)

§ 113A-259. Clean Water Management Trust Fund: Advisory Council.

There is established the Clean Water Management Trust Fund Advisory Council. The Council shall advise the Trustees with regard to allocations made from the Fund, and other issues as requested by the Trustees. The Council shall be composed of the following or its designees:

(1) Commissioner of Agriculture.

(2) Chair of the Wildlife Resources Commission.

(3) Secretary of Environment and Natural Resources.

(4) Secretary of the Department of Commerce. (1996, 2nd Ex. Sess., c. 18, s. 27.6(a); 1997-443, s. 11A.119(a); 2001-474, s. 11; 2003-340, s. 1.3.)

Chapter 113B.

North Carolina Energy Policy Act of 1975.

Article 1.

Energy Policy Council.

§ 113B-1. Legislative findings and purpose.

Upon investigation the General Assembly hereby finds that:

(1) Energy is essential to the health, safety and welfare of the people of this State and to the workings of the State economy. It is in the State's best interest to support the development of a reliable and adequate supply of energy for North Carolina that is secure, stable, and predictable in order to facilitate economic growth, job creation, and expansion of business and industry opportunities.

(2), (3) Repealed by Session Laws 2013-365, s. 8(a), effective July 29, 2013.

(3a) It is in the State's best interest to support the exploration, development, and production of domestic energy supplies, preferably from the resources within the State or region and most certainly from within the country.

(3b) It is the duty of State government to protect and preserve the State's natural resources, cultural heritage, and quality of life and, above all, the public health and safety of its residents during the exploration, development, and production of domestic energy resources.

(4) The State must provide the basis for development of a long-range unified energy policy to encompass comprehensive energy resource planning and efficient management of existing energy resources in relation to economic growth, to effectively meet an energy crisis, to encourage development of alternative sources of energy that are capable of achieving a positive benefit-to-cost ratio, and to ensure efficient utilization of energy resources in a manner consistent with assuring a reliable and adequate supply of energy for North Carolina, including active support and collaboration with the federal government to ensure access to the nation's energy resources located on the outer continental shelf directly adjacent to the State's coastal waters.

(5) It is the expressed intent of this Chapter to provide for development of such a unified domestic energy policy for the State of North Carolina as part of a nationwide effort for increased domestic energy production in the interest of national security and economic growth and stability. (1975, c. 877, s. 3; 2013-365, s. 8(a).)

§ 113B-2. Creation of Energy Policy Council; purpose of Council.

(a) The Energy Policy Council is created to advise and make recommendations on increasing domestic energy exploration, development, and production within the State and region to promote economic growth and job creation to the Governor and the General Assembly. The Energy Policy Council shall be located within the Department of Environment and Natural Resources.

(b) Except as otherwise provided in this Chapter, the powers, duties and functions of the Energy Policy Council shall be as prescribed by the Secretary of Environment and Natural Resources.

(c) The Energy Policy Council shall serve as the central energy policy planning body of the State and shall communicate and cooperate with federal, State, regional and local bodies and agencies to the end of effecting a coordinated energy policy. (1975, c. 877, s. 4; 1977, c. 23, ss. 1, 2; 2000-140, s. 76(a); 2009-446, s. 3; 2013-360, s. 15.22(l); 2013-365, s. 8(b).)

§ 113B-3. Composition of Council; appointments; terms of members; qualifications.

(a) The Energy Policy Council shall consist of 13 members to be appointed as follows:

(1), (2) Repealed by Session Laws 2013-365, s. 8(c), effective July 29, 2013.

(2a) The Secretary of Environment and Natural Resources.

(2b) The Secretary of Commerce.

(2c) The Lieutenant Governor.

(3) Ten public members who are citizens of the State of North Carolina and who are appointed in accordance with subsection (c) of this section.

(4) Repealed by Session Laws 2009-446, s. 4, effective August 7, 2009.

(b) Appointments to the Energy Policy Council shall be made by October 1, 2013. The terms of office of members of the Council are three years. The terms of members appointed under subdivisions (1), (4), and (6) of subsection (c) of this section shall expire on June 30 of years evenly divisible by three. The terms of members appointed under subdivisions (2), (5), (8), and (10) of subsection (c) of this section shall expire on June 30 of years that precede by one year those years that are evenly divisible by three. The terms of members appointed under subdivisions (3), (7), (11), and (12) of subsection (c) of this section shall expire on June 30 of years that follow by one year those years that are evenly divisible by three. Appointments made by the President Pro Tempore of the Senate and the Speaker of the House of Representatives shall be allowed when the General Assembly is not in session.

(c) The public members of the Energy Policy Council shall have the qualifications and shall be appointed as follows:

(1) Repealed by Session Laws 2013-365, s. 8(c), effective July 29, 2013.

(2) One member shall have experience in natural gas and associated hydrocarbon exploration, development, and production, to be appointed by the Governor.

(2a) Repealed by Session Laws 2013-365, s. 8(c), effective July 29, 2013.

(3) One member shall be a representative of an investor-owned natural gas public utility, to be appointed by the Speaker of the House of Representatives.

(4) One member shall be an energy economist or a person with experience in the financing or business development of an energy-related business, to be appointed by the President Pro Tempore of the Senate.

(5) One member shall have experience in energy policy, to be appointed by the President Pro Tempore of the Senate.

(6)   One member shall be an industrial energy consumer, to be appointed by the Speaker of the House of Representatives.

(7)   One member shall be knowledgeable of alternative and renewable sources of energy, to be appointed by the Governor.

(8)   One member shall have experience in trucking, rail, or shipping transportation, to be appointed by the Speaker of the House of Representatives.

(9)   Repealed by Session Laws 2009-446, s. 4, effective August 7, 2009.

(10)   One member shall have experience in energy research and development, to be appointed by the President Pro Tempore of the Senate.

(11)   One member shall have experience in environmental management, to be appointed by the Speaker of the House of Representatives.

(12)   One member shall be a representative of an investor-owned electric public utility, to be appointed by the President Pro Tempore of the Senate. (1975, c. 877, s. 4; 1977, c. 23, ss. 1, 5; c. 771, s. 4; 1979, c. 422; 1981, c. 701, ss. 4, 5; 1989, c. 727, s. 218(80); c. 751, s. 8(15); 1989 (Reg. Sess., 1990), c. 1004, s. 19(b); 1991, c. 739, s. 10; 1991 (Reg. Sess., 1992), c. 959, s. 27; 1997-443, s. 11A.119(a); 2009-446, s. 4; 2013-365, s. 8(c).)

§ 113B-4. Chairman of Council; replacement; reimbursement of members.

(a)   The Lieutenant Governor shall serve as chair of the Council.

(b)   In case of a vacancy in the membership on the Energy Policy Council prior to the expiration of a member's term, a successor shall be appointed within 30 days of such vacancy for the remainder of the unexpired term by the appropriate official pursuant to the provisions of G.S. 113B-3.

(c)   Members of the Energy Policy Council shall be reimbursed for their services pursuant to the provisions of G.S. 138-5. (1975, c. 877, s. 4; 1979, c. 514, s. 1; 2009-446, s. 5; 2013-365, s. 8(d).)

§ 113B-5. Organization of the Council; adoption of rules of procedure therefor.

(a) To facilitate the work of the Energy Policy Council and for administrative purposes, the chairman of the Energy Policy Council, with the consent and approval of the members, may organize the work of the Council so as to carry out the provisions of this Chapter and to insure the efficient operation of the Council.

(b) The Energy Policy Council shall adopt its own rules of procedure and shall meet regularly at such times and in such places as it may deem necessary to carry out its functions.

(c) The Energy Policy Council is authorized to create such advisory committees as will be needed to assist the Council in its efforts and to assure adequate citizen-consumer input into those efforts. Members of advisory committees shall be appointed by the Council for terms not to exceed the expiration date of terms of then present public members of the Council. (1975, c. 877, s. 4.)

§ 113B-6. General duties and responsibilities.

The goal of the Energy Policy Council is to identify and utilize all domestic energy resources in order to ensure a secure, stable, and predictable energy supply and to protect the economy of the State, promote job creation, and expand business and industry opportunities while ensuring the protection and preservation of the State's natural resources, cultural heritage, and quality of life. The Energy Policy Council may delegate its duties where appropriate to the Division of Energy, Mineral, and Land Resources of the Department of Environment and Natural Resources. The Council shall provide oversight and approval to the duties delegated to the Division. The Energy Policy Council shall have the following general duties and responsibilities:

(1) To develop and recommend to the Governor and the General Assembly a comprehensive State energy policy that addresses requirements in the short term (10 years), in the midterm (25 years), and in the long term (50 years) to achieve maximum effective management and use of present and future sources of energy, such policy to include but not be limited to energy efficiency, renewable and alternative sources of energy, research and development into alternative energy technologies, and improvements to the State's energy

infrastructure and energy economy, including smart grid and domestic energy resources that shall include at least natural gas, coal, hydroelectric power, solar, wind, nuclear energy, and biomass. For utilities regulated under Chapter 62 of the General Statutes, the policy developed under this subdivision shall be consistent with the analysis and plan developed under G.S. 62-110.1(c).

(2)   To conduct an ongoing assessment of the opportunities and constraints presented by various uses of all forms of energy to facilitate the expansion of the domestic energy supply and to encourage the efficient use of all such energy forms in a manner consistent with State energy policy.

(3)   To continually review and coordinate all State government research, education and management programs relating to energy matters, to continually educate and inform the general public regarding such energy matters, and to actively engage in discussions with the federal government, its agencies, and its leaders to identify opportunities to increase domestic energy supply within North Carolina and its adjacent offshore waters.

(4)   To recommend to the Governor and to the General Assembly needed energy legislation and rule making, and to recommend for implementation such modifications of energy policy, plans, and programs as the Council considers necessary and desirable.

(5)   Repealed by Session Laws 2009-446, s. 6, effective August 7, 2009. (1975, c. 877, s. 4; 2000-140, s. 76(b); 2003-284, s. 18.3; 2009-446, s. 6; 2013-365, s. 8(e).)

§ 113B-7. Energy Efficiency Program; components.

(a)   The Energy Policy Council shall prepare a recommended Energy Efficiency Program for transmittal to the Governor, the initial plan to be completed by January 30, 1976.

(b)   The Energy Efficiency Program shall be designed to assure the public health and safety of the people of North Carolina and to consider the conservation of energy through reducing wasteful, inefficient or uneconomical uses of energy resources.

(c)   The Energy Efficiency Program may include but not be limited to the following recommendations:

(1)   Recommendations to the Building Code Council for lighting, insulation, climate control systems and other building design and construction standards which increase the efficient use of energy and are economically feasible to implement;

(2)   Recommendations to the Building Code Council for per unit energy requirement allotments based upon square footage for various classes of buildings which would reduce energy consumption, yet are both technically and economically feasible and not injurious to public health and safety;

(3)   Recommendations for minimum levels of operating efficiency for all appliances whose use requires a significant amount of energy based upon both technical and economic feasibility considerations;

(4)   Recommendations for State government purchases of supplies, vehicles and equipment and such operating practices as will make possible more efficient use of energy;

(5)   Recommendations on energy conservation policies, programs and procedures for local units of government;

(6)   Any other recommendations which the Energy Policy Council considers to be a significant part of a statewide conservation effort and which include provisions for sufficient incentives to further energy conservation;

(7)   An economic and environmental impact analysis of the recommended program.

(d)   In addition to specific conservation recommendations, the Energy Efficiency Program shall contain proposals for implementation of such recommendations as can be carried out by executive order. Upon completion of a draft recommended program, the Council shall arrange for its distribution to interested parties and shall make the program available to the public and the Council further shall set a date for public hearing on said program.

(e)   Upon completion of the Energy Efficiency Program, the Council shall transmit said program, to be known as the State Energy Efficiency Program, to the Governor for approval or disapproval. Upon approval, the Governor shall assign administrative responsibility for such implementation as can be carried out by executive order to appropriate agencies of State government, and submit to the General Assembly such proposals which require legislative action for implementation. The Governor shall have the authority to accept, administer, and enforce federal programs, program measures and permissive delegations of authority delegated to the Governor by the President of the United States, Congress, or the United States Department of Energy, on behalf of the State of North Carolina, which pertain to the conservation of energy resources.

(f)   The Governor shall transmit the approved Energy Efficiency Program to the President Pro Tempore of the Senate, to the Speaker of the House of Representatives, to the heads of all State agencies and shall further seek to publicize such plan and make it available to all units of local government and to the public at large.

(g)   At least every five years and whenever such changes take place as would significantly affect energy supply or demand in North Carolina, the Energy Policy Council shall review and, if necessary, revise the Energy Efficiency Program, transmitting such revised plan to the Governor pursuant to the procedures contained in subsections (e) and (f) of this section. (1975, c. 877, s. 4; 1981, c. 701, s. 1; 2000-140, s. 76(c); 2013-365, s. 8(f).)

§ 113B-8. Energy Management Plan; components.

(a)   The Energy Policy Council shall prepare a recommended Energy Management Plan for transmittal to the Governor, the initial plan to be completed by June 30, 1976.

(b)   The Energy Management Plan shall be designed to encourage the most efficient use of all sources of energy available to meet the needs of the State and to avoid undue dependence upon relatively limited, unreliable or uneconomical sources of energy.

(c)   The Energy Management Plan shall include but not be limited to the following:

(1)   An analysis of the current pattern of consumption of energy throughout the State by category of energy user and by sources of energy supply;

(2) An assessment of the effect of demand and supply of different forms of energy upon the current pattern of consumption;

(3) An independent analysis, in five-, 10-and 20-year forecasts, of future energy production, supplies and consumption for North Carolina in relation to forecasts of statewide population growth and economic expansion;

(4) An analysis of the anticipated effects of recommended conservation measures upon the consumption of energy in the State;

(5) An assessment of the possible effects of national energy and economic policy and international economic and political conditions upon an adequate and reliable supply of different forms of energy for North Carolina;

(6) An assessment of the social, economic and environmental effects of alternative future consumption patterns on energy usage in North Carolina, including the potentially disruptive effects of supply limitations;

(7) Recommendations on the use of different future energy sources that seem most appropriate and feasible for North Carolina in meeting expected energy needs during the next five-, 10-and 20-year periods, with consideration given to growth trends in North Carolina industry and possible adverse economic impact on such trends.

(d) In addition to the above, the Energy Management Plan shall contain proposals for the implementation of such recommendations as can be carried out by executive order. Upon completion of a draft recommended plan, the Council shall arrange for its distribution to interested parties and shall make such plan available to the public and the Council further shall set a date for public hearing on said plan.

(e) Upon completion of the Energy Management Plan, the Council and the Governor shall follow the procedures as outlined in G.S. 113B-7(e) and (f).

(f) The Council shall update such plan upon a finding by it that an update is justified and shall follow the procedures for adoption pursuant to G.S. 113B-7(e) and (f).

(g) The Governor shall have the authority to accept, administer and enforce federal programs, program measures, and permissive delegations of authority delegated to the Governor by the President of the United States, Congress, or the United States Department of Energy, on behalf of the State of North Carolina, which pertain to management of energy resources.

(h) The Governor shall have the authority to accept, administer and enforce the delegation of authority delegated to the State by the Emergency Petroleum Allocation Act and the Emergency Energy Conservation Act of 1979 and any orders, rules, and regulations issued pursuant to those acts as well as any succeeding federal programs, program measures, laws, orders, or regulations relating to the allocation, conservation, consumption, management or rationing of energy resources. (1975, c. 877, s. 4; 1981, c. 701, s. 2.)

§ 113B-9. Emergency Energy Program; components.

(a) The Energy Policy Council shall, in accordance with the provisions of this Article, develop contingency and emergency plans to deal with possible shortages of energy to protect public health, safety and welfare, such plans to be compiled into an Emergency Energy Program.

(b) If required for an update of the program provided under subsection (j) of this section:

(1) Each electric utility and natural gas utility in the State shall prepare and submit to the Energy Policy Council a proposed emergency curtailment plan setting forth proposals for identifying priority loads or users in the event of the declaration of an energy crisis pursuant to G.S. 113B-20, and proposals for supply allocation to such priority loads or users. Utilities regulated under Chapter 62 of the General Statutes may satisfy this requirement by submitting the General Load Reduction and System Restoration Plan that is prepared annually for the Utilities Commission.

(2) Each major oil producer doing business in this State as determined by the Energy Policy Council shall prepare and submit to the Energy Policy Council an analysis of how any national supply curtailment pursuant to federal regulations shall affect the supply for North Carolina and how priority users will be determined and available supplies allocated to such users.

(c) The Energy Policy Council shall encourage the preparation of joint emergency curtailment plans and analyses. If such cooperative plans and analyses are developed between two or more utilities, major producers or by an association of such companies, the joint plans or analyses may be submitted to the Energy Policy Council in lieu of information required pursuant to subsection (b) of this section.

(d)   The Energy Policy Council shall collect from all relevant governmental agencies any existing contingency plans for dealing with sudden energy shortages or information related thereto.

(e)   The Energy Policy Council shall hold one or more public hearings, investigate and review the plans submitted pursuant to this section, and, within nine months after July 1, 1975, the Energy Policy Council shall approve and recommend to the Governor guidelines for emergency curtailment to be known as the Emergency Energy Program and to be implemented upon adoption by the Governor after the declaration of an energy crisis and pursuant to G.S. 113B-20 and 113B-23. Said program shall be based upon the plans presented to the Energy Policy Council, upon independent analysis and study by the Council, and upon information provided at the hearing or hearings, provided, however, that they are consistent with such federal programs and regulations as are already in effect at that time.

(f)   The Emergency Energy Program shall provide for the maintenance of essential services, the protection of public health, safety, and welfare, and the maintenance of a sound basic State economy. For utilities regulated under Chapter 62 of the General Statutes, the program shall be consistent with the General Load Reduction and System Restoration Plan that is prepared annually for the Utilities Commission. Provisions also shall be made in said program to differentiate curtailment of energy consumption by users on the basis of ability to accommodate such curtailments, and shall also include, but not be limited to, the following:

(1)   A variety of strategies and staged conservation measures of increasing intensity and authority to reduce energy use during an energy crisis, as defined in G.S. 113B-20 and guidelines and criteria for allocation of energy sources to priority users. The program shall contain alternative conservation actions and allocation plans to reasonably meet various foreseeable shortage circumstances and to allow a choice of appropriate responses;

(2)   Evidence that the program is consistent with requirements of federal emergency energy conservation and allocation laws and regulations;

(3)   Proposals to assist such individuals, institutions, agriculture and businesses which have engaged in energy saving measures;

(g)   The Energy Policy Council shall carry out such investigations and studies as are necessary to determine if and when potentially serious shortages of energy are likely to affect North Carolina and the Council shall make recommendations to the Governor concerning administrative and legislative actions required to avert such shortages, such recommendations to be included as a section of the Emergency Energy Program.

(h)   In addition to the above information and recommendations, the program shall contain proposals for implementation of such recommendations which include procedures, rules and regulations and agency administrative responsibilities for implementation, and shall further contain procedures for fair and equitable review of complaints and requests for special exemptions from emergency conservation measures or emergency allocations. Upon completion of a draft recommended plan, the Council shall arrange for its distribution to interested parties and shall make such plan available to the public and the Council further shall set a date for public hearing on said plan.

(i)   Upon completion of the Emergency Energy Allocation Program, the Council and the Governor shall follow the procedures as outlined in G.S. 113B-7(e) and (f).

(j)   The Council shall update the Emergency Energy Allocation Program upon finding that an update is justified. The Council shall follow the procedures for adoption pursuant to G.S. 113B-7(e) and (f).

(k)   The Governor shall have the authority to accept, administer and enforce federal programs, program measures and permissive delegations of authority delegated to the Governor by the President of the United States, Congress, or the United States Department of Energy, on behalf of the State of North Carolina, which pertain to actions necessary to deal with an actual or impending energy shortage. (1975, c. 877, s. 4; 1979, c. 514, s. 2; 1981; c. 701, s. 3; 2013-365, s. 8(g).)

§ 113B-10: Repealed by Session Laws 2009-446, s. 7, effective August 7, 2009.

§ 113B-11. Powers and authority.

(a)   The Energy Policy Council is authorized to secure directly from any officer, office, department, commission, board, bureau, institution and other agency of the State and its political subdivisions any information it deems necessary to carry out its functions; and all such officers and agencies shall cooperate with the Council and, to the extent permitted by law, furnish such information to the Council as it may request.

(b)   To assure the adequate development of relevant energy information, the Council may require all energy producers and major energy consumers, as determined by the Council, to file such reports and forecasts and at such dates as the Council may request; provided, however, that the Council may request only specific energy-related information which it deems necessary to carry out its duties as defined in Articles 1 and 2 of this Chapter.

(c)   The Council shall have authority to apply for and utilize grants, contributions and appropriations in order to carry out its duties as defined in Articles 1 and 2 of this Chapter, provided, however, that all such applications and requests are made through and administered by the Department of Environment and Natural Resources.

(d)   The Council shall have authority to request said Department to allocate and dispense any funds made available to the Council for energy research and related work efforts in such a manner as the Council desires subject only to the stipulation that said funds be reasonably used in furtherance of the purposes of this Article.

(e)   Staff support required by the Council shall be supplied by the Division of Energy, Mineral, and Land Resources of the Department of Environment and Natural Resources. The Department of Commerce and the Utilities Commission are hereby authorized to make their staff available to the Council to assist in the development of a State energy policy. (1975, c. 877, s. 4; 1977, c. 23, s. 1; 1989, c. 751, s. 7(10); 1991 (Reg. Sess., 1992), c. 959, s. 28; 2000-140, s. 76(d); 2009-446, s. 8; 2013-360, s. 15.22(m); 2013-365, s. 8(h).)

§ 113B-12. Annual reports; contents.

(a) Every two years the Energy Policy Council shall transmit to the Governor, the Speaker of the House of Representatives, the President Pro Tempore of the Senate, the Environmental Review Commission, the Joint Legislative Commission on Energy Policy, and the chairman of the Utilities Commission a comprehensive report providing a general overview of energy conditions in the State.

(b) The report shall include, but not be limited to, the following:

(1) An overview of statewide growth and development as they relate to future requirements for energy, including patterns of urban and metropolitan expansion, shifts in transportation modes, modifications in building types and design, and other trends and factors which, as determined by the Council, will significantly affect energy needs;

(2) The level of statewide and multi-county regional energy demand for a five, 10- and 20-year forecast period which, in the judgment of the Council, can reasonably be met, with proposals as to possible energy supply sources;

(3) An assessment of growth trends in energy consumption and production and an identification of potential adverse social, economic, or environmental impacts which might be imposed by continuation of the present trends, including energy costs to consumers, significant increases in air, water, and other forms of pollution, threats to public health and safety, and loss of scenic and natural areas;

(4) An analysis of the role of energy efficiency, renewable energy, improvements to the State's energy infrastructure, and other means in meeting the State's current and projected energy demand;

(5) Repealed by Session Laws 2009-446, s. 9, effective August 7, 2009.

(6) Recommendations to the Governor and the General Assembly for additional administrative and legislative actions on energy matters;

(7) A summary of the Council's activities since the last report, a description of major plans developed by the Council, an assessment of plan implementation, and a review of Council plans and programs for the coming biennium. (1975, c. 877, s. 4; 2009-446, s. 9; 2013-365, s. 8(i).)

§§ 113B-13 through 113B-19. Reserved for future codification purposes.

Article 2.

Energy Crisis Administration.

§ 113B-20. Definition; declaration of energy crisis.

(a) "Energy crisis". - An energy crisis exists when the health, welfare or safety of the citizens of North Carolina are threatened by reason of an actual or impending acute shortage in usable, necessary energy resources.

(b) Declaration by Governor. - Upon a finding by the Governor that the conditions stated in subsection (a) do exist, the Governor may declare the existence of an energy crisis. (1975, c. 877, s. 4.)

§ 113B-21. Creation of Legislative Committee on Energy Crisis Management.

(a) Upon the declaration of an energy crisis by the Governor, a Legislative Committee on Energy Crisis Management shall be created to consist of the Speaker, the Speaker Pro Tempore of the House of Representatives, the President Pro Tempore of the Senate, and the majority leader of the Senate. The Lieutenant Governor shall serve as chair and shall be a nonvoting ex officio member, provided, however, that the chair shall vote to break a tie.

(b) The Legislative Committee shall convene within 24 hours following the declaration of an energy crisis, as provided in G.S. 113B-20.

(c) Members of the Legislative Committee shall be reimbursed for their services pursuant to the provisions of G.S. 138-5. (1975, c. 877, s. 4; 1977, c. 23, s. 1; 1983 (Reg. Sess., 1984), c. 1034, s. 135; 2013-365, s. 8(j).)

§ 113B-22. Procedures for adopting emergency proposals; emergency powers.

(a) Upon the declaration of an energy crisis, the Governor shall submit to the Legislative Committee for its prompt consideration such emergency orders, rules and regulations as deemed necessary to alleviate the effects of the energy crisis.

(b) The Governor shall immediately consult with the Legislative Committee about the emergency proposals. The emergency orders, rules, or regulations shall become effective at a time specified by the Governor, but no earlier than 48 hours after submission to the Legislative Committee, provided that they may take effect at an earlier time if approved by a majority vote of the Council of State after the Council makes a finding that the crisis is of such immediacy as to make delay for legislative review cause for probable harm to the public.

(c) No order, rule, or regulation promulgated under the provisions of this section shall remain in effect for more than 30 days unless the Governor consults with the Legislative Committee. Such consultation is separate and apart from the consultation required by subsection (a) of this section, and may not take place until the order, rule, or regulation has been in effect for at least seven days.

(d) The Governor's orders, rules and regulations, promulgated, subject to consultation with the Legislative Committee, pursuant to this section, may also include, by way of further enumerated example rather than limitation, provisions for the establishment and implementation of programs, controls, standards, priorities, and quotas for the allocation, conservation and consumption of energy resources; the suspension and modification of existing standards and requirements affecting or affected by the use of energy resources, including those relating to air quality control and the hours and days during which public buildings may or may not be required to remain open; and the establishment and implementation of regional programs and agreements for the purposes of coordinating the energy resource programs and actions of the State with those of the federal government and of other states and localities. (1975, c. 877, s. 4; 1983 (Reg. Sess., 1984), c. 1034, ss. 136, 137.)

§ 113B-23. Administration of plans and procedures.

(a) Upon the declaration of an energy crisis, pursuant to G.S. 113B-20, the Energy Policy Council shall become the emergency energy coordinating body for the State and shall carry out the following duties:

(1) Identify and determine the nature and severity of expected energy shortages;

(2) Provide for daily communications with and gather information from significant energy producers, distributors, transporters and major consumers, as determined by the Energy Policy Council, to carry out its responsibilities pursuant to this section;

(3) Provide data, carry out continuing assessments of the crisis situation, and make recommendations to the Governor and to the Legislative Committee on Energy Crisis Management for further action.

(b) Upon the declaration of an energy crisis, the Governor shall order the Energy Policy Council, the Utilities Commission, the Attorney General and other appropriate State and local agencies to implement and enforce the Emergency Energy Program pursuant to G.S. 113B-9 and any emergency rules, orders or regulations approved pursuant to G.S. 113B-22.

(c) Upon the declaration of an energy crisis, the Governor may employ such measures and give such direction to State and local offices and agencies as may be reasonable and necessary for the purpose of securing compliance with the provisions of this Article and with emergency rules, orders and regulations issued pursuant to G.S. 113B-22. (1975, c. 877, s. 4; 1983 (Reg. Sess., 1984), c. 1034, s. 138; 2013-365, s. 8(k).)

§ 113B-24. Enforcement; penalties for violations.

(a) The Attorney General and the law-enforcement authorities of the State and its political subdivisions shall enforce the provisions of this Article and all orders, rules and regulations promulgated pursuant to G.S. 113B-22.

(b) Any person who violates this Article or any rules, orders or regulations promulgated pursuant to G.S. 113B-22 or knowingly or willfully submits false information in any report required herein shall be guilty of a Class 1 misdemeanor.

(c) The provisions of this Article or any rules, orders or regulations promulgated pursuant to G.S. 113B-22 may be enforced by bringing an action to enjoin such acts or practices as may be in violation and, upon a proper showing, a temporary restraining order or a preliminary or permanent injunction shall be issued. The relief sought may include a mandatory injunction commanding any person to comply with any such order, rule or regulation and restitution of money received in violation of any such order, rule or regulation. The Attorney General shall bring any action under this subsection upon the request of the Governor, the Legislative Committee on Energy Crisis Management, the Energy Policy Council, or upon his direction if he deems such action advisable and in the public interest. The Attorney General may institute such action in the Superior Court of Wake County, or, in his discretion, in the superior court of the county in which the acts or practices constituting a violation occurred, are occurring or may occur. (1975, c. 877, s. 4; 1993, c. 539, s. 878; 1994, Ex. Sess., c. 24, s. 14(c).)

Article 3.

Revenues From Offshore Energy Production.

§ 113B-30. (Contingent effective date - see notes) Allocation of revenues from offshore energy production; creation of Offshore Energy Management Fund.

(a) Any revenues and royalties paid to the State as a result of offshore leasing, exploration, development, and production of all energy resources shall be deposited in the Offshore Emergency Fund until the Fund reaches two hundred fifty million dollars ($250,000,000). The Offshore Energy Management Fund is an interest-bearing special revenue fund to be established within the State treasury. This Fund shall be used only for emergency preparation, emergency response, emergency environmental protection, or mitigation associated with a release of liquid hydrocarbons or associated fluids directly related to offshore energy exploration, development, production, or transmission. Once the Fund balance reaches the amount of two hundred fifty million dollars ($250,000,000), the funds shall be used as provided in subsection (b) of this section. If monies are withdrawn from this Fund to carry out the provisions in this section, all revenues and royalties paid to the State as a result of offshore leasing, exploration, development, and production of all energy resources shall be deposited in the Fund until a total of two hundred fifty million dollars ($250,000,000) is reestablished. Once the Fund balance reaches the amount of two hundred fifty million dollars ($250,000,000), the funds shall be used as provided in subsection (b) of this section.

(b) Any revenues and royalties paid to the State as a result of offshore leasing, exploration, development, and production of all energy resources in excess of the amount needed to establish the Fund created in subsection (a) of this section are annually appropriated and shall be used for the following purposes:

(1) Seventy-five percent (75%) of such revenues and royalties shall be credited to the General Fund.

(2) Five percent (5%) of such revenues and royalties shall be credited to the North Carolina Highway Trust Fund established under G.S. 136-176.

(3) Five percent (5%) of such revenues and royalties shall be transferred to the Community Colleges System Office to establish and manage a fund for curriculum development and implementation as well as financial assistance for students attending community college to receive vocational training through this curriculum in fields directly related to energy exploration and development and related energy infrastructure.

(4) Five percent (5%) of such revenues and royalties shall be transferred to the Board of Governors of The University of North Carolina System to establish and manage research and development funds for programs directly related to energy research and development.

(5) Five percent (5%) of such revenues and royalties shall be transferred to the Department of Environment and Natural Resources for conservation, protection, and mitigation, including, but not limited to, beach and inlet management projects, dredging operations, channel navigation and maintenance, public beach and water access, water quality management, and habitat restoration.

(6) Three percent (3%) of such revenues and royalties shall be transferred to the State Ports Authority for expansion and maintenance of State Port infrastructure associated with energy-related commerce.

(7) Two percent (2%) of such revenues and royalties shall be transferred to the Department of Commerce for recruitment of energy-related industries to the State. (2013-365, s. 6.)

Chapter 114.

Department of Justice.

Article 1.

Attorney General.

§ 114-1. Creation of Department of Justice under supervision of Attorney General.

There is hereby created a Department of Justice which shall be under the supervision and direction of the Attorney General, as authorized by Article III, Sec. 7, of the Constitution of North Carolina. (1939, c. 315, s. 1; 1973, c. 702, s. 1.)

§ 114-1.1. Common-law powers.

The General Assembly reaffirms that the Attorney General has had and continues to be vested with those powers of the Attorney General that existed at the common law, that are not repugnant to or inconsistent with the Constitution or laws of North Carolina. (1985, c. 479, s. 137.)

§ 114-2. Duties.

It shall be the duty of the Attorney General:

(1)   To defend all actions in the appellate division in which the State shall be interested, or a party, and to appear for the State in any other court or tribunal in any cause or matter, civil or criminal, in which the State may be a party or interested.

(2)   To represent all State departments, agencies, institutions, commissions, bureaus or other organized activities of the State which receive support in whole or in part from the State.

(3)   Repealed by Session Laws 1973, c. 702, s. 2.

(4) To consult with and advise the prosecutors, when requested by them, in all matters pertaining to the duties of their office.

(5) To give, when required, his opinion upon all questions of law submitted to him by the General Assembly, or by either branch thereof, or by the Governor, Auditor, Treasurer, or any other State officer.

(6) To pay all moneys received for debts due or penalties to the State immediately after the receipt thereof into the treasury.

(7) To compare the warrants drawn on the State treasury with the laws under which they purport to be drawn.

(8) Subject to the provisions of G.S. 62-20:

a. To intervene, when he deems it to be advisable in the public interest, in proceedings before any courts, regulatory officers, agencies and bodies, both State and federal, in a representative capacity for and on behalf of the using and consuming public of this State. He shall also have the authority to institute and originate proceedings before such courts, officers, agencies or bodies and shall have authority to appear before agencies on behalf of the State and its agencies and citizens in all matters affecting the public interest.

b. Upon the institution of any proceeding before any State agency by application, petition or other pleading, formal or informal, the outcome of which will affect a substantial number of residents of North Carolina, such agency or agencies shall furnish the Attorney General with copies of all such applications, petitions and pleadings so filed, and, when the Attorney General deems it advisable in the public interest to intervene in such proceedings, he is authorized to file responsive pleadings and to appear before such agency either in a representative capacity in behalf of the using and consuming public of this State or in behalf of the State or any of its agencies. (1868-9, c. 270, s. 82; 1871-2, c. 112, s. 2; Code, s. 3363; 1893, c. 379; 1901, c. 744; Rev., s. 5380; C.S., s. 7694; 1931, c. 243, s. 5; 1933, c. 134, s. 8; 1941, c. 97; 1967, c. 691, s. 51; 1969, c. 535; 1973, c. 702, s. 2; 1977, c. 468, s. 17; 1979, c. 107, s. 9; 1983, c. 913, s. 15.)

§ 114-2.1. Consent judgments.

In litigation in which the State is interested or is a party, no consent judgment shall be entered into by the State unless and no consent judgment shall be binding on the State except to the extent that the State's entire obligation for the current and for future fiscal years will be satisfied with funds that are available for that purpose for the current fiscal year, including funds that the Council of State agrees to allot from the Contingency and Emergency Fund, provided that for payments of tort claims and workers' compensation claims it shall not be binding on the State except to the extent that the State's entire obligation for the current and for future fiscal years can be satisfied with funds that are available for the current fiscal year, including funds that the Council of State agrees to allot from the Contingency and Emergency Fund. The Director of the Budget shall report to the appropriation committees of the General Assembly concerning all funds made available during the preceding fiscal year from the Contingency and Emergency Fund for the purpose of carrying out consent judgments. (1981 (Reg. Sess., 1982), c. 1282, s. 51; 1983 (Reg. Sess., 1984), c. 1034, s. 95; c. 1116, s. 85.)

§ 114-2.2. Attorney General to approve consent judgments.

(a)   To be effective against the State, a consent judgment entered into by the State, a State department, State agency, State institution, or a State officer who is a party in his official capacity must be signed personally by the Attorney General. This power of approval may not be delegated to a deputy or assistant Attorney General or to any other subordinate.

(b)   The provisions of this section are supplemental to G.S. 114-2.1.

(c)   Notwithstanding subsection (a) of this section, the Attorney General by rule may delegate to a deputy or assistant Attorney General or to another subordinate the power to sign consent judgments in condemnation or eminent domain actions brought under the provisions of Chapters 40A or 136 of the General Statutes and consent judgments under the provision of Article 31 of Chapter 143 (Tort Claims Act) and Chapter 97 (Workers' Compensation Act) of the General Statutes. (1983 (Reg. Sess., 1984), c. 1034, s. 95; c. 1116, s. 85.)

§ 114-2.3. Use of private counsel limited.

Every agency, institution, department, bureau, board, or commission of the State, authorized by law to retain private counsel, shall obtain written permission from the Attorney General prior to employing private counsel. This section does not apply to counties, cities, towns, other municipal corporations or political subdivisions of the State, or any agencies of these municipal corporations or political subdivisions, or to county or city boards of education. (1985, c. 479, s. 135.)

§ 114-2.4. Attorney General to render opinion on settlement agreements.

(a) The Attorney General shall review the terms of all proposed agreements entered into by the State or a State department, agency, institution, or officer to settle or resolve litigation or potential litigation, that involves the payment of public monies in the sum of seventy-five thousand dollars ($75,000) or more. In order for such an agreement or contract to be effective against the State, the Attorney General shall submit to the State or the State department, agency, institution, or officer a written opinion regarding the terms of the proposed agreement and the advisability of entering into the agreement, prior to entering into the agreement. The written opinion required by this section shall be maintained in the official file of the final settlement agreement. The Attorney General by rule may delegate to a deputy or assistant Attorney General or to another subordinate the authority to approve settlement agreements.

(b) The Attorney General shall report to the Joint Legislative Commission on Governmental Operations on all agreements entered into by the State or a State department, agency, institution, or officer to settle or resolve litigation or potential litigation, that involves the payment of public monies in the sum of seventy-five thousand dollars ($75,000) or more. (1997-443, s. 20.14(a).)

§ 114-2.5. Attorney General to report payment of public monies pursuant to settlement agreements and final court orders.

(a) Not less than 30 days prior to the disbursement of funds received by the State or a State agency pursuant to a settlement agreement or final order or judgment of the court where the amount of funds received exceeds seventy-five thousand dollars ($75,000), the Attorney General shall file a written report with the Joint Legislative Commission on Governmental Operations and the Chairs of the Appropriations Subcommittees on Justice and Public Safety of the Senate and House of Representatives on the payments received by the State or a State agency. The Attorney General shall also report on the terms or conditions of payment and of any disbursements set forth in the agreement or order. The Attorney General shall submit a written report to the Fiscal Research Division of the General Assembly.

(b) This section only applies to executed settlement agreements and final orders or judgments of the court and shall in no way affect the authority of the Attorney General to negotiate the settlement of cases in which the State or a State department, agency, institution, or officer is a party. (1998-212, s. 18.7(b); 1999-237, s. 19(b).)

§ 114-2.5A. Report by the Medicaid Fraud Control Unit required annually.

By September 1 of each year, the Medicaid Fraud Control Unit of the Department of Justice shall file a written report about its activities with the Chairs of the Appropriations Subcommittees on Justice and Public Safety and Health and Human Services of the Senate and House of Representatives and with the Fiscal Research Division of the Legislative Services Office. This report may be combined with the report required by G.S. 1-617 and shall include the following information about the Unit's activities during the previous fiscal year:

(1) The number of matters reported to the Unit.

(2) The number of cases investigated.

(3) The number of criminal convictions and civil settlements.

(4) The total amount of funds recovered in each case.

(5) The allocation of recovered funds in each case to (i) the federal government; (ii) the State Medical Assistance Program; (iii) the Civil Penalty and Forfeiture Fund; (iv) the Department of Justice; and (v) other victims. (2010-31, s. 16.1.)

§ 114-2.6. Attorney General to report on pending lawsuits in which State is a party.

By April 1 and October 1 of each year, the Attorney General shall submit a report to the Chairs of the Joint Legislative Commission on Governmental Operations, the Chairs of the Appropriations Committees of the Senate and House of Representatives, the Chairs of the Finance Committees of the Senate and House of Representatives, and the Fiscal Research Division of the Legislative Services Office on any lawsuit in which the constitutionality of a North Carolina law has been challenged and on any case in which plaintiffs seek in excess of one million dollars ($1,000,000) in damages. In addition, the Attorney General shall submit a written report to the Joint Legislative Commission on Governmental Operations, the Chairs of the Appropriations Committees of the Senate and House of Representatives, the Chairs of the Finance Committees of the Senate and House of Representatives, and the Fiscal Research Division of the Legislative Services Office within 30 days of a final judgment that orders the State to pay the sum of one million dollars ($1,000,000) or more. (2001-424, s. 23.11(a).)

§ 114-2.7. Reporting system and database on certain domestic-violence-related homicides; reports by law enforcement agencies required; annual report to the General Assembly.

The Attorney General's Office, in consultation with the North Carolina Council for Women/Domestic Violence Commission, the North Carolina Sheriffs' Association, and the North Carolina Association of Chiefs of Police, shall develop a reporting system and database that reflects the number of homicides in the State where the offender and the victim had a personal relationship, as defined by G.S. 50B-1(b). The information in the database shall also include the type of personal relationship that existed between the offender and the victim, whether the victim had obtained an order pursuant to G.S. 50B-3, and whether there was a pending charge for which the offender was on pretrial release pursuant to G.S. 15A-534.1. All State and local law enforcement agencies shall report information to the Attorney General's Office upon making a determination that a homicide meets the reporting system's criteria. The report shall be made in the format adopted by the Attorney General's Office. The Attorney General's Office shall report to the Joint Legislative Committee on Domestic Violence, no later than February 1 of each year, with the data collected for the previous calendar year. (2007-14, s. 2.)

§ 114-3. To devote whole time to duties.

The Attorney General shall devote his whole time to the duties of the office and shall not engage in the private practice of law. (1929, c. 1, s. 1.)

§ 114-4. Assistants; compensation; assignments.

The Attorney General shall be allowed to appoint from among his staff such number of assistant attorneys general as he shall deem advisable, and each of such assistant attorneys general shall be subject to all of the provisions of Chapter 126 of the General Statutes relating to the State Personnel System. Two assistant attorneys general shall be assigned to the State Department of Revenue. The other assistant attorneys general shall perform such duties as may be assigned by the Attorney General: Provided, however, the provisions of this section shall not be construed as preventing the Attorney General from assigning additional duties to the assistant attorneys general assigned to the State Department of Revenue. (1925, c. 207, s. 1; 1937, c. 357; 1945, c. 786; 1947, c. 182; 1967, c. 260, s. 1; 1973, c. 702, s. 3.)

§ 114-4.1. Repealed by Session Laws 1973, c. 702, s. 4.

§ 114-4.2. Assistant attorneys general and other attorneys to assist Department of Transportation.

The Attorney General is authorized to appoint from among his staff such assistant attorneys general and such other staff attorneys as he shall deem advisable to provide all legal assistance for the State highway functions of the Department of Transportation, and such assistant attorneys general and other attorneys shall also perform such additional duties as may be assigned to them by the Attorney General, and shall otherwise be subject to all provisions of the statutes relating to assistant attorneys general and other staff attorneys. There shall be appropriated from the State Highway Fund such sum as may be necessary to pay the salaries of said assistant attorneys general and other attorneys and necessary secretaries. The Department of Transportation shall provide adequate office space, equipment and supplies. (1957, c. 65, s. 9; 1965, c. 55, s. 16; c. 408, s. 1; 1973, c. 702, s. 5; 1975, c. 716, s. 7; 1977, c. 464, s. 36.)

§ 114-4.2A. Assistant attorney general assigned to State Insurance Department.

Such assistant attorneys general as are assigned to the Commissioner of Insurance and the State Insurance Department by the Attorney General shall perform such additional duties as may be assigned to them by the Attorney General, and shall otherwise be subject to all provisions of the statutes relating to assistant attorneys general. (1967, c. 1115, s. 1; 1973, c. 702, s. 6.)

§ 114-4.2B. Employment of attorney for University of North Carolina Hospitals at Chapel Hill.

The Attorney General is hereby authorized to employ an attorney to be assigned by him full time to the University of North Carolina Hospitals at Chapel Hill. Such attorney shall be subject to all the provisions of Chapter 126 of the General Statutes, relating to the State Personnel System. Such attorney shall also perform additional duties as may be assigned to him by the Attorney General.

The attorney employed by the Attorney General under provisions of this section shall be paid from the funds of the University of North Carolina Hospitals at Chapel Hill. (1975, c. 526, s. 1; 1989, c. 141, s. 3.)

§ 114-4.2C. Employment of attorney for the Real Estate Commission.

The Attorney General is hereby authorized to employ an attorney and assign him full time to the North Carolina Real Estate Commission. Such attorney shall be subject to all the provisions of Chapter 126 of the General Statutes relating to the State Personnel System. Such attorney shall also perform such additional duties as may be assigned to him by the Attorney General.

The North Carolina Real Estate Commission shall fully reimburse the North Carolina Department of Justice for the compensation of such attorney employed under the provisions of this section. (1975, c. 835, ss. 1, 2; 1983, c. 81, s. 1.)

§ 114-4.2D. Employment of attorney for Energy Policy Council of the Department of Environment and Natural Resources and the Energy Efficiency Program of the Department of Commerce.

The Attorney General shall assign an attorney to work full time with the Energy Policy Council of the Department of Environment and Natural Resources and the Energy Efficiency Program of the Department of Commerce. Such attorney shall be subject to all provisions of Chapter 126 of the General Statutes relating to the State Personnel System. Such attorney shall also perform such additional duties as may be assigned by the Attorney General. (1979, c. 942; 1989, c. 751, s. 7(11); 1991 (Reg. Sess., 1992), c. 959, s. 29; 2000-140, s. 76(e); 2010-142, s. 7; 2013-365, s. 8(l).)

§ 114-4.2E. Repealed by Session Laws 1981, c. 859, s. 13.10, effective July 1, 1981.

§ 114-4.2F. Designation of attorney specializing in the law of the handicapped.

The Attorney General is authorized to designate from his staff an attorney to specialize in the law of the handicapped. The attorney so designated shall act as advisor to the Division of Vocational Rehabilitation, the Division of Services for the Deaf and the Hard of Hearing, the North Carolina School for the Deaf and the Governor Morehead School. (1983, c. 850, s. 1; 1989, c. 533, s. 7.)

§ 114-4.2G: Repealed by Session Laws 2002-168, s. 6, effective October 1, 2002.

§ 114-4.3. Repealed by Session Laws 1973, c. 702, s. 7.

§ 114-4.4. Deputy attorneys general.

The Attorney General is hereby authorized to designate from among his staff such deputy attorneys general as he shall deem advisable to perform such duties and undertake such responsibilities as he may direct. (1963, c. 355; 1973, c. 702, s. 8.)

§ 114-5. Additional clerical help.

The Attorney General shall be allowed such additional clerical help as shall be necessary; the amount of such help and the salary therefor shall be fixed by the Department of Administration and the Attorney General. (1925, c. 207, s. 2; 1957, c. 269, s. 1.)

§ 114-6. Duties of Attorney General as to civil litigation.

The Attorney General shall continue to perform all duties now required of his office by law and to exercise the duties now prescribed by law as to civil litigation affecting the State, or any agency or department thereof, and shall assign to the members of the staff all duties to be performed in connection with criminal prosecutions and civil litigation authorized by this Article or by existing laws. (1939, c. 315, ss. 7, 8.)

§ 114-6.1. Biannual reporting on attorney activity.

Beginning on February 1, 2013, and every six months thereafter, the Attorney General shall report on the work of Department of Justice attorneys during the previous two quarters. The reports required by this section shall be filed with the Chairs of the House and Senate Appropriations Subcommittees on Justice and Public Safety and with the Fiscal Research Division of the General Assembly as follows:

(1) Agency-specific work. - A report on the work of Department of Justice attorneys for State agencies. This report shall include at least all of the following information:

a. The amount of time spent working for each State department and agency.

b. The amount of time spent on each case for each State department and agency.

c. The amount billed to each State agency for the legal services provided.

(2) Other work. - A report on the work of Department of Justice attorneys that is not on behalf of a particular State agency. The report required by this subdivision shall include all of the information required by subdivision (1) of this section. The report shall include at least all of the following information:

a. The amount of time spent by each unit of the Department of Justice.

b. The amount of time spent on each particular matter for each unit of the Department of Justice. (2012-142, s. 15.2)

§ 114-7. Salary of the Attorney General.

The salary of the Attorney General shall be set by the General Assembly in the Current Operations Appropriations Act. In addition to the salary set by the General Assembly in the Current Operations Appropriations Act, longevity pay shall be paid on the same basis as is provided to employees of the State who are subject to the North Carolina Human Resources Act. (1929, c. 1, s. 2; 1947, c. 1043; 1949, c. 1278; 1953, c. 1, s. 2; 1957, c. 1; 1963, c. 1178, s. 3; 1967, c. 1130; c. 1237, s. 3; 1969, c. 1214, s. 3; 1971, c. 912, s. 3; 1973, c. 778, s. 3; 1975, 2nd Sess., c. 983, s. 18; 1977, c. 802, s. 42.14; 1983, c. 761, s. 209; 1983 (Reg. Sess., 1984), c. 1034, s. 164; 1987, c. 738, s. 32(b); 2013-382, s. 9.1(c).)

§ 114-8. Repealed by Session Laws 1969, c. 44, s. 89.

§ 114-8.1. Attorney General interns.

The Attorney General may select interns to work in the Attorney General's Office from institutions of higher education, including the constituent institutions of The University of North Carolina. The Attorney General may adopt policies or rules to provide for the selection, tenure, duties, and compensation of these interns. (1985, c. 479, s. 140.)

§ 114-8.2. Charges for legal services.

The Department of Justice shall charge State boards and commissions that are totally supported by receipts from fees or surcharges for legal services rendered by the Department to the board or commission. Client State departments, agencies, boards, and commissions shall reimburse the Department of Justice for reasonable court fees, attorney travel and subsistence costs, and other costs directly related to litigation in which the Department of Justice is representing the department, agency, or board. (1989, c. 500, s. 60; 2011-145, s. 16.4.)

§ 114-8.3. Attorney General/General Counsel; review certain contracts.

(a) Except as provided in subsections (b) and (b1) of this section, the Attorney General or the Attorney General's designee shall perform the duties required pursuant to G.S. 143-49(3a) for proposed contracts for contractual services that exceed five million dollars ($5,000,000). The designee shall confirm that the proposed contracts are (i) in proper legal form, (ii) contain all clauses required by North Carolina law, (iii) are legally enforceable, and (iv) accomplish the intended purposes of the proposed contract. The designee's review does not constitute approval or disapproval of the policy merit or lack thereof of the proposed contract. For purposes of this subsection, the term "Attorney General's designee" includes any attorney approved by the Attorney General to review contracts as provided in this subsection. The Attorney General shall:

(1) Establish procedures regarding the review of contracts subject to this section and shall provide any attorney designated under G.S. 143-49(3a) with guidelines to be used in reviewing contracts.

(2) Advise and assist the Contract Management Section of the Division of Purchase and Contract, Department of Administration, in establishing procedures and guidelines for the review of contracts pursuant to G.S. 143-50.1.

(b) For the constituent institutions of The University of North Carolina, the General Counsel of each institution or the General Counsel's designee shall review all proposed contracts for supplies, materials, printing, equipment, and contractual services that exceed one million dollars ($1,000,000) to ensure that the proposed contracts are (i) in proper legal form, (ii) contain all clauses required by North Carolina law, (iii) are legally enforceable, and (iv) accomplish the intended purposes of the proposed contract. The term "review" as used in this section does not constitute approval or disapproval of the policy merit or lack thereof of the proposed contract. For purposes of this subsection, the term "General Counsel's designee" includes any attorney approved by the General Counsel to review contracts as provided in this subsection. The General Counsel shall establish procedures regarding the review of contracts subject to this section and shall require that any attorney designated under this subsection comply with any procedures established by the Attorney General or the Department of Administration regarding the review of contracts.

(b1) The General Counsel of the Department of State Treasurer or the General Counsel's designee shall review all proposed investment contracts, as defined in subdivision (4) of this subsection, and all proposed contracts for investment-related services entered pursuant to the State Treasurer's authority under G.S. 147-69.3 not constituting consulting contracts, to confirm that the proposed contracts (i) are in proper legal form, (ii) contain all clauses required by North Carolina law, (iii) are legally enforceable to the extent governed by North Carolina law, and (iv) accomplish the intended purposes of the proposed contract. The General Counsel shall establish, in consultation with the Attorney General and the Department of Administration, procedures regarding the review of contracts subject to this subsection. The following terms and requirements apply to contracts under this subsection:

(1) The term "review" as used in this section does not constitute approval or disapproval of the policy merit or lack thereof of the proposed contract.

(2) The term "General Counsel's designee" includes any attorney employed or retained by the General Counsel to review contracts as provided in this subsection.

(3) Any contract for services reviewed pursuant to this subsection must include the signature of the General Counsel or the General Counsel's designee confirming that the Department of State Treasurer has adhered to the procedures established by the General Counsel regarding the review of the contract. Except for a contract entered into as part of direct trading of bonds, instruments, equity securities, or other approved securities, a contract that has not been signed as required by this subdivision is voidable by the State, and any party or parties to the contract are entitled to receive the value of services rendered prior to the termination of the contract.

(4) For the purposes of this subsection, "investment contract" means any of the following:

a. Investments to be acquired, held, or sold, directly or indirectly, by or for the State Treasurer, the Department of State Treasurer, or an investment entity created by the Department of State Treasurer, either on its own behalf or on behalf of another beneficial owner.

b. Investments administered by the North Carolina Supplemental Retirement Board of Trustees.

(c) All State agencies, the constituent institutions of The University of North Carolina, or any person who will be entering into a contract on behalf of the State for supplies, materials, printing, equipment, or contractual services that exceeds one million dollars ($1,000,000) shall notify the Secretary of the Department of Administration or the Secretary's designee of the intent to enter into the contract and provide information as required by the Department for the purposes of maintaining a centralized log of contracts and identifying the location of the contract documents. (2010-194, s. 16; 2011-326, s. 15(p); 2013-234, s. 1.)

§ 114-8.4. Legislative assistance to agencies and local governments.

The Department of Justice may (i) prepare bills to be presented to the General Assembly at the request of the Governor and the officials and departments of the State and advise in connection therewith and (ii) advise with and assist counties, cities, and towns in the drafting of legislation to be submitted to the General Assembly. (2011-97, s. 2.)

§ 114-8.5. Itemized billing for legal services provided to State agencies.

Whenever the Department of Justice charges a State agency, board, or commission for legal services rendered by the Department, the Department shall do so by providing the agency, board, or commission with an invoice that includes at least all of the following information for all charges:

(1) The case or matter for which the agency, board, or commission is being charged.

(2) The name of each attorney who worked on each case or matter and the number of hours worked by each attorney.

(3) The hourly rate being charged by each attorney. (2012-142, s. 15.1.)

§ 114-8.6. Designation of State Crime Laboratory as Internet Crimes Against Children affiliated agency.

The Attorney General shall designate the North Carolina State Crime Laboratory as a North Carolina Internet Crimes Against Children (ICAC) affiliated agency. (2013-360, s. 17.6(p).)

§ 114-8.7. Reserved for future codification purposes.

Article 2.

Division of Legislative Drafting and Codification of Statutes.

§§ 114-9, 114-9.1: Recodified as Article 7D of Chapter 120, G.S. 120-36.21 and G.S. 120-36.22, by Session Laws 2011-97, s. 1, effective June 1, 2011.

Article 3.

Division of Criminal Information.

§ 114-10. Division of Criminal Information.

The Attorney General shall set up in the Department of Justice a division to be designated as the Division of Criminal Information. There shall be assigned to this Division by the Attorney General duties as follows:

(1) To collect and correlate information in criminal law administration, including crimes committed, arrests made, dispositions on preliminary hearings, prosecutions, convictions, acquittals, punishment, appeals, together with the age, race, and sex of the offender, the necessary data to make a trace regarding all firearms seized, forfeited, found, or otherwise coming into the possession of any State or local law enforcement agency of the State that are believed to have been used in the commission of a crime, and such other information concerning crime and criminals as may appear significant or helpful. To correlate such information with the operations of agencies and institutions charged with the supervision of offenders on probation, in penal and correctional institutions, on parole and pardon, so as to show the volume, variety and tendencies of crime and criminals and the workings of successive links in the machinery set up for the administration of the criminal law in connection with the arrests, trial, punishment, probation, prison parole and pardon of all criminals in North Carolina.

(2) To collect, correlate, and maintain access to information that will assist in the performance of duties required in the administration of criminal justice throughout the State. This information may include, but is not limited to, motor vehicle registration, drivers' licenses, wanted and missing persons, stolen property, warrants, stolen vehicles, firearms registration, sexual offender registration as provided under Article 27A of Chapter 14 of the General Statutes, drugs, drug users and parole and probation histories. In performing this function, the Division may arrange to use information available in other agencies and units of State, local and federal government, but shall provide security measures to insure that such information shall be made available only to those whose duties, relating to the administration of justice, require such information.

(2a) Recodified as G.S. 114-10.1 by Session Laws 2002-159, s. 18(a).

(3) To make scientific study, analysis and comparison from the information so collected and correlated with similar information gathered by federal agencies, and to provide the Governor and the General Assembly with the information so collected biennially, or more often if required by the Governor.

(4) To perform all the duties heretofore imposed by law upon the Attorney General with respect to criminal statistics.

(5) To perform such other duties as may be from time to time prescribed by the Attorney General.

(6) To promulgate rules and regulations for the administration of this Article. (1939, c. 315, s. 2; 1955, c. 1257, ss. 1, 2; 1969, c. 1267, s. 1; 1995, c. 545, s. 2; 1999-26, s. 1; 1999-225, s. 1; 2000-67, s. 17.2(a); 2001-424, s. 23.7(a); 2002-159, s. 18(a); 2012-182, s. 1.)

§ 114-10.01. Collection of traffic law enforcement statistics.

(a) In addition to the duties set forth in G.S. 114-10, the Division of Criminal Information shall collect, correlate, and maintain the following information regarding traffic law enforcement by law enforcement officers:

(1) The number of drivers stopped for routine traffic enforcement by law enforcement officers, the officer making each stop, the date each stop was made, the agency of the officer making each stop, and whether or not a citation or warning was issued.

(2) Identifying characteristics of the drivers stopped, including the race or ethnicity, approximate age, and sex.

(3) The alleged traffic violation that led to the stop.

(4) Whether a search was instituted as a result of the stop.

(5) Whether the vehicle, personal effects, driver, or passenger or passengers were searched, and the race or ethnicity, approximate age, and sex of each person searched.

(6) Whether the search was conducted pursuant to consent, probable cause, or reasonable suspicion to suspect a crime, including the basis for the request for consent, or the circumstances establishing probable cause or reasonable suspicion.

(7) Whether any contraband was found and the type and amount of any such contraband.

(8) Whether any written citation or any oral or written warning was issued as a result of the stop.

(9) Whether an arrest was made as a result of either the stop or the search.

(10) Whether any property was seized, with a description of that property.

(11) Whether the officers making the stop encountered any physical resistance from the driver or passenger or passengers.

(12) Whether the officers making the stop engaged in the use of force against the driver, passenger, or passengers for any reason.

(13) Whether any injuries resulted from the stop.

(14) Whether the circumstances surrounding the stop were the subject of any investigation, and the results of that investigation.

(15) The geographic location of the stop; if the officer making the stop is a member of the State Highway Patrol, the location shall be the Highway Patrol District in which the stop was made; for all other law enforcement officers, the location shall be the city or county in which the stop was made.

(b) For purposes of this section, "law enforcement officer" means any of the following:

(1) All State law enforcement officers.

(2) Law enforcement officers employed by county sheriffs or county police departments.

(3) Law enforcement officers employed by police departments in municipalities with a population of 10,000 or more persons.

(4) Law enforcement officers employed by police departments in municipalities employing five or more full-time sworn officers for every 1,000 in population, as calculated by the Division for the calendar year in which the stop was made.

(c) The information required by this section need not be collected in connection with impaired driving checks under G.S. 20-16.3A or other types of roadblocks, vehicle checks, or checkpoints that are consistent with the laws of this State and with the State and federal constitutions, except when those stops result in a warning, search, seizure, arrest, or any of the other activity described in subdivisions (4) through (14) of subsection (a) of this section.

(d) Each law enforcement officer making a stop covered by subdivision (1) of subsection (a) of this section shall be assigned an anonymous identification number by the officer's employing agency. The anonymous identifying number shall be public record and shall be reported to the Division to be correlated along with the data collected under subsection (a) of this section. The correlation between the identification numbers and the names of the officers shall not be a public record, and shall not be disclosed by the agency except when required by order of a court of competent jurisdiction to resolve a claim or defense properly before the court.

(d1) Any agency subject to the requirements of this section shall submit information collected under subsection (a) of this section to the Division within 60 days of the close of each month. Any agency that does not submit the information as required by this subsection shall be ineligible to receive any law enforcement grants available by or through the State until the information which is reasonably available is submitted.

(e) The Division shall publish and distribute by December 1 of each year a list indicating the law enforcement officers that will be subject to the provisions of this section during the calendar year commencing on the following January 1. (1939, c. 315, s. 2; 1955, c. 1257, ss. 1, 2; 1969, c. 1267, s. 1; 1995, c. 545, s. 2; 1999-26, s. 1; 1999-225, s. 1; 2000-67, s. 17.2(a); 2001-424, s. 23.7(a); 2002-159, s. 18(a), (b); 2009-544, s. 1; 2012-182, s. 1.)

§ 114-10.02. Collection of statistics on the use of deadly force by law enforcement officers.

(a) In addition to the duties set forth in G.S. 114-10, the Division of Criminal Information shall collect, maintain, and annually publish the number of deaths, by law enforcement agency, resulting from the use of deadly force by law enforcement officers in the course and scope of their official duties.

(b) For purposes of this section, "law enforcement officer" means sworn law enforcement officers with the power of arrest, both State and local. (2009-106, s. 1; 2012-182, s. 1.)

§ 114-10.1. Police Information Network.

(a) The Division of Criminal Information is authorized to establish, devise, maintain and operate a system for receiving and disseminating to participating agencies information collected, maintained and correlated under authority of G.S. 114-10 of this Article. The system shall be known as the Division of Criminal Information Network.

(b) The Division of Criminal Information is authorized to cooperate with the Division of Motor Vehicles, Department of Administration, the Department of Public Safety, and other State, local and federal agencies and organizations in carrying out the purpose and intent of this section, and to utilize, in cooperation with other State agencies and to the extent as may be practical, computers and related equipment as may be operated by other State agencies.

(c) The Division of Criminal Information, after consultation with participating agencies, shall adopt rules and regulations governing the organization and administration of the Division of Criminal Information Network, including rules and regulations governing the types of information relating to the administration of criminal justice to be entered into the system, and who shall have access to such information. The rules and regulations governing access to the Division of Criminal Information Network shall not prohibit an attorney who has entered a criminal proceeding in accordance with G.S. 15A-141 from obtaining information relevant to that criminal proceeding. The rules and regulations governing access to the Division of Criminal Information Network shall not prohibit an attorney who represents a person in adjudicatory or dispositional proceedings for an infraction from obtaining the person's driving record or criminal history.

(d) The Division of Criminal Information may impose an initial set up fee of two thousand six hundred fifty dollars ($2,650) for agencies to participate in the

Division of Criminal Information Network. This one-time fee shall be used to offset the cost of the router and data circuit needed to access the Network.

The Division of Criminal Information may also impose monthly fees on participating agencies. The monthly fees collected under this subsection shall be used to offset the cost of operating and maintaining the Police Information Network

(1) The Division of Criminal Information may impose a monthly circuit fee on agencies that access the Division of Criminal Information Network through a circuit maintained and operated by the Department of Justice. The amount of the monthly fee is three hundred dollars ($300.00) plus an additional fee amount for each device linked to the Network. The additional fee amount varies depending upon the type of device. For a desktop device after the first seven desktop devices, the additional monthly fee is twenty-five dollars ($25.00) per device. For a mobile device, the additional monthly fee is twelve dollars ($12.00) per device.

(2) The Division of Criminal Information may impose a monthly device fee on agencies that access the Police Information Network through some other approved means. The amount of the monthly device fee varies depending upon the type of device. For a desktop device, the monthly fee is twenty-five dollars ($25.00) per device. For a mobile device, the fee is twelve dollars ($12.00) per device. (1969, c. 1267, s. 2; 1975, c. 716, s. 5; 1977, c. 836; 1993, c. 39, s. 1; 2005-276, ss. 43.4(a), 43.4(b); 2011-145, s. 19.1(h); 2012-83, s. 36; 2012-182, s. 1.)

§ 114-11. Repealed by Session Laws 1969, c. 1190, s. 57.

§ 114-11.1. Repealed by Session Laws 1965, c. 310, s. 4.

§§ 114-11.2 through 114-11.5. Reserved for future codification purposes.

Article 3A.

Special Prosecution Division.

§ 114-11.6. Division established; duties.

There is hereby established in the office of the Attorney General of North Carolina, a Special Prosecution Division. The attorneys assigned to this Division shall be available to prosecute or assist in the prosecution of criminal cases when requested to do so by a district attorney and the Attorney General approves. In addition, these attorneys assigned to this Division shall serve as legal advisers to the State Bureau of Investigation and the Police Information Network and perform any other duties assigned to them by the Attorney General. (1973, c. 47, s. 2; c. 813.)

Article 4.

State Bureau of Investigation.

Part 1. General Powers and Duties of the State Bureau of Investigation.

§ 114-12. Bureau of Investigation created; powers and duties.

In order to secure a more effective administration of the criminal laws of the State, to prevent crime, and to procure the speedy apprehension of criminals, the Attorney General shall set up in the Department of Justice a division to be designated as the State Bureau of Investigation. The Division shall have charge of and administer the agencies and activities herein set up for the identification of criminals, for their apprehension, and investigation and preparation of evidence to be used in criminal courts; and the said Bureau shall have charge of investigation of criminal matters herein especially mentioned, and of such other crimes and criminal procedure as the Governor may direct.

In the personnel of the Bureau shall be included a sufficient number of persons of training and skill in the investigation of crime and in the preparation of evidence as to be of service to local enforcement officers, under the direction of the Governor, in criminal matters of major importance.

The State radio system shall be made available to the Bureau Laboratory for use in its work. (1937, c. 349, s. 1; 1939, c. 315, s. 6; 2003-214, s. 1(1); 2013-360, s. 17.6(l).)

§ 114-12.1. Minority sensitivity training for law enforcement personnel.

(a) The Department of Justice shall develop guidelines for minority sensitivity training for all law enforcement personnel throughout the State. The Department shall ensure that all persons who work with minority juveniles in the juvenile justice system are taught how to communicate effectively with minority juveniles and how to recognize and address the needs of those juveniles. The Department shall also advise all law enforcement and professionals who work within the juvenile justice system of ways to improve the treatment of minority juveniles so that all juveniles receive equal treatment. Except where local law enforcement has existing minority sensitivity training that meets the Department guidelines, the Department shall conduct the minority sensitivity training annually. Prior to the training each year, the Department shall assess whether minorities are receiving fair and equal treatment in the juvenile justice system with regard to the administration of predisposition procedures, of diversion methods, of dispositional alternatives, and of treatment and post-release supervision plans.

(b) The Division of Juvenile Justice of the Department of Public Safety shall ensure that all juvenile court counselors and other Division personnel receive the minority sensitivity training specified in subsection (a) of this section. (1998-202, s. 17; 2000-137, s. 4(i); 2003-214, s. 1; 2011-145, s. 19.1(l).)

§ 114-13. Director of the Bureau; personnel.

The Attorney General shall appoint a Director of the Bureau of Investigation, who shall serve at the will of the Attorney General, and whose salary shall be fixed by the Department of Administration under G.S. 143-36 et seq. He may further appoint a sufficient number of assistants and stenographic and clerical help, who shall be competent and qualified to do the work of the Bureau. The salaries of such assistants shall be fixed by the Department of Administration under G.S. 143-36 et seq. The salaries of clerical and stenographic help shall be the same as now provided for similar employees in other State departments and bureaus. (1937, c. 349, s. 4; 1939, c. 315, s. 6; 1955, c. 1185, s. 1; 1957, c. 269, s. 1; 1979, 2nd Sess., c. 1272, s. 3; 2003-214, s. 1(1); 2011-145, s. 19.1(q1); 2011-391, s. 43(g).)

§ 114-14. General powers and duties of Director and assistants.

The Director of the Bureau and his assistants are given the same power of arrest as is now vested in the sheriffs of the several counties, and their jurisdiction shall be statewide. The Director of the Bureau and his assistants shall, at the request of the Governor, give assistance to sheriffs, police officers, district attorneys, and judges when called upon by them and so directed. They shall also give assistance, when requested, to the Department of Public Safety in the investigation of cases pending before the parole office and of complaints lodged against parolees, when so directed by the Governor. (1937, c. 349, s. 5; 1973, c. 47, s. 2; c. 1262, s. 10; 2003-214, s. 1(1); 2011-145, s. 19.1(h), (q1); 2011-391, s. 43(g); 2012-83, s. 37.)

§ 114-14.1. Transfer of personnel.

The Director of the State Bureau of Investigation shall have authority to transfer members of the Bureau from one locality in the State to another as he may deem necessary. When any member of the State Bureau of Investigation is transferred from one point to another for the convenience of the State, or otherwise than upon the request of the employee, the Bureau shall be responsible for transporting the household goods, furniture, and personal effects of the employee and members of his household. (1955, c. 1185, s. 2; 2003-214, s. 1(1); 2011-145, s. 19.1(q1); 2011-391, s. 43(g).)

§ 114-15. Investigations of lynchings, election frauds, etc.; services subject to call of Governor; witness fees and mileage for Director and assistants.

(a) The Bureau shall, through its Director and upon request of the Governor, investigate and prepare evidence in the event of any lynching or mob violence in the State; shall investigate all cases arising from frauds in connection with elections when requested to do so by the Board of Elections, and when so directed by the Governor. Such investigation, however, shall in nowise interfere with the power of the Attorney General to make such investigation as the Attorney General is authorized to make under the laws of the State. The Bureau is authorized further, at the request of the Governor, to investigate cases of frauds arising under the Social Security Laws of the State, of violations of the gaming laws, and lottery laws, and matters of similar kind when called upon by the Governor so to do. In all such cases it shall be the duty of the Department to keep such records as may be necessary and to prepare evidence in the cases investigated, for the use of enforcement officers and for the trial of causes. The services of the Director of the Bureau, and of the Director's assistants, may be required by the Governor in connection with the investigation of any crime committed anywhere in the State when called upon by the enforcement officers of the State, and when, in the judgment of the Governor, such services may be rendered with advantage to the enforcement of the criminal law. The State Bureau of Investigation is hereby authorized to investigate without request the attempted arson of, or arson of, damage of, theft from, or theft of, or misuse of, any State-owned personal property, buildings, or other real property or any assault upon or threats against any legislative officer named in G.S. 147-2(1), (2), or (3), any executive officer named in G.S. 147-3(c), or any court officer as defined in G.S. 14-16.10(1). The Bureau also is authorized at the request of the Governor to conduct a background investigation on a person that the Governor plans to nominate for a position that must be confirmed by the General Assembly, the Senate, or the House of Representatives. The background investigation of the proposed nominee shall be limited to an investigation of the person's criminal record, educational background, employment record, records concerning the listing and payment of taxes, and credit record, and to a requirement that the person provide the information contained in the statements of economic interest required to be filed by persons subject to Chapter 138A of the General Statutes. The Governor must give the person being investigated written notice that the Governor intends to request a background investigation at least 10 days prior to the date that the Governor requests the State Bureau of Investigation to conduct the background investigation. The written notice shall be sent by regular mail, and there is created a rebuttable presumption that the person received the notice if the Governor has a copy of the notice.

(b)   The State Bureau of Investigation is further authorized, upon request of the Governor or the Attorney General, to investigate the commission or attempted commission of the crimes defined in the following statutes:

(1)   All sections of Article 4A of Chapter 14 of the General Statutes;

(2)   G.S. 14-277.1;

(3)   G.S. 14-277.2;

(4)   G.S. 14-283;

(5)   G.S. 14-284;

(6) G.S. 14-284.1;

(7) G.S. 14-288.2;

(8) G.S. 14-288.7;

(9) G.S. 14-288.8;

(10) G.S. 14-288.20;

(11) G.S. 14-284.2;

(12) G.S. 14-399(e);

(12a) G.S. 15A-287 and G.S. 15A-288;

(13) G.S. 130A-26.1;

(14) G.S. 143-215.6B;

(15) G.S. 143-215.88B; and

(16) G.S. 143-215.114B.

(b1) The State Bureau of Investigation is further authorized, upon request of the Governor or Attorney General, to investigate the solicitation, commission, or attempted commission, by means of a computer, computer network, computer system, electronic mail service provider, or the Internet, of the crimes defined in the following statutes:

(1) G.S. 14-190.6;

(2) G.S. 14-190.7;

(3) G.S. 14-190.8;

(4) G.S. 14-190.14;

(5) G.S. 14-190.15;

(6) G.S. 14-190.16;

(7) G.S. 14-190.17;

(8) G.S. 14-190.17A;

(9) G.S. 14-190.18;

(10) G.S. 14-190.19;

(11) G.S. 14-202.3;

Upon determining the location of the criminal violation, the State Bureau of Investigation shall promptly notify the sheriff and local law enforcement of its investigation.

(c) All records and evidence collected and compiled by the Director of the Bureau and his assistants shall, upon request, be made available to the district attorney of any district if the same concerns persons or investigations in his district.

(d) In all cases where the cost is assessed against the defendant and paid by him, there shall be assessed in the bill of cost, mileage and witness fees to the Director and any of his assistants who are witnesses in cases arising in courts of this State. The fees so assessed, charged and collected shall be forwarded by the clerks of the court to the Treasurer of the State of North Carolina, and there credited to the Bureau of Identification and Investigation Fund. (1937, c. 349, s. 6; 1947, c. 280; 1965, c. 772; 1973, c. 47, s. 2; 1981, c. 822, s. 2; 1987, c. 858, s. 1; c. 867, s. 3; 1991, c. 725, s. 2; 1993, c. 461, s. 2; 1995, c. 407, s. 2; 1999-398, s. 2; 2003-214, s. 1(1); 2005-121, s. 3; 2008-213, s. 88; 2011-145, s. 19.1(q1); 2011-391, s. 43(g).)

§ 114-15.1. Department heads to report possible violations of criminal statutes involving misuse of State property to State Bureau of Investigation.

Any person employed by the State of North Carolina, its agencies or institutions, who receives any information or evidence of an attempted arson, or arson, damage of, theft from, or theft of, or embezzlement from, or embezzlement of, or misuse of, any state-owned personal property, buildings or other real property, shall as soon as possible, but not later than three days from receipt of the information or evidence, report such information or evidence to his immediate supervisor, who shall in turn report such information or evidence to the head of the respective department, agency, or institution. The head of any department, agency, or institution receiving such information or evidence shall, within a reasonable time but no later than 10 days from receipt thereof, report such information in writing to the Director of the State Bureau of Investigation.

Upon receipt of notification and information as provided for in this section, the State Bureau of Investigation shall, if appropriate, conduct an investigation.

The employees of all State departments, agencies and institutions are hereby required to cooperate with the State Bureau of Investigation, its officers and agents, as far as may be possible, in aid of such investigation.

If such investigation reveals a possible violation of the criminal laws, the results thereof shall be reported by the State Bureau of Investigation to the district attorney of any district if the same concerns persons or offenses in his district. (1977, c. 763; 2003-214, s. 1(1); 2011-145, s. 19.1(q1); 2011-391, s. 43(g).)

§ 114-15.2. Use of private investigators limited.

No State executive officer, department, agency, institution, commission, bureau, or other organized activity of the State that receives support in whole or in part from the State except for counties, cities, towns, other municipal corporations or political subdivisions of the State or any agencies of these subdivisions, or county or city boards of education may employ a private investigator without the consent of the Attorney General. If the Attorney General determines that it is impracticable for the Bureau to conduct the investigation, the Attorney General shall employ a private investigator and shall fix the compensation for his services. The cost of the private investigator shall be paid from funds credited to the entity requesting the investigation or from the Contingency and Emergency Fund. (1985, c. 479, s. 138; 2003-214, s. 1(1).)

§ 114-15.3. Investigations of child sexual abuse in child care.

The Director of the Bureau may form a task force to investigate and gather evidence following a notification by the director of a county department of social services, pursuant to G.S. 7B-301, that child sexual abuse may have occurred in a child care facility. (1991, c. 593, s. 3; 1991 (Reg. Sess., 1992), c. 923, s. 5; 1997-506, s. 37; 1998-202, s. 13(z); 2003-214, s. 1(1); 2011-145, s. 19.1(q1); 2011-391, s. 43(g).)

§§ 114-16 through 114-16.2: Recodified as Article 9 of Chapter 114, G.S. 114-60 through 114-62, by Session Laws 2013-360, s. 17.6(d), effective July 1, 2013.

§ 114-17. Cooperation of local enforcement officers.

All local enforcement officers are hereby required to cooperate with the said Bureau, its officers and agents, as far as may be possible, in aid of such investigations and arrest and apprehension of criminals as the outcome thereof. (1937, c. 349, s. 8; 2003-214, s. 1(1).)

§ 114-17.1: Repealed by Session Laws 1995, c. 507, s. 6.

§ 114-18. Governor authorized to transfer activities of Central Prison Identification Bureau to the new Bureau; photographing and fingerprinting records.

The records and equipment of the Identification Bureau now established at Central Prison shall be made available to the said Bureau of Investigation, and the activities of the Identification Bureau now established at Central Prison may, in the future, if the Governor deem advisable, be carried on by the Bureau hereby established; except that the Bureau established by this Article shall have authority to make rules and regulations whereby the photographing and fingerprinting of persons confined in the Central Prison, or clearing through the Central Prison, or sentenced by any of the courts of this State to service upon the roads, may be taken and filed with the Bureau. (1937, c. 349, s. 2; 1939, c. 315, s. 6; 2003-214, s. 1(1).)

§ 114-18.1: Repealed by Session Laws 2000-119, s. 6, effective December 1, 2000.

§ 114-19. Criminal statistics.

(a)   It shall be the duty of the State Bureau of Investigation to receive and collect police information, to assist in locating, identifying, and keeping records of criminals in this State, and from other states, and to compare, classify, compile, publish, make available and disseminate any and all such information to the sheriffs, constables, police authorities, courts or any other officials of the State requiring such criminal identification, crime statistics and other information respecting crimes local and national, and to conduct surveys and studies for the purpose of determining so far as is possible the source of any criminal conspiracy, crime wave, movement or cooperative action on the part of the criminals, reporting such conditions, and to cooperate with all officials in detecting and preventing.

(b)   Repealed by Session Laws 2000-119, s. 7, effective December 1, 2000. (1965, c. 1049, s. 1; 1973, c. 1286, s. 19; 1989, c. 772, s. 3; 1989 (Reg. Sess., 1990), c. 814, s. 9; 2000-119, s. 7; 2003-214, s. 1(1).)

Part 2. Criminal History Record Checks.

§ 114-19.01. Study and report on use of pseudoephedrine products to make methamphetamine.

The State Bureau of Investigation shall study issues regarding the use of pseudoephedrine products to make methamphetamine, including any data on the use of particular pseudoephedrine products in that regard, pertinent law enforcement statistics, trends observed, and other relevant information, and report annually to the Commission for Mental Health, Developmental Disabilities, and Substance Abuse Services, the Legislative Commission on Methamphetamine Abuse, and the Joint Governmental Operations Subcommittee on Justice and Public Safety. (2005-434, s. 8.)

§ 114-19.1. Criminal history background investigations; fees.

(a) When the Department of Justice determines that any person is entitled by law to receive information, including criminal records, from the State Bureau of Investigation, for any purpose other than the administration of criminal justice, the State Bureau of Investigation shall charge the recipient of such information a reasonable fee for retrieving such information. The fee authorized by this section shall not exceed the actual cost of locating, editing, researching and retrieving the information, and may be budgeted for the support of the State Bureau of Investigation.

(b) As used in this section, "administration of criminal justice" means the performance of any of the following activities: the detection, apprehension, detention, pretrial release, post-trial release, prosecution, adjudication, correctional supervision, or rehabilitation of persons suspected of, accused of or convicted of a criminal offense. The term also includes screening for suitability for employment, appointment or retention of a person as a law enforcement or criminal justice officer or for suitability for appointment of a person who must be appointed or confirmed by the General Assembly, the Senate, or the House of Representatives.

(c) In providing criminal history record checks, the Department of Justice shall process requests in the following priority order:

(1) Administration of criminal justice record checks,

(2) Mandatory noncriminal justice criminal history record checks,

(3) Voluntary noncriminal justice criminal history record checks.

(d) Nothing in this section shall be construed as enlarging any right to receive any record of the State Bureau of Investigation. Such rights are and shall be controlled by G.S. 114-15, G.S. 114-19, G.S. 120-19.4A, and other applicable statutes. (1979, c. 816; 1981, c. 832, s. 1; 1987, c. 867, s. 1; 1995 (Reg. Sess., 1996), c. 606, s. 4; 2002-126, s. 29A.12(a); 2003-214, s. 1(2).)

§ 114-19.2. Criminal record checks of school personnel.

(a) The Department of Justice may provide a criminal record check to the local board of education of a person who is employed in a public school in that local school district or of a person who has applied for employment in a public school in that local school district, if the employee or applicant consents to the record check. The Department may also provide a criminal record check of school personnel as defined in G.S. 115C-332 by fingerprint card to the local board of education from National Repositories of Criminal Histories, in accordance with G.S. 115C-332. The information shall be kept confidential by the local board of education as provided in Article 21A of Chapter 115C of the General Statutes.

(a1)   The Department of Justice may provide a criminal history record check to the board of directors of a regional school of a person who is employed at a regional school or of a person who has applied for employment at a regional school if the employee or applicant consents to the record check. The Department may also provide a criminal history record check of school personnel as defined in G.S. 115C-238.56N by fingerprint card to the board of directors of the regional school from the National Repositories of Criminal Histories, in accordance with G.S. 115C-238.56N. The information shall be kept confidential by the board of directors of the regional school as provided in G.S. 115C-238.56N.

(b)   The Department of Justice may provide a criminal record check to the employer of a person who is employed in a nonpublic school or of a person who has applied for employment in a nonpublic school, if the employee or applicant consents to the record check. For purposes of this subsection, the term nonpublic school is one that is subject to the provisions of Article 39 of Chapter 115C of the General Statutes, but does not include a home school as defined in that Article.

(c)   The Department of Justice shall charge a reasonable fee for conducting a criminal record check under this section. The fee shall not exceed the actual cost of locating, editing, researching, and retrieving the information.

(c1)   The Department of Justice may provide a criminal record check to the schools within the Department of Health and Human Services of a person who is employed, applies for employment, or applies to be selected as a volunteer, if the employee or applicant consents to the record check. The Department of Health and Human Services shall keep all information pursuant to this subsection confidential, as provided in Article 7 of Chapter 126 of the General Statutes.

(d)   The Department of Justice shall adopt rules to implement this section. (1991, c. 705, s. 1; 1993, c. 350, s. 1; 1995, c. 373, s. 2; 1997-443, s. 11A.118(a); 2003-214, s. 1(2); 2011-241, s. 2.)

§ 114-19.3. Criminal record checks of providers of treatment for or services to children, the elderly, mental health patients, the sick, and the disabled.

(a)   Authority. - The Department of Justice may provide to any of the following entities a criminal record check of an individual who is employed by that entity, has applied for employment with that entity, or has volunteered to provide direct care on behalf of that entity:

(1)   Hospitals licensed under Chapter 131E of the General Statutes.

(2),   (3) Repealed by Session Laws 2000-154, s. 5, effective January 1, 2001.

(4)   Hospices licensed under Chapter 131E of the General Statutes.

(5)   Child placing agencies licensed under Chapter 131D of the General Statutes.

(6)   Residential child care facilities licensed under Chapter 131D of the General Statutes.

(7)   Hospitals licensed under Chapter 122C of the General Statutes.

(8)   Repealed by Session Laws 2000-154, s. 5, effective January 1, 2001.

(9)   Licensed child care facilities and nonlicensed child care homes regulated by the State.

(10)   Any other organization or corporation, whether for profit or nonprofit, that provides direct care or services to children, the sick, the disabled, or the elderly.

(b)   Procedure. - A criminal record check may be conducted by using an individual's fingerprint or any information required by the Department of Justice to identify that individual. A criminal record check shall be provided only if the individual whose record is checked consents to the record check. The information shall be kept confidential by the entity that receives the information. Upon the disclosure of confidential information under this section by the entity, the Department may refuse to provide further criminal record checks to that entity.

(c)   Repealed by Session Laws 1995 (Regular Session, 1996), c. 606, s. 1.

(d)   Foster or Adoptive Parent. - The Department of Justice, at the request of a child placing agency licensed under Chapter 131D of the General Statutes or a local department of social services, may provide a criminal record check of a prospective foster care or adoptive parent if the prospective parent consents to the record check. The information shall be kept confidential and upon the disclosure of confidential information under this section by the agency or department, the Department may refuse to provide further criminal record checks to that agency or department.

(e)   Fee. - The Department may charge a fee to offset the cost incurred by it to conduct a criminal record check under this section. The fee may not exceed fourteen dollars ($14.00). (1993, c. 403, s. 1; 1995, c. 453, s. 1; 1995 (Reg. Sess., 1996), c. 606, s. 1; 1997-506, s. 38; 2000-154, s. 5; 2003-214, s. 1(2).)

§ 114-19.4. Criminal record checks for foster care.

The Department of Justice may provide to the Division of Social Services, Department of Health and Human Services, the criminal history from the State and National Repositories of Criminal Histories as defined in G.S. 131D-10.2(6a). The Division shall provide to the Department of Justice, along with the request, the fingerprints of the individual to be checked, any additional information required by the Department of Justice, and a form consenting to the check of the criminal record and to the use of fingerprints and other identifying information required by the State or National Repositories signed by the individual to be checked. The fingerprints of the individual shall be forwarded to the State Bureau of Investigation for a search of the State's criminal history record file, and the State Bureau of Investigation shall forward a set of fingerprints to the Federal Bureau of Investigation for a national criminal history record check. The Division shall keep all information pursuant to this section privileged, as provided in G.S. 131D-10.3A(g). The Department of Justice shall charge a reasonable fee only for conducting the checks of the national criminal history records authorized by this section. (1995, c. 507, s. 23.26(c); 1997-140, s. 3; 1997-443, s. 11A.118(a); 2003-214, s. 1(2).)

§ 114-19.5. Criminal record checks of child care providers.

The Department of Justice may provide to the Division of Child Development, Department of Health and Human Services, the criminal history from the State and National Repositories of Criminal Histories in accordance with G.S. 110-90.2, of any child care provider, as defined in G.S. 110-90.2. The Division shall provide to the Department of Justice, along with the request, the fingerprints of the provider to be checked, any additional information required by the Department of Justice, and a form consenting to the check of the criminal record and to the use of fingerprints and other identifying information required by the State or National Repositories signed by the child care provider to be checked. The Division shall keep all information pursuant to this section privileged, as provided in G.S. 110-90.2(e). The Department of Justice shall charge a reasonable fee only for conducting the checks of the national criminal history records authorized by this section. (1995, c. 507, s. 23.25(b); 1997-443, s. 11A.118(a); 1997-506, s. 39; 2003-214, s. 1(2).)

§ 114-19.6. Criminal history record checks of employees of and applicants for employment with the Department of Health and Human Services, and the Division of Juvenile Justice of the Department of Public Safety.

(a) Definitions. - As used in this section, the term:

(1) "Covered person" means any of the following:

a. An applicant for employment or a current employee in a position in the Division of Juvenile Justice of the Department of Public Safety who provides direct care for a client, patient, student, resident or ward of the Division.

b. A person who supervises positions in the Division of Juvenile Justice of the Department of Public Safety providing direct care for a client, patient, student, resident or ward of the Division.

c. An applicant for employment or a current employee in a position in the Department of Health and Human Services.

d. An independent contractor or an employee of an independent contractor that has contracted to provide services to the Department of Health and Human Services.

e. A person who has been approved to perform volunteer services for the Department of Health and Human Services.

f. An independent contractor or an employee of an independent contractor who has contracted with the Division of Juvenile Justice of the Department of Public Safety to provide direct care for a client, patient, student, resident, or ward of the Division.

g. A person who has been approved to perform volunteer services in or for the Division of Juvenile Justice of the Department of Public Safety to provide direct care for a client, patient, student, resident, or ward of the Division.

(2) "Criminal history" means a State or federal history of conviction of a crime, whether a misdemeanor or felony, that bears upon a covered person's fitness for employment in the Department of Health and Human Services or the Division of Juvenile Justice of the Department of Public Safety. The crimes include, but are not limited to, criminal offenses as set forth in any of the following Articles of Chapter 14 of the General Statutes: Article 5, Counterfeiting and Issuing Monetary Substitutes; Article 5A, Endangering Executive and Legislative Officers; Article 6, Homicide; Article 7A, Rape and Other Sex Offenses; Article 8, Assaults; Article 10, Kidnapping and Abduction; Article 13, Malicious Injury or Damage by Use of Explosive or Incendiary Device or Material; Article 14, Burglary and Other Housebreakings; Article 15, Arson and Other Burnings; Article 16, Larceny; Article 17, Robbery; Article 18, Embezzlement; Article 19, False Pretenses and Cheats; Article 19A, Obtaining Property or Services by False or Fraudulent Use of Credit Device or Other Means; Article 19B, Financial Transaction Card Crime Act; Article 20, Frauds; Article 21, Forgery; Article 26, Offenses Against Public Morality and Decency; Article 26A, Adult Establishments; Article 27, Prostitution; Article 28, Perjury; Article 29, Bribery; Article 31, Misconduct in Public Office; Article 35, Offenses Against the Public Peace; Article 36A, Riots, Civil Disorders, and Emergencies; Article 39, Protection of Minors; Article 40, Protection of the Family; Article 59, Public Intoxication; and Article 60, Computer-Related Crime. The crimes also include possession or sale of drugs in violation of the North Carolina Controlled Substances Act, Article 5 of Chapter 90 of the General Statutes, and alcohol-related offenses such as sale to underage persons in violation of G.S. 18B-302, or driving while impaired in violation of G.S. 20-138.1 through G.S. 20-138.5.

(b) When requested by the Department of Health and Human Services or the Division of Juvenile Justice of the Department of Public Safety, the North Carolina Department of Justice may provide to the requesting department a covered person's criminal history from the State Repository of Criminal Histories. Such requests shall not be due to a person's age, sex, race, color, national origin, religion, creed, political affiliation, or handicapping condition as defined by G.S. 168A-3. For requests for a State criminal history record check only, the requesting department shall provide to the Department of Justice a form consenting to the check signed by the covered person to be checked and any additional information required by the Department of Justice. National criminal record checks are authorized for covered applicants who have not resided in the State of North Carolina during the past five years. For national checks the Department of Health and Human Services or the Division of Juvenile Justice of the Department of Public Safety shall provide to the North Carolina Department of Justice the fingerprints of the covered person to be checked, any additional information required by the Department of Justice, and a form signed by the covered person to be checked consenting to the check of the criminal record and to the use of fingerprints and other identifying information required by the State or National Repositories. The fingerprints of the individual shall be forwarded to the State Bureau of Investigation for a search of the State criminal history record file and the State Bureau of Investigation shall forward a set of fingerprints to the Federal Bureau of Investigation for a national criminal history record check. The Department of Health and Human Services and the Division of Juvenile Justice of the Department of Public Safety shall keep all information pursuant to this section confidential. The Department of Justice shall charge a reasonable fee for conducting the checks of the criminal history records authorized by this section.

(c) All releases of criminal history information to the Department of Health and Human Services or the Division of Juvenile Justice of the Department of Public Safety shall be subject to, and in compliance with, rules governing the dissemination of criminal history record checks as adopted by the North Carolina Division of Criminal Information. All of the information either department receives through the checking of the criminal history is privileged information and for the exclusive use of that department.

(d) If the covered person's verified criminal history record check reveals one or more convictions covered under subsection (a) of this section, then the conviction shall constitute just cause for not selecting the person for employment, or for dismissing the person from current employment with the Department of Health and Human Services or the Division of Juvenile Justice of the Department of Public Safety. The conviction shall not automatically prohibit employment; however, the following factors shall be considered by the Department of Health and Human Services or the Division of Juvenile Justice of the Department of Public Safety in determining whether employment shall be denied:

(1)   The level and seriousness of the crime;

(2)   The date of the crime;

(3)   The age of the person at the time of the conviction;

(4)   The circumstances surrounding the commission of the crime, if known;

(5)   The nexus between the criminal conduct of the person and job duties of the person;

(6)   The prison, jail, probation, parole, rehabilitation, and employment records of the person since the date the crime was committed; and

(7)   The subsequent commission by the person of a crime listed in subsection (a) of this section.

(e)   The Department of Health and Human Services and the Division of Juvenile Justice of the Department of Public Safety may deny employment to or dismiss a covered person who refuses to consent to a criminal history record check or use of fingerprints or other identifying information required by the State or National Repositories of Criminal Histories. Any such refusal shall constitute just cause for the employment denial or the dismissal from employment.

(f)   The Department of Health and Human Services and the Division of Juvenile Justice of the Department of Public Safety may extend a conditional offer of employment pending the results of a criminal history record check authorized by this section. (1997-260, s. 1; 1997-443, s. 11A.118(b); 1998-202, s. 4(f); 2000-137, s. 4(h); 2003-214, s. 1(2); 2005-114, s. 4; 2011-145, s. 19.1(l); 2012-12, s. 2(nn); 2012-83, s. 5.)

§ 114-19.7. Criminal record checks required prior to placement for adoption of a minor who is in the custody or placement responsibility of a county department of social services.

The Department of Justice may provide to the Division of Social Services, Department of Health and Human Services, the criminal history from the State and National Repositories of Criminal Histories as defined in G.S. 48-1-101(5a). The Division shall provide to the Department of Justice, along with the request, the fingerprints of any individual to be checked, any additional information required by the Department of Justice, and a form consenting to the check of the criminal record and to the use of fingerprints and other identifying information required by the State or National Repositories signed by the individual to be checked. The fingerprints of the individual shall be forwarded to the State Bureau of Investigation for a search of the State's criminal history record file, and the State Bureau of Investigation shall forward a set of fingerprints to the Federal Bureau of Investigation for a national criminal history record check. The Division shall keep all information pursuant to this section privileged, as provided in G.S. 48-3-309(f). The Department of Justice shall charge a reasonable fee only for conducting the checks of the national criminal history records authorized by this section. (1998-229, s. 16; 2003-214, s. 1(2); 2005-114, s. 3.)

§ 114-19.8. Criminal record checks of applicants for auctioneer, apprentice auctioneer, or auction firm license.

The Department of Justice may provide to the North Carolina Auctioneers Commission from the State and National Repositories of Criminal Histories the criminal history of any applicant for an auctioneer's license under Chapter 85B of the General Statutes. Along with the request, the Commission shall provide to the Department of Justice the fingerprints of the applicant, a form signed by the applicant consenting to the criminal record check and the use of fingerprints and other identifying information required by the State or National Repositories, and any additional information required by the Department of Justice. The applicant's fingerprints shall be forwarded to the State Bureau of Investigation for a check of the State's criminal history record file, and the State Bureau of Investigation shall forward a set of fingerprints to the Federal Bureau of Investigation for a national criminal history record check. The Commission shall keep all information obtained pursuant to this section confidential. The Department of Justice may charge a fee to offset the cost incurred by it to conduct a criminal record check under this section. The fee shall not exceed the actual cost of locating, editing, researching, and retrieving the information. (1999-142, s. 9; 2000-140, s. 59(c); 2003-214, s. 1(2).)

§ 114-19.9. Criminal record checks of McGruff House Program volunteers.

(a)   Authority. - The Department of Justice and the Federal Bureau of Investigation may provide to any local law enforcement agency a criminal record check of any individual who applies as a volunteer for the McGruff House Program in that community and a criminal record check of all persons 18 years of age or older who live in the applying household. The North Carolina criminal record check may also be done by a certified DCI operator within the local law enforcement agency.

(b)   Procedure. - A criminal record check must be conducted by using an individual's fingerprints and all identification information required by the Department of Justice to identify that individual. A criminal record check shall be provided only if: (i) the individual whose record is checked consents to the record check, and (ii) every individual who is 18 years of age or older who lives in the household also consents to the record check. Refusal to give consent is considered withdrawal of the application. The information shall be kept confidential by the local law enforcement agency that receives the information. If the confidential information is disclosed under this section, the Department may refuse to provide further criminal record checks to that local law enforcement agency. (1999-214, s. 1; 2003-214, s. 1(2).)

§ 114-19.10. Criminal record checks for adult care homes, nursing homes, home care agencies, and providers of mental health, developmental disabilities, and substance abuse services.

The Department of Justice may provide to the following entities the criminal history from the State and National Repositories of Criminal Histories:

(1)   Nursing homes or combination homes licensed under Chapter 131E of the General Statutes.

(2)   Adult care homes licensed under Chapter 131D of the General Statutes.

(3) Home care agencies licensed under Chapter 131E of the General Statutes.

(4) Providers licensed under Chapter 122C of the General Statutes, including a contract agency of a provider that is subject to the provisions of Article 4 of that Chapter.

The criminal history shall be provided to nursing homes and home care agencies in accordance with G.S. 131E-265, to adult care homes in accordance with G.S. 131D-40, and to a provider in accordance with G.S. 122C-80. The requesting entity shall provide to the Department of Justice, along with the request, the fingerprints of the individual to be checked if a national criminal history record check is required, any additional information required by the Department of Justice, and a form signed by the individual to be checked consenting to the check of the criminal record and to the use of fingerprints and other identifying information required by the State or National Repositories of Criminal Histories. If a national criminal history record check is required, the fingerprints of the individual shall be forwarded to the State Bureau of Investigation for a search of the State's criminal history record file, and the State Bureau of Investigation shall forward a set of fingerprints to the Federal Bureau of Investigation for a national criminal history record check. All information received by the entity shall be kept confidential in accordance with G.S. 131E-265, 131D-40, and 122C-80, as applicable. The Department of Justice shall charge a reasonable fee for conducting the checks authorized by this section. The fee for the State check may not exceed fourteen dollars ($14.00). (2000-154, s. 1; 2003-214, s. 1(2); 2005-4, s. 5(b).)

§ 114-19.11. Criminal record checks of applicants for licensure as registered nurses or licensed practical nurses.

The Department of Justice may provide to the North Carolina Board of Nursing from the State and National Repositories of Criminal Histories the criminal history of any applicant for licensure as a registered nurse or licensed practical nurse under Article 9A of Chapter 90 of the General Statutes. Along with the request, the Board shall provide to the Department of Justice the fingerprints of the applicant, a form signed by the applicant consenting to the criminal record check and use of fingerprints and other identifying information required by the State and National Repositories, and any additional information required by the Department of Justice. The applicant's fingerprints shall be forwarded to the

State Bureau of Investigation for a search of the State's criminal history record file and the State Bureau of Investigation shall forward a set of fingerprints to the Federal Bureau of Investigation for a national criminal history record check. The Board shall keep all information obtained pursuant to this section confidential. The Department of Justice may charge a fee to offset the cost incurred by it to conduct a criminal record check under this section. The fee shall not exceed the actual cost of locating, editing, researching, and retrieving the information. (2001-371, s. 1; 2003-214, s. 1(2).)

§ 114-19.11A. Criminal record checks of applicants for registration, certification, or licensure as a substance abuse professional.

The Department of Justice may provide to the North Carolina Substance Abuse Professional Practice Board from the State and National Repositories of Criminal Histories the criminal history of any applicant for registration, certification, or licensure pursuant to Article 5C of Chapter 90 of the General Statutes. Along with the request, the Board shall provide to the Department of Justice the fingerprints of the applicant, a form signed by the applicant consenting to the criminal record check and use of fingerprints and other identifying information required by the State and National Repositories, and any additional information required by the Department of Justice. The applicant's fingerprints shall be forwarded to the State Bureau of Investigation for a search of the State's criminal history record file, and the State Bureau of Investigation shall forward a set of fingerprints to the Federal Bureau of Investigation for a national criminal history record check. The Board shall keep all information obtained pursuant to this section confidential. The Department of Justice may charge a fee to offset the cost incurred by it to conduct a criminal record check under this section. The fee shall not exceed the actual cost of locating, editing, researching, and retrieving the information. (2005-431, s. 2.)

§ 114-19.11B. Criminal record checks of applicants for licensure as massage and bodywork therapists.

The Department of Justice may provide to the North Carolina Board of Massage and Bodywork Therapy from the State and National Repositories of Criminal Histories the criminal history of any applicant for licensure pursuant to Article 36 of Chapter 90 of the General Statutes. Along with the request, the Board shall provide to the Department of Justice the fingerprints of the applicant, a form signed by the applicant consenting to the criminal record check and use of fingerprints and other identifying information required by the State and National Repositories, and any additional information required by the Department of Justice. The applicant's fingerprints shall be forwarded to the State Bureau of Investigation for a search of the State's criminal history record file, and the State Bureau of Investigation shall forward a set of fingerprints to the Federal Bureau of Investigation for a national criminal history record check. The Board shall keep all information obtained pursuant to this section confidential. The Department of Justice may charge a fee to offset the cost incurred by it to conduct a criminal record check under this section. The fee shall not exceed the actual cost of locating, editing, researching, and retrieving the information. (2008-224, s. 20.)

§ 114-19.12. Criminal history record checks of applicants to fire departments and emergency medical services.

(a) Definitions. - The following definitions apply in this section:

(1) Applicant. - A person who applies for a paid or volunteer position with a fire department or an emergency medical service.

(2) Criminal history. - A State or federal history of conviction of a crime, whether a misdemeanor or felony, that bears upon a covered person's fitness for holding a paid or volunteer position with a fire department. The crimes include, but are not limited to, criminal offenses as set forth in any of the following Articles of Chapter 14 of the General Statutes: Article 5, Counterfeiting and Issuing Monetary Substitutes; Article 5A, Endangering Executive and Legislative Officers; Article 6, Homicide; Article 7A, Rape and Other Sex Offenses; Article 8, Assaults; Article 10, Kidnapping and Abduction; Article 13, Malicious Injury or Damage by Use of Explosive or Incendiary Device or Material; Article 14, Burglary and Other Housebreakings; Article 15, Arson and Other Burnings; Article 16, Larceny; Article 17, Robbery; Article 18, Embezzlement; Article 19, False Pretenses and Cheats; Article 19A, Obtaining Property or Services by False or Fraudulent Use of Credit Device or Other Means; Article 19B, Financial Transaction Card Crime Act; Article 20, Frauds; Article 21, Forgery; Article 26, Offenses Against Public Morality and Decency; Article 26A, Adult Establishments; Article 27, Prostitution; Article 28, Perjury; Article 29, Bribery; Article 31, Misconduct in Public Office; Article 35, Offenses

Against the Public Peace; Article 36A, Riots, Civil Disorders, and Emergencies; Article 39, Protection of Minors; Article 40, Protection of the Family; Article 59, Public Intoxication; and Article 60, Computer-Related Crime. The crimes also include possession or sale of drugs in violation of the North Carolina Controlled Substances Act, Article 5 of Chapter 90 of the General Statutes, and alcohol-related offenses such as sale to underage persons in violation of G.S. 18B-302, or driving while impaired in violation of G.S. 20-138.1 through G.S. 20-138.5.

(b)   When requested by a designated local Homeland Security director a local fire chief, a county fire marshal, or an emergency services director or, when there is no designated local Homeland Security director, local fire chief, county fire marshal, or emergency services director, by a local law enforcement agency, the North Carolina Department of Justice may provide to the requesting director, chief, marshal, director, or agency an applicant's criminal history from the State and National Repositories of Criminal Histories. The local Homeland Security director, local fire chief, marshal, director, or local law enforcement agency shall provide to the North Carolina Department of Justice the fingerprints of the applicant to be checked, any additional information required by the Department of Justice, and a form signed by the applicant to be checked consenting to the check of the criminal record and to the use of fingerprints and other identifying information required by the State or National Repositories. The fingerprints of the individual shall be forwarded to the State Bureau of Investigation for a search of the State criminal history record file, and the State Bureau of Investigation shall forward a set of fingerprints to the Federal Bureau of Investigation for a national criminal history record check. The local Homeland Security director, local fire chief, county fire marshal, emergency services director, or local law enforcement agency shall keep all information pursuant to this section confidential. The Department of Justice shall charge a reasonable fee for conducting the checks of the criminal history records authorized by this section.

(c)   All releases of criminal history information to the local Homeland Security director, local fire chief, county fire marshal, emergency services director, or local law enforcement agency shall be subject to, and in compliance with, rules governing the dissemination of criminal history record checks as adopted by the North Carolina Division of Criminal Information. All of the information the local Homeland Security director, local fire chief, county fire marshal, emergency services director, or local law enforcement agency receives through the checking of the criminal history is privileged information and for the exclusive use of that director, chief, marshal, or agency.

(d) If the applicant's verified criminal history record check reveals one or more convictions covered under subdivision (a)(2) of this section, then the conviction shall constitute just cause for not selecting the applicant for the position or for dismissing the person from a current position with the local fire department or emergency medical services. The conviction shall not automatically prohibit volunteering or employment; however, the following factors shall be considered by the local Homeland Security director, local fire chief, county fire marshal, emergency services director, or local law enforcement agency in determining whether the position shall be denied:

(1) The level and seriousness of the crime;

(2) The date of the crime;

(3) The age of the person at the time of the conviction;

(4) The circumstances surrounding the commission of the crime, if known;

(5) The nexus between the criminal conduct of the person and the duties of the person;

(6) The prison, jail, probation, parole, rehabilitation, and employment records of the person since the date the crime was committed; and

(7) The subsequent commission by the person of a crime listed in subsection (a) of this section.

(e) The local fire department or emergency medical services may deny the applicant the position or dismiss an applicant who refuses to consent to a criminal history record check or use of fingerprints or other identifying information required by the State or National Repositories of Criminal Histories. This refusal constitutes just cause for the denial of the position or the dismissal from the position.

(f) The local fire department or emergency medical services may extend a conditional offer of the position pending the results of a criminal history record check authorized by this section.

(g) For purposes of this section, "local fire chief" shall include only fire chiefs who are paid employees of a city; "county fire marshal" shall include only fire marshals who are paid employees of a county; and "emergency services director" shall include only emergency services directors who are paid employees of a city or county. (2003-182, s. 1; 2007-479, s. 1; 2012-12, s. 2(oo).)

§ 114-19.13. Criminal record checks of applicants for manufactured home manufacturer, dealer, salesperson, or set-up contractor licensure.

The Department of Justice may provide to the North Carolina Manufactured Housing Board from the State and National Repositories of Criminal Histories the criminal history of any applicant for licensure as a manufactured home manufacturer, dealer, salesperson, or set-up contractor under Article 9A of Chapter 143 of the General Statutes. Along with the request, the Board shall provide to the Department of Justice the fingerprints of the applicant, a form signed by the applicant consenting to the criminal record check, and use of fingerprints and other identifying information required by the State and National Repositories, and any additional information required by the Department of Justice. The applicant's fingerprints shall be forwarded to the State Bureau of Investigation for a search of the State's criminal history record file, and the State Bureau of Investigation shall forward a set of fingerprints to the Federal Bureau of Investigation for a national criminal history record check. The Board shall keep all information obtained pursuant to this section confidential. The Department of Justice may charge a fee to offset the cost incurred by it to conduct a criminal record check under this section. The fee shall not exceed the actual cost of locating, editing, researching, and retrieving the information. (2003-400, s. 12.)

§ 114-19.14. Criminal record checks for municipalities and county governments.

The Department of Justice may provide to a city or county from the State and National Repositories of Criminal Histories the criminal history of any person who applies for employment with the city or county. The city or county shall provide to the Department of Justice, along with the request, the fingerprints of the applicant, a form signed by the applicant consenting to the criminal record check and use of fingerprints and other identifying information required by the State and National Repositories, and any additional information required by the Department of Justice. The applicant's fingerprints shall be forwarded to the

State Bureau of Investigation for a search of the State's criminal history record file, and the State Bureau of Investigation shall forward a set of fingerprints to the Federal Bureau of Investigation for a national criminal history record check. The city or county shall keep all information obtained pursuant to this section confidential. The Department of Justice may charge a fee to offset the cost incurred by it to conduct a criminal record check under this section. The fee shall not exceed the actual cost of locating, editing, researching, and retrieving the information. (2003-214, s. 4; 2005-358, s. 1.)

§ 114-19.15. Criminal record checks of applicants for locksmith licensure or apprentice designation.

The Department of Justice may provide to the North Carolina Locksmith Licensing Board from the State and National Repositories of Criminal Histories the criminal history of any applicant for licensure as a locksmith or an apprentice under Chapter 74F of the General Statutes. Along with the request, the Board shall provide to the Department of Justice the fingerprints of the applicant, a form signed by the applicant consenting to the criminal record check and use of fingerprints and other identifying information required by the State and National Repositories, and any additional information required by the Department of Justice. The applicant's fingerprints shall be forwarded to the State Bureau of Investigation for a search of the State's criminal history record file, and the State Bureau of Investigation shall forward a set of fingerprints to the Federal Bureau of Investigation for a national criminal history record check. The Board shall keep all information obtained pursuant to this section confidential. The Department of Justice may charge a fee to offset the cost incurred by it to conduct a criminal record check under this section. The fee shall not exceed the actual cost of locating, editing, researching, and retrieving the information. (2003-350, s. 12.)

§ 114-19.16. Criminal record checks for the North Carolina State Lottery Commission and its Director.

The Department of Justice may provide to the North Carolina State Lottery Commission and to its Director from the State and National Repositories of Criminal Histories the criminal history of any prospective employee of the Commission and any potential contractor. The North Carolina State Lottery

Commission or its Director shall provide to the Department of Justice, along with the request, the fingerprints of the prospective employee of the Commission, or of the potential contractor, a form signed by the prospective employee of the Commission, or of the potential contractor consenting to the criminal record check and use of fingerprints and other identifying information required by the State and National Repositories, and any additional information required by the Department of Justice. The fingerprints of the prospective employee of the Commission, or potential contractor, shall be forwarded to the State Bureau of Investigation for a search of the State's criminal history record file, and the State Bureau of Investigation shall forward a set of fingerprints to the Federal Bureau of Investigation for a national criminal history record check. The North Carolina State Lottery Commission and its Director shall remit any fingerprint information retained by the Commission to alcohol law enforcement agents appointed under Article 5 of Chapter 18B of the General Statutes and shall keep all information obtained pursuant to this section confidential. The Department of Justice shall charge a reasonable fee only for conducting the checks of the criminal history records authorized by this section. (2005-344, s. 6; 2005-276, s. 31.1(w); 2006-259, s. 8(g); 2006-264, s. 91(c); 2009-570, s. 32(e).)

§ 114-19.17. Criminal record checks of applicants for permit or license to conduct exploration, recovery, or salvage operations and archaeological investigations.

The Department of Justice may provide to the Department of Cultural Resources from the State and National Repositories of Criminal Histories the criminal history of any applicant for a permit or license under Article 3 of Chapter 121 of the General Statutes or Article 2 of Chapter 70 of the General Statutes. Along with the request, the Department of Cultural Resources shall provide to the Department of Justice the fingerprints of the applicant, a form signed by the applicant consenting to the criminal history record check and use of fingerprints and other identifying information required by the State and National Repositories, and any additional information required by the Department of Justice. The applicant's fingerprints shall be forwarded to the State Bureau of Investigation for a search of the State's criminal history record file, and the State Bureau of Investigation shall forward a set of fingerprints to the Federal Bureau of Investigation for a national criminal history record check. The Department of Cultural Resources shall keep all information obtained under this section confidential. The Department of Justice may charge a fee to offset the cost incurred by it to conduct a criminal record check under this section. The fee shall not exceed the actual cost of locating, editing, researching, and retrieving the information. (2005-367, s. 1.)

§ 114-19.18. Criminal record checks of applicants for licensure and licensees.

The Department of Justice may provide to the North Carolina Psychology Board from the State and National Repositories of Criminal Histories the criminal history of any applicant for licensure or reinstatement of a license to practice psychology or a licensed psychologist or psychological associate under Article 18A of Chapter 90 of the General Statutes. Along with the request, the Board shall provide to the Department of Justice the fingerprints of the applicant or licensee, a form signed by the applicant or licensee consenting to the criminal record check and use of fingerprints and other identifying information required by the State and National Repositories, and any additional information required by the Department of Justice. The applicant's or licensee's fingerprints shall be forwarded to the State Bureau of Investigation for a search of the State's criminal history record file, and the State Bureau of Investigation shall forward a set of fingerprints to the Federal Bureau of Investigation for a national criminal history record check. The Board shall keep all information obtained pursuant to this section confidential. The Department of Justice may charge each applicant or licensee a fee to offset the cost incurred by it to conduct a criminal record check under this section. The fee shall not exceed the actual cost of locating, editing, researching, and retrieving the information. (2006-175, s. 3; 2006-259, s. 42.)

§ 114-19.19. Criminal record checks for the Judicial Department.

(a) The Department of Justice may provide to the Judicial Department from the State and National Repositories of Criminal Histories the criminal history of any current or prospective employee, volunteer, or contractor of the Judicial Department. The Judicial Department shall provide to the Department of Justice, along with the request, the fingerprints of the current or prospective employee, volunteer, or contractor, a form signed by the current or prospective employee, volunteer, or contractor consenting to the criminal record check and use of fingerprints and other identifying information required by the State and National Repositories, and any additional information required by the Department of Justice. The fingerprints of the current or prospective employee, volunteer, or contractor shall be forwarded to the State Bureau of Investigation for a search of the State's criminal history record file, and the State Bureau of Investigation shall forward a set of fingerprints to the Federal Bureau of Investigation for a national criminal history record check. The Judicial Department shall keep all information obtained pursuant to this section confidential.

(b)   The Department of Justice may charge a fee to offset the cost incurred by it to conduct a criminal record check under this section. The fee shall not exceed the actual cost of locating, editing, researching, and retrieving the information. (2006-187, s. 3(a); 2006-259, s. 42.)

§ 114-19.20. Criminal record checks for the Office of Information Technology Services.

(a)   The Department of Justice may provide to the Office of Information Technology Services from the State and National Repositories of Criminal Histories the criminal history of any current or prospective employee, volunteer, or contractor of the Office of Information Technology Services. The Office of Information Technology Services shall provide to the Department of Justice, along with the request, the fingerprints of the current or prospective employee, volunteer, or contractor, a form signed by the current or prospective employee, volunteer, or contractor consenting to the criminal record check and use of fingerprints and other identifying information required by the State and National Repositories, and any additional information required by the Department of Justice. The fingerprints of the current or prospective employee, volunteer, or contractor shall be forwarded to the State Bureau of Investigation for a search of the State's criminal history record file, and the State Bureau of Investigation shall forward a set of fingerprints to the Federal Bureau of Investigation for a national criminal history record check. The Office of Information Technology Services shall keep all information obtained pursuant to this section confidential.

(b)   The Department of Justice may charge a fee to offset the cost incurred by it to conduct a criminal record check under this section. The fee shall not exceed the actual cost of locating, editing, researching, and retrieving the information. (2007-155, s. 3; 2007-189, ss. 3, 5.1.)

§ 114-19.21. Criminal record checks of EMS personnel.

The Department of Justice may provide to the Department of Health and Human Services the criminal history from the State and National Repositories of Criminal Histories of an individual who applies for EMS credentials, seeks to renew EMS credentials, or holds EMS credentials, when the criminal history is requested by the Department. The Department of Health and Human Services shall provide to the Department of Justice the request for the criminal history, the fingerprints of the individual to be checked, any additional information required by the Department of Justice, and a form consenting to the check of the criminal record and to the use of fingerprints and other identifying information required by the State or National Repositories signed by the individual to be checked. The Department of Health and Human Services and Emergency Medical Services Disciplinary Committee, established by G.S. 143-519, shall keep all information obtained pursuant to this section confidential. The Department of Justice shall charge a reasonable fee to offset the costs incurred by it to conduct the checks of criminal history records authorized by this section. (2007-411, s. 2.)

§ 114-19.22. Criminal record checks of applicants for licensure as chiropractic physicians.

The Department of Justice may provide to the State Board of Chiropractic Examiners from the State and National Repositories of Criminal Histories the criminal history of any applicant for licensure pursuant to Article 8 of Chapter 90 of the General Statutes. Along with the request, the Board shall provide to the Department of Justice the fingerprints of the applicant, a form signed by the applicant consenting to the criminal record check and use of fingerprints and other identifying information required by the State and National Repositories, and any additional information required by the Department of Justice. The applicant's fingerprints shall be forwarded to the State Bureau of Investigation for a search of the State's criminal history record file, and the State Bureau of Investigation shall forward a set of fingerprints to the Federal Bureau of Investigation for a national criminal history record check. The Board shall keep all information obtained pursuant to this section confidential. The Department of Justice may charge a fee to offset the cost incurred by it to conduct a criminal record check under this section. The fee shall not exceed the actual cost of locating, editing, researching, and retrieving the information. (2007-525, s. 2.)

§ 114-19.23. Criminal history record checks of employees of and applicants for employment with the Department of Public Instruction.

(a) Definitions. - As used in this section, the term:

(1) "Covered person" means any of the following:

a. An applicant for employment or a current employee in a position in the Department of Public Instruction.

b. An independent contractor or an employee of an independent contractor that has contracted to provide services to the Department of Public Instruction.

(2) "Criminal history" means a State or federal history of conviction of a crime, whether a misdemeanor or felony, that bears upon a covered person's fitness for employment in the Department of Public Instruction. The crimes include, but are not limited to, criminal offenses as set forth in any of the following Articles of Chapter 14 of the General Statutes: Article 5, Counterfeiting and Issuing Monetary Substitutes; Article 5A, Endangering Executive and Legislative Officers; Article 6, Homicide; Article 7A, Rape and Other Sex Offenses; Article 8, Assaults; Article 10, Kidnapping and Abduction; Article 13, Malicious Injury or Damage by Use of Explosive or Incendiary Device or Material; Article 14, Burglary and Other Housebreakings; Article 15, Arson and Other Burnings; Article 16, Larceny; Article 17, Robbery; Article 18, Embezzlement; Article 19, False Pretenses and Cheats; Article 19A, Obtaining Property or Services by False or Fraudulent Use of Credit Device or Other Means; Article 19B, Financial Transaction Card Crime Act; Article 20, Frauds; Article 21, Forgery; Article 26, Offenses Against Public Morality and Decency; Article 26A, Adult Establishments; Article 27, Prostitution; Article 28, Perjury; Article 29, Bribery; Article 31, Misconduct in Public Office; Article 35, Offenses Against the Public Peace; Article 36A, Riots, Civil Disorders, and Emergencies; Article 39, Protection of Minors; Article 40, Protection of the Family; Article 59, Public Intoxication; and Article 60, Computer-Related Crime. The crimes also include possession or sale of drugs in violation of the North Carolina Controlled Substances Act, Article 5 of Chapter 90 of the General Statutes, and alcohol-related offenses such as sale to underage persons in violation of G.S. 18B-302, or driving while impaired violation of G.S. 20-138.1 through G.S. 20-138.5.

(b) When requested by the Department of Public Instruction, the North Carolina Department of Justice may provide to the requesting department a covered person's criminal history from the State Repository of Criminal

Histories. Such request shall not be due to a person's age, sex, race, color, national origin, religion, creed, political affiliation, or handicapping condition as defined by G.S. 168A-3. For requests for a State criminal history record check only, the requesting department shall provide to the Department of Justice a form consenting to the check, signed by the covered person to be checked and any additional information required by the Department of Justice. National criminal record checks are authorized for covered applicants who have not resided in the State of North Carolina during the past five years. For national checks the Department of Public Instruction shall provide to the North Carolina Department of Justice the fingerprints of the covered person to be checked, any additional information required by the Department of Justice, and a form signed by the covered person to be checked, consenting to the check of the criminal record and to the use of fingerprints and other identifying information required by the State or National Repositories. The fingerprints of the individual shall be forwarded to the State Bureau of Investigation for a search of the State criminal history record file and the Federal Bureau of Investigation for a national criminal history record check. The Department of Public Instruction shall keep all information pursuant to this section confidential. The Department of Justice shall charge a reasonable fee for conducting the checks of the criminal history records authorized by this section.

(c) All releases of criminal history information to the Department of Public Instruction shall be subject to, and in compliance with, rules governing the dissemination of criminal history record checks as adopted by the North Carolina Division of Criminal Information. All of the information the department receives through the checking of the criminal history is privileged information and for the exclusive use of the department.

(d) If the covered person's verified criminal history record check reveals one or more convictions covered under subsection (a) of this section, then the conviction shall constitute just cause for not selecting the person for employment, or for dismissing the person from current employment with the Department of Public Instruction. The conviction shall not automatically prohibit employment; however, the following factors shall be considered by the Department of Public Instruction in determining whether employment shall be denied:

(1) The level and seriousness of the crime;

(2) The date of the crime;

(3) The age of the person at the time of the conviction;

(4) The circumstances surrounding the commission of the crime, if known;

(5) The nexus between the criminal conduct of the person and job duties of the person;

(6) The prison, jail, probation, parole, rehabilitation, and employment records of the person since the date the crime was committed; and

(7) The subsequent commission by the person of a crime listed in subsection (a) of this section.

(e) The Department of Public Instruction may deny employment to or dismiss a covered person who refuses to consent to a criminal history record check or use of fingerprints or other identifying information required by the State or National Repositories of Criminal Histories. Any such refusal shall constitute just cause for the employment denial or the dismissal from employment.

(f) The Department of Public Instruction may extend a conditional offer of employment pending the results of a criminal history record check authorized by this section. (2007-516, s. 1; 2012-12, s. 2(pp).)

§ 114-19.24. Criminal record checks of applicants and of current employees who are involved in the manufacture or production of drivers licenses and identification cards.

(a) The Department of Justice may, upon request, provide to the Department of Transportation, Division of Motor Vehicles, the criminal history from the State and National Repositories of Criminal Histories of the following individuals if the individual (i) is or will be involved in the manufacture or production of drivers licenses and identification cards, or (ii) has or will have the ability to affect the identity information that appears on drivers licenses or identification cards:

(1) An applicant for employment.

(2) A current employee.

(3) A contractual employee or applicant.

(4) An employee of a contractor.

(b) Along with the request, the Division of Motor Vehicles shall provide the following to the Department of Justice:

(1) The fingerprints of the person who is the subject of the record check.

(2) A form signed by the person who is the subject of the record check consenting to:

a. The criminal record check.

b. The use of fingerprints.

c. Any other identifying information required by the State and National Repositories.

d. Any additional information required by the Department of Justice.

(c) The fingerprints shall be forwarded to the State Bureau of Investigation for a search of the State's criminal history record file, and the State Bureau of Investigation shall forward a set of fingerprints to the Federal Bureau of Investigation for a national criminal history record check.

(d) The Division of Motor Vehicles shall keep all information obtained pursuant to this section confidential.

(e) The Department of Justice may charge a fee to offset the cost incurred by it to conduct a criminal record check under this section. The fee shall not exceed the actual cost of locating, editing, researching, and retrieving the information. (2008-202, s. 1.)

§ 114-19.25. Criminal history record checks of applicants for licensure as nursing home administrators.

(a) The Department of Justice may provide to the North Carolina State Board of Examiners for Nursing Home Administrators from the State and

National Repositories of Criminal Histories the criminal history of any applicant for licensure as a nursing home administrator under Article 20 of Chapter 90 of the General Statutes. Along with the request, the Board shall provide to the Department of Justice the fingerprints of the applicant, a form signed by the applicant consenting to the criminal history record check and use of fingerprints and other identifying information required by the State and National Repositories, and any additional information required by the Department of Justice. The applicant's fingerprints shall be forwarded to the State Bureau of Investigation for a search of the State's criminal history record file, and the State Bureau of Investigation shall forward a set of fingerprints to the Federal Bureau of Investigation for a national criminal history record check. The Board shall keep all information obtained pursuant to this section confidential.

(b)   The Department of Justice may charge a fee to offset the cost incurred by it to conduct a criminal history record check under this section. The fee shall not exceed the actual cost of locating, editing, researching, and retrieving the information. (2008-183, s. 2.)

§ 114-19.26. Criminal record checks of applicants for licensure as professional counselors.

The Department of Justice may provide to the North Carolina Board of Licensed Professional Counselors from the State and National Repositories of Criminal Histories the criminal history of any applicant for licensure or reinstatement of a license or licensee under Article 24 of Chapter 90 of the General Statutes. Along with the request, the Board shall provide to the Department of Justice the fingerprints of the applicant or licensee, a form signed by the applicant or licensee consenting to the criminal record check and use of fingerprints and other identifying information required by the State and National Repositories, and any additional information required by the Department of Justice. The applicant or licensee's fingerprints shall be forwarded to the State Bureau of Investigation for a search of the State's criminal history record file, and the State Bureau of Investigation shall forward a set of fingerprints to the Federal Bureau of Investigation for a national criminal history record check. The Board shall keep all information obtained pursuant to this section confidential. The Department of Justice may charge a fee to offset the cost incurred by it to conduct a criminal record check under this section. The fee shall not exceed the actual cost of locating, editing, researching, and retrieving the information. (2009-367, s. 10.)

§ 114-19.27. Criminal history record checks of applicants for licensure as marriage and family therapists and marriage and family therapy associates.

The Department of Justice may provide to the North Carolina Marriage and Family Therapy Licensure Board from the State and National Repositories of Criminal Histories the criminal history of any applicant for licensure or reinstatement of a license or licensee under Article 18C of Chapter 90 of the General Statutes. Along with the request, the Board shall provide to the Department of Justice the fingerprints of the applicant or licensee, a form signed by the applicant or licensee consenting to the criminal history record check and use of fingerprints and other identifying information required by the State and National Repositories, and any additional information required by the Department of Justice. The applicant's or licensee's fingerprints shall be forwarded to the State Bureau of Investigation for a search of the State's criminal history record file, and the State Bureau of Investigation shall forward a set of fingerprints to the Federal Bureau of Investigation for a national criminal history record check. The Board shall keep all information obtained pursuant to this section confidential. The Department of Justice may charge a fee to offset the cost incurred by the Department to conduct a criminal history record check under this section. The fee shall not exceed the actual cost of locating, editing, researching, and retrieving the information. (2009-393, s. 18.)

§ 114-19.28. Criminal record checks of petitioners for restoration of firearms rights.

(a) A person who petitions the court to have the person's firearms rights restored shall submit a full set of the petitioner's fingerprints, to be administered by the sheriff. The petitioner shall also submit to the sheriff a form signed by the petitioner consenting to the criminal record check and use of fingerprints and other identifying information required by the State and National Repositories, and any additional information required by the State Bureau of Investigation or the Federal Bureau of Investigation. The sheriff shall forward the set of fingerprints and the signed consent form to the State Bureau of Investigation for a records check of State and national databases.

(b) Upon receipt of the fingerprints and consent form forwarded by the sheriff pursuant to subsection (a) of this section, the State Bureau of Investigation shall conduct a search of the State criminal history record file and shall forward a set of the fingerprints and a copy of the signed consent form to the Federal Bureau of Investigation for a national criminal history record check.

(c) The State Bureau of Investigation shall provide a copy of the information obtained pursuant to this section to the clerk of superior court, which shall be kept confidential in the court file for the petition for restoration of firearms rights.

(d) The Department of Justice may charge a fee to offset the cost incurred by it to conduct a criminal record check under this section. The fee shall not exceed the actual cost of locating, editing, researching, and retrieving the information. (2010-108, s. 2; 2011-2, ss. 1, 2.)

§ 114-19.29. Criminal record checks of applicants for certification by the Department of Agriculture and Consumer Services as euthanasia technicians.

The Department of Justice may provide a criminal record check to the Department of Agriculture and Consumer Services for a person who has applied for a new or renewal certification as a euthanasia technician. The Department of Agriculture and Consumer Services shall provide the Department of Justice a request for the criminal record check, the fingerprints of the individual to be checked, any additional information required by the Department of Justice, and a form signed by the person seeking certification consenting to the check of the criminal record. The fingerprints shall be forwarded to the State Bureau of Investigation for a search of the State's criminal history record file, and the State Bureau of Investigation shall forward a set of fingerprints to the Federal Bureau of Investigation for a national criminal history record check. The Department of Agriculture and Consumer Services shall keep all information pursuant to this section privileged, in accordance with applicable State law and federal guidelines, and the information shall be confidential and shall not be a public record under Chapter 132 of the General Statutes. The Department of Justice may charge each applicant a fee for conducting the checks of criminal history records authorized by this section. (2010-127, s. 4.)

§ 114-19.30. Criminal history record checks of applicants for trainee registration, appraiser licensure, appraiser certification, or registrants for registration as real estate appraisal management companies.

The Department of Justice may provide to the North Carolina Appraisal Board from the State and National Repositories of Criminal Histories the criminal history of any applicant or registrant for registration under Article 1 and Article 2 of Chapter 93E of the General Statutes. Along with the request, the Board shall provide to the Department of Justice the fingerprints of the applicant or registrant, a form signed by the applicant or registrant consenting to the criminal history record check and use of fingerprints and other identifying information required by the State and National Repositories, and any additional information required by the Department of Justice. The applicant's or registrant's fingerprints shall be forwarded to the State Bureau of Investigation for a search of the State's criminal history record file, and the State Bureau of Investigation shall forward a set of fingerprints to the Federal Bureau of Investigation for a national criminal history record check. The Board shall keep all information obtained pursuant to this section confidential. The Department of Justice may charge a fee to offset the cost incurred by the Department to conduct a criminal history record check under this section. The fee shall not exceed the actual cost of locating, editing, researching, and retrieving the information. (2010-141, s. 2; 2013-403, s. 8.)

§ 114-19.31. Criminal history record checks of applicants for a restoration of a revoked drivers license.

The Department of Justice may provide to the Division of Motor Vehicles, from the State and National Repositories of Criminal Histories, the criminal history record of any applicant for a restoration of a revoked drivers license. Along with the request, the Division shall provide to the Department of Justice the fingerprints of the applicant, a form signed by the applicant consenting to the criminal history record check and use of fingerprints, other identifying information required by the State and National Repositories, and any additional information required by the Department of Justice. The applicant's fingerprints shall be forwarded to the State Bureau of Investigation for a search of the State's criminal history record file, and the State Bureau of Investigation shall forward a set of fingerprints to the Federal Bureau of Investigation for a national criminal history record check. The Division shall keep all information obtained pursuant to this section confidential. The Department of Justice may charge a fee to offset the cost incurred by it to conduct a criminal history record check under this section. The fee shall not exceed the actual cost of locating, editing, researching, and retrieving the information. Fees and other costs incurred by the Division under this statute may be charged to the applicant. (2011-381, s. 5.)

§ 114-19.32. Criminal history record checks of applicants for and current holders of certificate to transport household goods.

The Department of Justice may provide to the Utilities Commission from the State and National Repositories of Criminal Histories the criminal history of any applicant for or current holder of a certificate to transport household goods. Along with the request, the Commission shall provide to the Department of Justice the fingerprints of the applicant or current holder, a form signed by the applicant or current holder consenting to the criminal history record check and use of fingerprints and other identifying information required by the State and National Repositories of Criminal Histories, and any additional information required by the Department of Justice. The applicant's or current holder's fingerprints shall be forwarded to the State Bureau of Investigation for a search of the State's criminal history record file, and the State Bureau of Investigation shall forward a set of fingerprints to the Federal Bureau of Investigation for a national criminal history record check. The Utilities Commission shall keep all information obtained pursuant to this section confidential. The Department of Justice may charge a fee to offset the cost incurred by it to conduct a criminal history record check under this section. The fee shall not exceed the actual cost of locating, editing, researching, and retrieving the information. The Department of Justice shall send a copy of the results of the criminal history record checks directly to the Utilities Commission Chief Clerk. (2012-9, s. 2.)

§ 114-19.33. Criminal history record checks of applicants for licensure as physical therapists or physical therapist assistants.

The Department of Justice may provide to the North Carolina Board of Physical Therapy Examiners a criminal history record from the State and National Repositories of Criminal Histories for applicants for licensure by the Board. Along with a request for criminal history records, the Board shall provide to the Department of Justice the fingerprints of the applicant or subject, a form signed by the applicant consenting to the criminal history record check and use of the fingerprints and other identifying information required by the Repositories, and any additional information required by the Department. The fingerprints shall be forwarded to the State Bureau of Investigation for a search of the State's criminal history record file, and the State Bureau of Investigation shall forward a set of fingerprints to the Federal Bureau of Investigation for a national criminal history record check. The Board shall keep all information obtained pursuant to this section confidential. The Department of Justice may charge a fee to offset the cost incurred by the Department of Justice to conduct a criminal history record check under this section, but the fee shall not exceed the actual cost of locating, editing, researching, and retrieving the information. (2013-312, s. 6.)

§ 114-19.34. Criminal record checks of applicants and recipients of programs of public assistance.

(a)   Upon receipt of a request from a county department of social services pursuant to G.S. 108A-26.1, the Department of Justice shall, to the extent allowed by federal law, provide to the county department of social services the criminal history from the State or National Repositories of Criminal Histories of an applicant for, or recipient of, program assistance under Part 2 or Part 5 of Article 2 of Chapter 108A of the General Statutes.

(b)   The county department of social services shall provide to the Department of Justice, along with the request, any information required by the Department of Justice and a form signed by the individual to be checked consenting to the check of the criminal record and to the use of any necessary identifying information required by the State or National Repositories. The county department of social services shall keep all information pursuant to this section confidential and privileged, except as provided in G.S. 108A-26.1.

(c)   The Department of Justice may charge a reasonable fee only for conducting the checks of the criminal history records authorized by this section. (2013-417, s. 3.)

§ 114-19.35: Reserved for future codification purposes.

§ 114-19.36: Reserved for future codification purposes.

§ 114-19.37: Reserved for future codification purposes.

§ 114-19.38: Reserved for future codification purposes.

§ 114-19.39: Reserved for future codification purposes.

§ 114-19.40: Reserved for future codification purposes.

§ 114-19.41: Reserved for future codification purposes.

§ 114-19.42: Reserved for future codification purposes.

§ 114-19.43: Reserved for future codification purposes.

§ 114-19.44: Reserved for future codification purposes.

§ 114-19.45: Reserved for future codification purposes.

§ 114-19.46: Reserved for future codification purposes.

§ 114-19.47: Reserved for future codification purposes.

§ 114-19.48: Reserved for future codification purposes.

§ 114-19.49: Reserved for future codification purposes.

§ 114-19.50. The National Crime Prevention and Privacy Compact.

The National Crime Prevention and Privacy Compact is enacted into law and entered into with all jurisdictions legally joining in the compact in the form substantially as set forth in this section, as follows:

Preamble.

Whereas, it is in the interest of the State to facilitate the dissemination of criminal history records from other states for use in North Carolina as authorized by State law; and

Whereas, the National Crime Prevention and Privacy Compact creates a legal framework for the cooperative exchange of criminal history records for noncriminal justice purposes; and

Whereas, the compact provides for the organization of an electronic information-sharing system among the federal government and the states to exchange criminal history records for noncriminal justice purposes authorized by federal or state law, such as background checks for governmental licensing and employment; and

Whereas, under the compact, the FBI and the party states agree to maintain detailed databases of their respective criminal history records, including arrests and dispositions, and to make them available to the federal government and party states for authorized purposes; and

Whereas, the FBI shall manage the federal data facilities that provide a significant part of the infrastructure for the system; and

Whereas, entering into the compact would facilitate the interstate and federal-state exchange of criminal history information to streamline the processing of background checks for noncriminal justice purposes; and

Whereas, release and use of information obtained through the system for noncriminal justice purposes would be governed by the laws of the receiving state; and

Whereas, entering into the compact will provide a mechanism for establishing and enforcing uniform standards for record accuracy and for the confidentiality and privacy interests of record subjects.

Article I.

Definitions.

As used in this compact, the following definitions apply:

(1)   "Attorney General" means the Attorney General of the United States.

(2)   "Compact officer" means:

a.   With respect to the federal government, an official so designated by the director of the FBI; and

b.   With respect to a party state, the chief administrator of the state's criminal history record repository or a designee of the chief administrator who is a regular, full-time employee of the repository.

(3)   "Council" means the compact council established under Article VI.

(4)   "Criminal history record repository" means the State Bureau of Investigation's Division of Criminal Information.

(5)   "Criminal history records" means information collected by criminal justice agencies on individuals consisting of identifiable descriptions and notations of arrests, detentions, indictments, or other formal criminal charges and any disposition arising therefrom, including acquittal, sentencing, correctional supervision, or release. The term does not include identification information such as fingerprint records if the information does not indicate involvement of the individual with the criminal justice system.

(6)   "Criminal justice" includes activities relating to the detection, apprehension, detention, pretrial release, posttrial release, prosecution, adjudication, correctional supervision, or rehabilitation of accused persons or criminal offenders. The administration of criminal justice includes criminal identification activities and the collection, storage, and dissemination of criminal history records.

(7)   "Criminal justice agency" means: (i) courts; and (ii) a governmental agency or any subunit of an agency that performs the administration of criminal justice pursuant to a statute or executive order and allocates a substantial part of its annual budget to the administration of criminal justice. The term includes federal and state inspector general offices.

(8)   "Criminal justice services" means services provided by the FBI to criminal justice agencies in response to a request for information about a particular individual or as an update to information previously provided for criminal justice purposes.

(9)   "Direct access" means access to the national identification index by computer terminal or other automated means not requiring the assistance of or intervention by any other party or agency.

(10) "Executive order" means an order of the President of the United States or the chief executive officer of a state that has the force of law and that is promulgated in accordance with applicable law.

(11) "FBI" means the Federal Bureau of Investigation.

(12) "III system" means the interstate identification index system, which is the cooperative federal-state system for the exchange of criminal history records. The term includes the national identification index, the national fingerprint file, and, to the extent of their participation in the system, the criminal history record repositories of the states and the FBI.

(13) "National fingerprint file" means a database of fingerprints or of other uniquely personal identifying information that relates to an arrested or charged individual and that is maintained by the FBI to provide positive identification of record subjects indexed in the III system.

(14) "National identification index" means an index maintained by the FBI consisting of names, identifying numbers, and other descriptive information relating to record subjects about whom there are criminal history records in the III system.

(15) "National indices" means the national identification index and the national fingerprint file.

(16) "Noncriminal justice purposes" means uses of criminal history records for purposes authorized by federal or state law other than purposes relating to criminal justice activities, including employment suitability, licensing determinations, immigration and naturalization matters, and national security clearances.

(17) "Nonparty state" means a state that has not ratified this compact.

(18) "Party state" means a state that has ratified this compact.

(19) "Positive identification" means a determination, based upon a comparison of fingerprints or other equally reliable biometric identification techniques, that the subject of a record search is the same person as the subject of a criminal history record or records indexed in the III system. Identifications based solely upon a comparison of subjects' names or other

nonunique identification characteristics or numbers, or combinations thereof, does not constitute positive identification.

(20) "Sealed record information" means:

a. With respect to adults, that portion of a record that is:

1. Not available for criminal justice uses;

2. Not supported by fingerprints or other accepted means of positive identification; or

3. Subject to restrictions on dissemination for noncriminal justice purposes pursuant to a court order related to a particular subject or pursuant to a federal or state statute that requires action on a sealing petition filed by a particular record subject; and

b. With respect to juveniles, whatever each state determines is a sealed record under its own law and procedure.

(21) "State" means any state, territory, or possession of the United States, the District of Columbia, and the Commonwealth of Puerto Rico.

Article II.

Purposes.

The purposes of this compact are to:

(1) Provide a legal framework for the establishment of a cooperative federal-state system for the interstate and federal-state exchange of criminal history records for noncriminal justice uses;

(2) Require the FBI to permit use of the national identification index and the national fingerprint file by each party state and to provide, in a timely fashion, federal and state criminal history records to requesting states, in accordance

with the terms of this compact and with rules, procedures, and standards established by the council under Article VI;

(3) Require party states to provide information and records for the national identification index and the national fingerprint file and to provide criminal history records, in a timely fashion, to criminal history record repositories of other states and the federal government for noncriminal justice purposes, in accordance with the terms of this compact and with rules, procedures, and standards established by the council under Article VI;

(4) Provide for the establishment of a council to monitor III system operations and to prescribe system rules and procedures for the effective and proper operation of the III system for noncriminal justice purposes; and

(5) Require the FBI and each party state to adhere to III system standards concerning record dissemination and use, response times, system security, data quality, and other duly established standards, including those that enhance the accuracy and privacy of such records.

Article III.

Responsibilities of Compact Parties.

(a) The director of the FBI shall:

(1) Appoint an FBI compact officer who shall:

a. Administer this compact within the Department of Justice and among federal agencies and other agencies and organizations that submit search requests to the FBI pursuant to Article V(c);

b. Ensure that compact provisions and rules, procedures, and standards prescribed by the council under Article VI are complied with by the Department of Justice and federal agencies and other agencies and organizations referred to in sub-subdivision (a)(1)a. of this Article III; and

c. Regulate the use of records received by means of the III system from party states when such records are supplied by the FBI directly to other federal agencies;

(2) Provide to federal agencies and to state criminal history record repositories criminal history records maintained in its database for the noncriminal justice purposes described in Article IV, including:

a. Information from nonparty states; and

b. Information from party states that is available from the FBI through the III system but is not available from the party states through the III system;

(3) Provide a telecommunications network and maintain centralized facilities for the exchange of criminal history records for both criminal justice purposes and the noncriminal justice purposes described in Article IV and ensure that the exchange of records for criminal justice purposes has priority over exchange for noncriminal justice purposes; and

(4) Modify or enter into user agreements with nonparty state criminal history record repositories to require them to establish record request procedures conforming to those prescribed in Article V.

(b) Each party state shall:

(1) Appoint a compact officer who shall:

a. Administer this compact within that state;

b. Ensure that compact provisions and rules, procedures, and standards established by the council under Article VI are complied with in the state; and

c. Regulate the in-state use of records received by means of the III system from the FBI or from other party states;

(2) Establish and maintain a criminal history record repository, which shall provide:

a. Information and records for the national identification index and the national fingerprint file; and

b. The state's III system-indexed criminal history records for noncriminal justice purposes described in Article IV;

(3) Participate in the national fingerprint file; and

(4) Provide and maintain telecommunications links and related equipment necessary to support the criminal justice services set forth in this compact.

(c) In carrying out their responsibilities under this compact, the FBI and each party state shall comply with III system rules, procedures, and standards duly established by the council concerning record dissemination and use, response times, data quality, system security, accuracy, privacy protection, and other aspects of III system operation.

(d) Use of the III system for noncriminal justice purposes authorized in this compact must be managed so as not to diminish the level of services provided in support of criminal justice purposes. Administration of compact provisions may not reduce the level of service available to authorized noncriminal justice users on the effective date of this compact.

Article IV.

Authorized Record Disclosures.

(a) To the extent authorized by section 552a of Title 5, United States Code (commonly known as the Privacy Act of 1974), the FBI shall provide on request criminal history records, excluding sealed record information, to state criminal history record repositories for noncriminal justice purposes allowed by federal statute, federal executive order, or a state statute that has been approved by the Attorney General to ensure that the state statute explicitly authorizes national indices checks.

(b) The FBI, to the extent authorized by section 552a of Title 5, United States Code (commonly known as the Privacy Act of 1974), and state criminal history record repositories shall provide criminal history records, excluding sealed record information, to criminal justice agencies and other governmental or nongovernmental agencies for noncriminal justice purposes allowed by federal statute, federal executive order, or a state statute that has been approved by the Attorney General to ensure that the state statute explicitly authorizes national indices checks.

(c) Any record obtained under this compact may be used only for the official purposes for which the record was requested. Each compact officer shall establish procedures consistent with this compact and with rules, procedures, and standards established by the council under Article VI, which procedures shall protect the accuracy and privacy of the records and shall:

(1) Ensure that records obtained under this compact are used only by authorized officials for authorized purposes;

(2) Require that subsequent record checks are requested to obtain current information whenever a new need arises; and

(3) Ensure that record entries that may not legally be used for a particular noncriminal justice purpose are deleted from the response and, if no information authorized for release remains, that an appropriate "no record" response is communicated to the requesting official.

Article V.

Record Request Procedures.

(a) Subject fingerprints or other approved forms of positive identification must be submitted with all requests for criminal history record checks for noncriminal justice purposes.

(b) Each request for a criminal history record check utilizing the national indices made under any approved state statute must be submitted through that state's criminal history record repository. A state criminal history record repository shall process an interstate request for noncriminal justice purposes through the national indices only if the request is transmitted through another state criminal history record repository or the FBI.

(c) Each request for criminal history record checks utilizing the national indices made under federal authority must be submitted through the FBI or, if the state criminal history record repository consents to process fingerprint submissions, through the criminal history record repository in the state in which the request originated. Direct access to the national identification index by entities other than the FBI and state criminal history record repositories may not be permitted for noncriminal justice purposes.

(d) A state criminal history record repository or the FBI:

(1) May charge a fee, in accordance with applicable law, for handling a request involving fingerprint processing for noncriminal justice purposes; and

(2) May not charge a fee for providing criminal history records in response to an electronic request for a record that does not involve a request to process fingerprints.

(e) (1) If a state criminal history record repository cannot positively identify the subject of a record request made for noncriminal justice purposes, the request, together with fingerprints or other approved identifying information, must be forwarded to the FBI for a search of the national indices.

(2) If, with respect to a request forwarded by a state criminal history record repository under subdivision (e)(1) of this Article V, the FBI positively identifies the subject as having a III system-indexed record or records:

a. The FBI shall so advise the state criminal history record repository; and

b. The state criminal history record repository is entitled to obtain the additional criminal history record information from the FBI or other state criminal history record repositories.

Article VI.

Establishment of Compact Council.

(a) There is established a council to be known as the compact council which has the authority to promulgate rules and procedures governing the use of the III system for noncriminal justice purposes, not to conflict with FBI administration of the III system for criminal justice purposes. The council shall:

(1) Continue in existence as long as this compact remains in effect;

(2) Be located, for administrative purposes, within the FBI; and

(3) Be organized and hold its first meeting as soon as practicable after the effective date of this compact.

(b) The council must be composed of 15 members, each of whom must be appointed by the Attorney General, as follows:

(1) Nine members, each of whom shall serve a two-year term, who must be selected from among the compact officers of party states based on the recommendation of the compact officers of all party states, except that in the absence of the requisite number of compact officers available to serve, the chief administrators of the criminal history record repositories of nonparty states must be eligible to serve on an interim basis;

(2) Two at-large members, nominated by the director of the FBI, each of whom shall serve a three-year term, of whom:

a. One must be a representative of the criminal justice agencies of the federal government and may not be an employee of the FBI; and

b. One must be a representative of the noncriminal justice agencies of the federal government;

(3) Two at-large members, nominated by the chair of the council once the chair is elected pursuant to subsection (c) of this Article VI, each of whom shall serve a three-year term, of whom:

a. One must be a representative of state or local criminal justice agencies; and

b. One must be a representative of state or local noncriminal justice agencies;

(4) One member who shall serve a three-year term and who shall simultaneously be a member of the FBI's advisory policy board on criminal justice information services, nominated by the membership of that policy board; and

(5) One member, nominated by the director of the FBI, who shall serve a three-year term and who must be an employee of the FBI.

(c) From its membership, the council shall elect a chair and a vice-chair of the council. Both the chair and vice-chair of the council: (i) must be a compact officer, unless there is no compact officer on the council who is willing to serve, in which case the chair may be an at-large member and (ii) shall serve two-year terms and may be reelected to only one additional two-year term. The vice-chair of the council shall serve as the chair of the council in the absence of the chair.

(d) The council shall meet at least once each year at the call of the chair. Each meeting of the council must be open to the public. The council shall provide prior public notice in the federal register of each meeting of the council, including the matters to be addressed at the meeting. A majority of the council or any committee of the council shall constitute a quorum of the council or of a committee, respectively, for the conduct of business. A lesser number may meet to hold hearings, take testimony, or conduct any business not requiring a vote.

(e) The council shall make available for public inspection and copying at the council office within the FBI and shall publish in the federal register any rules, procedures, or standards established by the council.

(f) The council may request from the FBI reports, studies, statistics, or other information or materials that the council determines to be necessary to enable the council to perform its duties under this compact. The FBI, to the extent authorized by law, may provide assistance or information upon a request.

(g) The chair may establish committees as necessary to carry out this compact and may prescribe their membership, responsibilities, and duration.

Article VII.

Ratification of Compact.

This compact takes effect upon being entered into by two or more states as between those states and the federal government. When additional states subsequently enter into this compact, it becomes effective among those states and the federal government and each party state that has previously ratified it. When ratified, this compact has the full force and effect of law within the ratifying jurisdictions. The form of ratification must be in accordance with the laws of the executing state.

Article VIII.

Miscellaneous Provisions.

(a) Administration of this compact may not interfere with the management and control of the director of the FBI over the FBI's collection and dissemination of criminal history records and the advisory function of the FBI's advisory policy board chartered under the Federal Advisory Committee Act (5 U.S.C. App.) for all purposes other than noncriminal justice.

(b) Nothing in this compact may require the FBI to obligate or expend funds beyond those appropriated to the FBI.

(c) Nothing in this compact may diminish or lessen the obligations, responsibilities, and authorities of any state, whether a party state or a nonparty state, or of any criminal history record repository or other subdivision or component thereof under the Departments of State, Justice, and Commerce, the Judiciary, and Related Agencies Appropriation Act, 1973 (Public Law 92-544) or regulations and guidelines promulgated thereunder, including the rules and procedures promulgated by the council under Article VI(a), regarding the use and dissemination of criminal history records and information.

Article IX.

Renunciation.

(a) This compact shall bind each party state until renounced by the party state.

(b) Any renunciation of this compact by a party state must:

(1) Be effected in the same manner by which the party state ratified this compact; and

(2) Become effective 180 days after written notice of renunciation is provided by the party state to each other party state and to the federal government.

Article X.

Severability.

The provisions of this compact must be severable. If any phrase, clause, sentence, or provision of this compact is declared to be contrary to the constitution of any participating state or to the Constitution of the United States or if the applicability of any phrase, clause, sentence, or provision of this compact to any government, agency, person, or circumstance is held invalid, the validity of the remainder of this compact and the applicability of the remainder of the compact to any government, agency, person, or circumstance may not be affected by the severability. If a portion of this compact is held contrary to the constitution of any party state, all other portions of this compact must remain in full force and effect as to the remaining party states and in full force and effect as to the party state affected, as to all other provisions.

Article XI.

Adjudication of Disputes.

(a) The council:

(1) Has initial authority to make determinations with respect to any dispute regarding:

a. Interpretation of this compact;

b. Any rule or standard established by the council pursuant to Article VI; and

c. Any dispute or controversy between any parties to this compact; and

(2) Shall hold a hearing concerning any dispute described in subdivision (a)(1) of this Article XI at a regularly scheduled meeting of the council and only render a decision based upon a majority vote of the members of the council. The decision must be published pursuant to the requirements of Article VI(e).

(b) The FBI shall exercise immediate and necessary action to preserve the integrity of the III system, to maintain system policy and standards, to protect the accuracy and privacy of records, and to prevent abuses until the council holds a hearing on the matters.

(c) The FBI or a party state may appeal any decision of the council to the Attorney General and after that appeal may file suit in the appropriate district court of the United States that has original jurisdiction of all cases or controversies arising under this compact. Any suit arising under this compact and initiated in a state court must be removed to the appropriate district court of the United States in the manner provided by section 1446 of Title 28, United States Code, or other statutory authority. (2003-214, s. 2; 2004-199, s. 28.)

Part 3. Protection of Public Officials.

§ 114-20. Authority to provide protection to certain public officials.

The North Carolina State Bureau of Investigation is authorized to provide protection to public officials who request it, and who, in the discretion of the Director of the Bureau with the approval of the Attorney General, demonstrate a need for such protection. The bureau shall not provide protection for any individual other than the Governor for a period greater than 30 days without review and reapproval by the Attorney General. This review and reapproval shall be required at the end of each 30-day period. (1977, c. 571; 2003-214, s. 1(3); 2011-145, s. 19.1(q1); 2011-391, s. 43(g).)

§ 114-20.1. Authority to designate areas for protection of public officials.

(a) The Attorney General is authorized to designate buildings and grounds which constitute temporary residences or temporary offices of any public official being protected under authority of G.S. 114-20, or any area that will be visited by any such official, a public building or facility during the time of such use.

(b) The Attorney General or the Director of the State Bureau of Investigation may, with the consent of the official to be protected, make rules governing ingress to or egress from such buildings, grounds or areas designated under this section. (1981, c. 499, s. 1; 2003-214, s. 1(3); 2011-145, s. 19.1(q1); 2011-391, s. 43(g).)

§ 114-21: Recodified as G.S. 114-12.1 by Session Laws 2003-214, s. 1(4), effective June 19, 2003.

§§ 114-22 through 114-25. Reserved for future codification purposes.

Article 5.

Law Enforcement Officers' Minimum Salary Act.

§§ 114-26 through 114-39: Repealed by Session Laws 1983, c. 781.

Article 6.

Office of the Inspector General.

§§ 114-40 through 114-42: Repealed by Session Laws 2001-424, s. 23.10, effective January 1, 2002.

Article 7.

Methamphetamine Watch Program.

§ 114-43. Methamphetamine Watch Program - good faith actions immune from civil and criminal liability.

Anyone who, in good faith, does any of the acts listed in subdivisions (1) through (3) of this section as part of a Methamphetamine Watch Program approved by the Department of Justice is immune from any civil or criminal liability that might otherwise be incurred or imposed for that action. In any proceeding involving liability, good faith is presumed. The actions for which immunity is granted under this section are as follows:

(1) The person files a report with a law enforcement agency concerning the purchase or theft of ingredients used to manufacture methamphetamine.

(2) The person cooperates in any law enforcement investigation concerning the manufacture of methamphetamine.

(3) The person testifies in any judicial proceeding concerning the manufacture of methamphetamine. (2004-178, s. 9.)

§ 114-44. Reserved for future codification purposes.

§ 114-45. Reserved for future codification purposes.

§ 114-46. Reserved for future codification purposes.

§ 114-47. Reserved for future codification purposes.

§ 114-48. Reserved for future codification purposes.

§ 114-49. Reserved for future codification purposes.

Article 8.

Financial Literacy Council.

§ 114-50. Financial Literacy Council established; purpose.

There is established within the Department of Justice the North Carolina Financial Literacy Council (Council). The Council shall monitor and assist the Department of Public Instruction in the coordination of statewide delivery of financial education within the public school system, shall identify programs designed to increase the financial literacy of North Carolinians outside the public school system, and shall work to expand access to financial education resources and programs in communities across North Carolina. (2009-265, s. 1.)

§ 114-51. Membership; terms; quorum.

(a) The Council shall consist of 18 members appointed by and serving at the pleasure of the Governor. The Governor shall designate a chair from among the members of the Council. Membership shall be as follows:

(1) Ten members from government agencies with responsibility for programs and services related to financial education, financial services, and related economic stability efforts. At least one representative shall come from each of the following government agencies:

a. Community College System.

b. Department of Commerce.

c. Department of Justice.

d. Department of Labor.

e. Department of Public Instruction.

f. Department of the Secretary of State.

g. Department of State Treasurer.

h. Office of the Commissioner of Banks.

i. The University of North Carolina.

(2) Two public members with experience in the financial services industry.

(3) Two public members who represent employers with experience in providing financial education to their employees.

(4) Four public members with experience in consumer advocacy or nonprofit financial education.

(b) Members of the Council shall be appointed for terms of three years and shall serve until their successors are appointed and qualified.

(c) A majority of the Council's members shall constitute a quorum. (2009-265, s. 1.)

§ 114-52. Staffing.

The Department of Justice shall provide administrative and staff support to the Council. (2009-265, s. 1.)

§ 114-53. Duties.

The Council shall meet at least quarterly and shall perform the following duties:

(1) Study and document current financial education programs in North Carolina and best practices across the country.

(2) Coordinate activities related to financial education and asset building that occur within various government agencies, private enterprise, and the nonprofit sector to ensure dissemination of resources and information to households across the State.

(3) Propose public and private policy, organizational changes, and systemic changes to ensure all North Carolinians have access to training about necessary financial skills and experience with financial services.

(4) Consider and make recommendations specifically to address the following issues:

a. Current personal financial literacy programs in the public schools and how to integrate financial education in K-12 to ensure that young people are prepared for financial success.

b. Unique financial issues facing students in higher education and how to address those issues through the community colleges and public and private university systems.

c. Creation of and access to financial products that provide hands-on learning of financial skills.

(5) Monitor the outcomes of financial education programs, focusing specifically on the following indicators: improved financial knowledge, improved financial behaviors, and increased access to and use of affordable financial services.

(6) Use the talents, expertise, and resources within the State, especially those of the public schools, community colleges, and public and private university systems, as well as the bank and credit union industries, to further its mission.

(7) Report annually to the General Assembly and the Governor on the performance of its prescribed duties and on the impact of the financial education activities conducted by State agencies. (2009-265, s. 1.)

§ 114-54. Compensation and expenses of members.

Public members of the Financial Literacy Council may receive subsistence and travel expenses at the rates set forth in G.S. 138-5 or G.S. 138-6, as appropriate. (2009-265, s. 1.)

§ 114-55. State officers, etc., upon request, to furnish data and information to the Council.

Except as provided in G.S. 105-259, all officers, agents, agencies, and departments of the State are required to give to the Council, upon request, all information and all data that are within their possession or ascertainable from their records and that are pertinent to financial education activities. (2009-265, s. 1.)

§ 114-56: Reserved for future codification purposes.

§ 114-57: Reserved for future codification purposes.

§ 114-58: Reserved for future codification purposes.

§ 114-59: Reserved for future codification purposes.

Article 9.

North Carolina State Crime Laboratory.

§ 114-60. Laboratory and clinical facilities; employment of criminologists; services of scientists, etc., employed by State; radio system.

In the Department of Justice there shall be provided laboratory facilities for the analysis of evidences of crime, including the determination of presence, quantity and character of poisons, the character of bloodstains, microscopic and other examination material associated with the commission of crime, examination and analysis of projectiles of ballistic imprints and records which might lead to the determination or identification of criminals, the examination and identification of fingerprints, and other evidence leading to the identification, apprehension, or conviction of criminals. A sufficient number of persons skilled in such matters shall be employed to render a reasonable service to the public through the criminal justice system and to the criminal justice system in the discharge of their duties.

The laboratory and clinical facilities of the institutions of the State, both educational and departmental, shall be made available to the Laboratory, and scientists and doctors now working for the State through its institutions and departments may be called upon by the Governor to aid the Laboratory in the evaluation, preparation, and preservation of evidence in which scientific methods are employed, and a reasonable fee may be allowed by the Governor for such service. (1937, c. 349, s. 7; 2003-214, s. 1(1); 2011-19, s. 10; 2013-360, s. 17.6(d), (m).)

§ 114-61. Forensic Science Advisory Board.

(a) Creation and Membership. - The North Carolina Forensic Science Advisory Board (Board) is hereby established as an advisory board within the Department of Justice. The Board shall consist of 16 members, consisting of the State Crime Laboratory Director, and 15 members appointed by the Attorney General as follows:

(1) A forensic scientist or any other person with an advanced degree who has received substantial education, training, or experience in the subject of laboratory standards or quality assurance regulation and monitoring.

(2) The Chief Medical Examiner of the State.

(3) A forensic scientist with an advanced degree who has received substantial education, training, or experience in the discipline of molecular biology.

(4) A forensic scientist with an advanced degree who has experience in the discipline of population genetics.

(5) A scientist with an advanced degree who has experience in the discipline of forensic chemistry.

(6) A scientist with an advanced degree who has experience in the discipline of forensic biology.

(7) A forensic scientist or any other person with an advanced degree who has received substantial education, training, or experience in the discipline of trace evidence.

(8) A scientist with a doctoral degree who has experience in the discipline of forensic toxicology and is certified by the American Board of Forensic Toxicologists.

(9) A member of the International Association for Identification.

(10) A member of the Association of Firearms and Toolmark Examiners.

(11) A member of the International Association for Chemical Testing.

(12) A director of a private or federal forensic laboratory located in the State.

(13) A member of the American Society of Crime Laboratory Directors.

(14) A member of the Academy of Forensic Sciences.

(15) A member of the American Statistical Association.

A chairman shall be elected from among the members appointed, and staff shall be provided by the Department of Justice.

(b) Meetings. - The Board shall meet quarterly and at such other times and places as it determines. Members of the Board cannot designate a proxy to vote in their absence.

(c) Terms. - Members of the Board initially appointed shall serve the following terms: five members shall serve a term of two years; five members shall serve a term of three years; and five members shall serve a term of four years. Thereafter, all appointments shall be for a term of four years. A vacancy other than by expiration of term shall be filled by the Attorney General for the unexpired term. Members of the Board cannot designate a proxy to vote in their absence.

(d) Terms. - Expenses. - Members of the Board shall be paid reasonable and necessary expenses incurred in the performance of their duties. Members of the Board who are State officers or employees shall receive no compensation for serving on the Board but may be reimbursed for their expenses in accordance with G.S. 138-6. Members of the Board who are full-time salaried public officers or employees other than State officers or employees shall receive no compensation for serving on the Board but may be reimbursed for their expenses in accordance with G.S. 138-5(b). All other members of the Board may receive compensation and reimbursement for expenses in accordance with G.S. 138-5.

(e) Functions. - The Board may review State Crime Laboratory operations and make recommendations concerning the services furnished to user agencies. The Board shall review and make recommendations as necessary to the Laboratory Director concerning any of the following:

(1) New scientific programs, protocols, and methods of testing.

(2) Plans for the implementation of new programs; sustaining existing programs and improving upon them where possible; and the elimination of programs which are no longer needed.

(3) Protocols for testing and examination methods and guidelines for the presentation of results in court.

(4) Qualification standards for the various forensic scientists of the Laboratory.

(f) Review Process. - Upon request of the Laboratory Director, the Board shall review analytical work, reports, and conclusions of scientists employed by the Laboratory. Records reviewed by this Board retain their confidential status and continue to be considered records of a criminal investigation as defined in G.S. 132-1.4. These records shall be reviewed only in a closed session meeting pursuant to G.S. 143-318.11 of the Board, and each member of the Board shall, prior to receiving any documents to review, sign a confidentiality agreement agreeing to maintain the confidentiality of and not to disclose the documents nor the contents of the documents reviewed. The Board shall recommend to the Laboratory a review process to use when there is a request that the Laboratory retest or reexamine evidence that has been previously examined by the Laboratory. (2011-19, s. 2; 2013-360, s. 17.6(d).)

§ 114-62. North Carolina State Crime Laboratory Ombudsman.

The position of ombudsman is created in the North Carolina State Crime Laboratory within the North Carolina Department of Justice. The primary purpose of this position shall be to work with defense counsel, prosecutorial agencies, criminal justice system stakeholders, law enforcement officials, and the general public to ensure all processes, procedures, practices, and protocols at the State Crime Laboratory are consistent with State and federal law, best forensic law practices, and in the best interests of justice in this State. The ombudsman shall mediate complaints brought to the attention of the ombudsman between the Crime Laboratory and defense counsel, prosecutorial agencies, law enforcement agencies, and the general public. The ombudsman shall ensure all criminal justice stakeholders and the general public are aware of the availability, responsibilities, and role of the ombudsman and shall regularly attend meetings of the Conferences of the District Attorneys, District and Superior Court Judges, Public Defenders, the Advocates for Justice, and Bar Criminal Law Sections. The ombudsman shall make recommendations on a regular basis to the Director of the State Crime Laboratory and the Attorney General of North Carolina as to policies, procedures, practices, and training of employees needed at the Laboratory to ensure compliance with State and federal law, best forensic law practices, and to resolve any meritorious systemic complaints received by the ombudsman. (2011-19, s. 6(a); 2013-360, s. 17.6(d), (n).)

§ 114-63. Transfer of personnel.

The Director of the North Carolina State Crime Laboratory shall have authority to transfer employees of the Crime Laboratory from one Crime Laboratory location in the State to another as the Director may deem necessary. When any member of the Crime Laboratory is transferred from one location to another for the convenience of the Crime Laboratory, or otherwise than upon the request of the employee, the Crime Laboratory shall be responsible for transporting the household goods, furniture, and personal effects of the employee and members of his or her household. (2013-360, s. 17.6(q).)

§ 114-64: Reserved for future codification purposes.

§ 114-65: Reserved for future codification purposes.

§ 114-66: Reserved for future codification purposes.

§ 114-67: Reserved for future codification purposes.

§ 114-68: Reserved for future codification purposes.

§ 114-69: Reserved for future codification purposes.

Article 10.

North Carolina Human Trafficking Commission.

§ 114-70. North Carolina Human Trafficking Commission.

(a)   Establishment. - There is established in the Department of Justice the North Carolina Human Trafficking Commission. For purposes of this section, "Commission" means the North Carolina Human Trafficking Commission.

(b)   Membership. - The Commission shall consist of 12 members as follows:

(1)   The President Pro Tempore of the Senate shall appoint one representative from each of the following:

a.   The public at large.

b.   A county sheriff's office.

c.   A city or town police department.

d.   Legal Aid of North Carolina.

(2)   The Speaker of the House of Representatives shall appoint one representative from each of the following:

a.   The public at large.

b.   North Carolina Coalition Against Human Trafficking.

c.   A faith-based shelter or benefits organization providing services to victims of human trafficking.

d.   A district attorney.

office

(3) The Governor shall appoint one representative from each of the following:

a. The Department of Labor.

b. The Department of Justice.

c. The Department of Public Safety.

d. A health care representative.

(c) Powers. - The Commission shall have the following powers:

(1) To apply for and receive, on behalf of the State, funding from federal, public or private initiatives, grant programs, or donors that will assist in examining and countering the problem of human trafficking in North Carolina.

(2) To commission, fund, and facilitate quantitative and qualitative research to explore the specific ways human trafficking is occurring in North Carolina and the links to international and domestic human trafficking, and to assist in creating measurement, assessment, and accountability mechanisms.

(3) To contribute to efforts to inform and educate law enforcement personnel, social services providers, and the general public about human trafficking so that human traffickers can be prosecuted and victim-survivors can receive appropriate services.

(4) To suggest new policies, procedures, or legislation to further the work of eradicating human trafficking and to provide assistance and review with new policies, procedures, and legislation.

(5) To assist in developing regional response teams or other coordinated efforts to counter human trafficking at the level of law enforcement, legal services, social services, and nonprofits.

(6) To identify gaps in law enforcement or service provision and recommend solutions to those gaps.

(7) To consider whether human trafficking should be added to the list of criminal convictions that require registration under the sex offender and public protection registration program.

(d) Terms and Chair. - Members shall serve two-year terms, with no prohibition against being reappointed. Any individual appointed to serve on the Commission shall serve until his or her successor is appointed and qualified. The chair shall be appointed biennially by the Governor from among the membership of the Commission.

(e) Meetings. - The chair shall convene the Commission. Meetings shall be held as often as necessary, but not less than four times a year.

(f) A majority of the members of the Commission shall constitute a quorum for the transaction of business. The affirmative vote of a majority of the members present at meetings of the Commission shall be necessary for action to be taken by the Commission.

(g) Vacancies. - A vacancy on the Commission or as chair of the Commission resulting from the resignation of a member or otherwise shall be filled in the same manner in which the original appointment was made, and the term shall be for the balance of the unexpired term.

(h) Removal. - The Commission may remove a member for misfeasance, malfeasance, nonfeasance, or neglect of duty.

(i) Compensation. - Commission members shall receive no per diem for their services but shall be entitled to receive travel allowances in accordance with the provisions of G.S. 138-5 or G.S. 138-6, as appropriate.

(j) Staffing. - The Department of Justice shall be responsible for staffing the Commission.

(k) Funding. - From funds available to the Department of Justice, the Attorney General shall allocate monies to fund the work of the Commission. (2012-142, s. 15.3A(a)-(k); 2012-194, s. 55.5; 2013-368, ss. 23, 24.)

§§ 115-1 through 115-410: Repealed by 1981, c. 423, s. 1.

Chapter 115A.

Community Colleges, Technical Institutes, and Industrial Education Centers.

§§ 115A-1 through 115A-42. Repealed by Session Laws 1979, c. 462, s. 1.

Chapter 115B.

Tuition and Fee Waivers.

§ 115B-1. Definitions.

The following definitions apply in this Chapter:

(1)   Employer. - The State of North Carolina and its departments, agencies, and institutions; or a county, city, town, or other political subdivision of the State.

(2)   Firefighter or volunteer firefighter. - The same as provided in G.S. 58-86-25 for "eligible firemen".

(3)   Law enforcement officer. - An employee or volunteer of an employer who possesses the power of arrest, who has taken the law enforcement oath administered under the authority of the State as prescribed by G.S. 11-11, and who is certified as a law enforcement officer under the provisions of Chapter 17C of the General Statutes or certified as a deputy sheriff under the provisions of Chapter 17E of the General Statutes. "Law enforcement officer" also means the sheriff of the county.

(4)   Permanently and totally disabled as a direct result of a traumatic injury sustained in the line of duty. - A person: (i) who as a law enforcement officer, firefighter, volunteer firefighter, or rescue squad worker suffered a disabling injury while in active service or training for active service, (ii) who at the time of active service or training was a North Carolina resident, and (iii) who has been determined to be permanently and totally disabled for compensation purposes by the North Carolina Industrial Commission.

(5)   Rescue squad worker. - The same as provided in G.S. 58-86-30 for "eligible rescue squad worker".

(6) Survivor. - Any person whose parent or spouse: (i) was a law enforcement officer, a firefighter, a volunteer firefighter, or a rescue squad worker, (ii) was killed while in active service or training for active service or died as a result of a service-connected disability, and (iii) at the time of active service or training was a North Carolina resident. The term does not include the widow or widower of a law enforcement officer, firefighter, volunteer firefighter, or a rescue squad worker if the widow or widower has remarried.

(7) Tuition. - The amount charged for registering for a credit hour of instruction and shall not be construed to mean any other fees or charges or costs of textbooks. (1975, c. 606, s. 1; 1977, c. 981, s. 1; 1997-505, s. 2; 2003-230, s. 1.)

§ 115B-2. Tuition waiver authorized.

(a) The constituent institutions of The University of North Carolina and the community colleges as defined in G.S. 115D-2(2) shall permit the following persons to attend classes for credit or noncredit purposes without the required payment of tuition:

(1) Repealed by Session Laws 2009-451, s. 8.11(a), effective July 1, 2009.

(2) Any person who is the survivor of a law enforcement officer, firefighter, volunteer firefighter, or rescue squad worker killed as a direct result of a traumatic injury sustained in the line of duty.

(3) The spouse of a law enforcement officer, firefighter, volunteer firefighter, or rescue squad worker who is permanently and totally disabled as a direct result of a traumatic injury sustained in the line of duty.

(4) Any child, if the child is at least 17 years old but not yet 24 years old, whose parent is a law enforcement officer, firefighter, volunteer firefighter, or rescue squad worker who is permanently and totally disabled as a direct result of a traumatic injury sustained in the line of duty. However, a child's eligibility for a waiver of tuition under this Chapter shall not exceed: (i) 54 months, if the child is seeking a baccalaureate degree, or (ii) if the child is not seeking a baccalaureate degree, the number of months required to complete the educational program to which the child is applying.

(5) Any child, if the child (i) is at least 17 years old but not yet 24 years old, (ii) is a ward of North Carolina or was a ward of the State at the time the child reached the age of 18, (iii) is a resident of the State; and (iv) is eligible for services under the Chaffee Education and Training Vouchers Program; but the waiver shall only be to the extent that there is any tuition still payable after receipt of other financial aid received by the student.

(6) Any child enrolled in a regional school established pursuant to Part 10 of Article 16 of Chapter 115C of the General Statutes who enrolls in classes at a constituent institution or community college which has a written agreement with the regional school.

(b) Persons eligible for the tuition waiver under subsection (a) of this section must meet admission and other standards considered appropriate by the educational institution. In addition, the constituent institutions of The University of North Carolina shall accept these persons only on a space available basis. (1975, c. 606, s. 2; 1977, c. 981, s. 2; 1997-505, s. 3; 2003-230, ss. 1, 2; 2005-276, s. 9.30(a); 2009-451, s. 8.11(a); 2010-31, s. 9.26; 2011-241, s. 3.)

§ 115B-2.1: Repealed by Session Laws 2009-451, s. 8.11(b), effective July 1, 2009.

§ 115B-3. Rules.

The Board of Governors of The University of North Carolina and the State Board of Community Colleges shall each, with respect to the institutions governed by it, promulgate rules necessary for the implementation of this Chapter. (1975, c. 606, s. 3; 1977, c. 981, s. 3; 2003-230, s. 3.)

§ 115B-4. Enrollment computation for funding purposes.

Persons attending classes under the provisions of this Chapter, without payment of tuition, shall be counted in the computation of enrollment for funding purposes. (1975, c. 606, s. 4; 1977, c. 981, s. 4.)

§ 115B-5. Proof of eligibility.

(a) Repealed by Session Laws 2009-451, s. 8.11(c), effective July 1, 2009.

(b) The officials of the institutions charged with administration of this Chapter shall require the following proof to insure that a person applying to the institution and who requests a tuition waiver under G.S. 115B-2(2), (3), or (4) is eligible for the benefits provided by this Chapter.

(1) The parent-child relationship shall be verified by a birth certificate, legal adoption papers, or other documentary evidence deemed appropriate by the institution.

(2) The marital relationship shall be verified by a marriage certificate or other documentary evidence deemed appropriate by the institution.

(3) The cause of death of the law enforcement officer, firefighter, volunteer firefighter, or rescue squad worker shall be verified by certification from the records of the Department of State Treasurer, the appropriate city or county law enforcement agency that employed the deceased, the administrative agency for the fire department or fire protection district recognized for funding under the Department of State Auditor, or the administrative agency having jurisdiction over any paid firefighters of all counties and cities.

(4) The permanent and total disability shall be verified by documentation deemed necessary by the institution from the North Carolina Industrial Commission.

(c) The officials of the institutions charged with administration of this Chapter may require proof to verify that a person applying to the institution under G.S. 115B-2(5) is eligible for the benefits provided by this Chapter. (1975, c. 606, s. 5; 1977, c. 981, s. 5; 1997-505, s. 4; 2003-230, s. 1; 2005-276, s. 9.30(b); 2009-451, s. 8.11(c).)

§ 115B-5.1. Student to be credited for scholarship value.

If a person obtains a tuition waiver under G.S. 115B-2(2), (3), or (4) and the person also receives a cash scholarship paid or payable to the institution, from whatever source, the amount of the scholarship shall be applied to the credit of the person in the payment of incidental expenses of the person's attendance at the institution, and any balance, if the terms of the scholarship permit, shall be returned to the student. (1997-505, s. 5; 2003-230, s. 1; 2009-570, s. 13.)

§ 115B-5A: Recodified as G. S. 115B-5.1 by Session Laws 2009-570, s. 13, effective August 28, 2009.

§ 115B-6. Misrepresentation of eligibility.

Any applicant who willfully misrepresents his eligibility for the tuition benefits provided under this Chapter, or any person who knowingly aids or abets such applicant in misrepresenting his eligibility for such benefits, shall be deemed guilty of a Class 3 misdemeanor. (1975, c. 606, s. 6; 1977, c. 981, s. 6; 1993, c. 539, s. 879; 1994, Ex. Sess., c. 24, s. 14(c).)

Chapter 115C.

Elementary and Secondary Education.

SUBCHAPTER I. GENERAL PROVISIONS.

Article 1.

Definitions and Preliminary Provisions.

§ 115C-1. General and uniform system of schools.

A general and uniform system of free public schools shall be provided throughout the State, wherein equal opportunities shall be provided for all students, in accordance with the provisions of Article IX of the Constitution of North Carolina. Tuition shall be free of charge to all children of the State, and to every person of the State less than 21 years old, who has not completed a standard high school course of study. There shall be operated in every local school administrative unit a uniform school term of nine months, without the levy of a State ad valorem tax therefor. (1955, c. 1372, art. 1, s. 1; 1963, c. 448, s. 24; 1971, c. 704, s. 1; c. 1231, s. 1; 1981, c. 423, s. 1; 1983 (Reg. Sess., 1984), c. 1034, s. 21; 1985, c. 780, s. 1.)

§ 115C-2. Administrative procedure.

All action of agencies taken pursuant to this Chapter, as agency is defined in G.S. 150B-2, is subject to the requirements of the Administrative Procedure Act, Chapter 150B of the General Statutes. (1981, c. 423, s. 1; 1987, c. 827, s. 1.)

§ 115C-3. Access to information and public records.

Except as otherwise provided in this Chapter, access to information gathered and public records made pursuant to the provisions of this Chapter must be in conformity with the requirements of Chapter 132 of the General Statutes. (1981, c. 423, s. 1.)

§ 115C-4. Open meetings law.

Meetings of governmental bodies held pursuant to the provisions of this Chapter must be in conformity with the requirements of Article 33C of Chapter 143 of the General Statutes. (1981, c. 423, s. 1.)

§ 115C-5. Definitions.

As used in this Chapter unless the context requires otherwise:

(1)   The State Board of Education may be referred to as the "Board" or as the "State Board."

(2)   The governing board of a city administrative unit is "the_____ city board of education."

(3)   The governing board of a county administrative unit is "the_____ county board of education."

(4)   The term "school district" means any district defined by G.S. 115C-69.

(5) "Local board" or "board" means a city board of education, county board of education, or a city-county board of education.

(6) "Local school administrative unit" means a subdivision of the public school system which is governed by a local board of education. It may be a city school administrative unit, a county school administrative unit, or a city-county school administrative unit.

(7) The executive head of a school shall be called "principal."

(8) The executive officer of a local school administrative unit shall be called "superintendent." "Superintendent" means the superintendent of schools of a public school system or, in his absence, the person designated to fulfill his functions.

(9) "Supervisor" means a person paid on the supervisor salary schedule who supervises the instructional program in one or more schools and is under the immediate supervision of the superintendent or his designee.

(10) The term "tax-levying authority" means the board of county commissioners of the county or counties in which an administrative unit is located or such other unit of local government as may be granted by local act authority to levy taxes on behalf of a local school administrative unit. (1955, c. 664; c. 1372, art. 1, ss. 8, 9; 1965, c. 584, s. 2; 1967, c. 223, s. 1; 1971, c. 883; c. 1188, s. 2; 1973, c. 315, s. 1; c. 782, ss. 1-30; 1975, c. 437, s. 10; 1979, c. 864, s. 2; 1981, c. 423, s. 1; 1985 (Reg. Sess., 1986), c. 975, s. 2; 1997-456, s. 27.)

§ 115C-6. Reserved for future codification purposes.

§ 115C-7. Reserved for future codification purposes.

§ 115C-8. Reserved for future codification purposes.

§ 115C-9. Reserved for future codification purposes.

SUBCHAPTER II. ADMINISTRATIVE ORGANIZATION OF STATE AND LOCAL EDUCATION AGENCIES.

Article 2.

State Board of Education.

§ 115C-10. Appointment of Board.

The State Board of Education shall consist of the Lieutenant Governor, the State Treasurer, and 11 members appointed by the Governor, subject to confirmation by the General Assembly in joint session. Not more than two public school employees paid from State or local funds may serve as appointive members of the State Board of Education. No spouse of any public school employee paid from State or local funds and no spouse of any employee of the Department of Public Instruction may serve as an appointive member of the State Board of Education. Of the appointive members of the State Board of Education, one shall be appointed from each of the eight educational districts and three shall be appointed as members at large. Appointments shall be for terms of eight years and shall be made in four classes. Appointments to fill vacancies shall be made by the Governor for the unexpired terms and shall not be subject to confirmation.

The Governor shall transmit to the presiding officers of the Senate and the House of Representatives, on or before the sixtieth legislative day of the General Assembly, the names of the persons appointed by the Governor and submitted to the General Assembly for confirmation; thereafter, pursuant to joint resolution, the Senate and the House of Representatives shall meet in joint session for consideration of an action upon such appointments. (1955, c. 1372, art. 1, s. 2; 1971, c. 704, s. 2; 1981, c. 423, s. 1; 1985, c. 479, s. 36; 1989, c. 46; 2009-2, s. 1.)

§ 115C-11. Organization and internal procedures of Board.

(a) Presiding Officer. - The State Board of Education shall elect from its membership a chairman and vice-chairman. A majority of the Board shall constitute a quorum for the transaction of business. Per diem and expenses of the appointive members of the Board shall be provided by the General Assembly. The chairman of the Board shall preside at all meetings of the Board.

In the absence of the chairman, the vice-chairman shall preside; in the absence of both the chairman and the vice-chairman, the Board shall name one of its own members as chairman pro tempore.

(a1) Student advisors. - The Governor is hereby authorized to appoint two high school students who are enrolled in the public schools of North Carolina as advisors to the State Board of Education. The student advisors shall participate in State Board deliberations in an advisory capacity only. The State Board may, in its discretion, exclude the student advisors from executive sessions.

The Governor shall make initial appointments of student advisors to the State Board as follows:

(1) One high school junior shall be appointed for a two-year term beginning September 1, 1986, and expiring June 14, 1988; and

(2) One high school senior shall be appointed for a one-year term beginning September 1, 1986, and expiring June 14, 1987. When an initial or subsequent term expires, the Governor shall appoint a high school junior for a two-year term beginning June 15 of that year. If a student advisor is no longer enrolled in the public schools of North Carolina or if a vacancy otherwise occurs, the Governor shall appoint a student advisor for the remainder of the unexpired term.

Student advisors shall receive per diem and necessary travel and subsistence expenses in accordance with the provisions of G.S. 138-5.

(a2) State Teacher of the Year Advisor. - Each State Teacher of the Year, as designated by the Department of Public Instruction, shall serve ex officio as advisor to the State Board of Education. Each State Teacher of the Year shall begin service as advisory member to the State Board at the commencement of the teacher's term as State Teacher of the Year and shall serve for two years. The State Teachers of the Year shall participate in State Board deliberations and committee meetings in an advisory capacity only. The State Board may, in its discretion, exclude the State Teachers of the Year from executive sessions.

In the event a vacancy occurs in the State Teacher of the Year's advisory position, the teacher who was next runner-up to that State Teacher of the Year shall serve as the advisory member to the Board for the remainder of the unexpired term. The State Teacher of the Year advisors to the State Board shall receive per diem and necessary travel and subsistence expenses in accordance with the provisions of G.S. 138-5.

(a3)   Superintendent Advisor. - The Governor shall appoint a superintendent of a local school administrative unit as an advisor to the State Board of Education. The superintendent advisor shall serve for a term of one year. The superintendent advisor shall participate in State Board deliberations and committee meetings in an advisory capacity only. The State Board may, in its discretion, exclude the superintendent advisor from executive sessions.

In the event that a superintendent advisor ceases to be a superintendent in a local school administrative unit, the position of superintendent advisor shall be deemed vacant. In the event that a vacancy occurs in the position for whatever reason, the Governor shall appoint a superintendent advisor for the remainder of the unexpired term. The superintendent advisor to the State Board shall receive per diem and necessary travel and subsistence expenses in accordance with the provisions of G.S. 138-5.

(a4)   State Principal of the Year Advisor. - Each State Principal of the Year, as designated by the Department of Public Instruction, shall serve ex officio as an advisor to the State Board of Education. Each State Principal of the Year shall begin service as an advisory member to the State Board at the commencement of the principal's term as State Principal of the Year and shall serve for one year. The State Principal of the Year shall participate in State Board deliberations and committee meetings in an advisory capacity only. The State Board may, in its discretion, exclude the State Principal of the Year from executive sessions.

In the event a vacancy occurs in the State Principal of the Year's advisory position, the principal who was next runner-up to that State Principal of the Year shall serve as the advisory member to the State Board for the remainder of the unexpired term. The State Principal of the Year advisor to the State Board shall receive per diem and necessary travel and subsistence expenses in accordance with the provisions of G.S. 138-5.

(a5)   Local Board of Education Advisor. - The current Raleigh Dingman Award winner shall serve as an advisor to the State Board of Education. The local board of education advisor shall serve for a term of one year. The local board of education advisor shall participate in State Board deliberations and committee meetings in an advisory capacity only. The State Board may, in its discretion, exclude the local board of education advisor from executive sessions.

In the event that the Raleigh Dingman Award winner ceases to be a local board of education member or notifies the State Board of Education that he or she is unable to fulfill his or her duties as a local board of education advisor member, the position of local board of education member shall be deemed vacant. In the event that a vacancy occurs in the position for whatever reason, the President of the North Carolina School Boards Association shall serve as the advisory member to the State Board for the remainder of the unexpired term. The local board of education advisor to the State Board shall receive per diem and necessary travel and subsistence expenses in accordance with the provisions of G.S. 138-5.

(b)   Regular Meetings of Board. - The regular meetings of the Board shall be held each month on a day certain, as determined by the Board. The Board shall determine the hour of the meeting, which may be adjourned from day to day, or to a day certain, until the business before the Board has been completed.

(b1)   Annual meeting with the State Board of Community Colleges and the Board of Governors of The University of North Carolina. The State Board of Education shall meet with the State Board of Community Colleges and the Board of Governors of The University of North Carolina at least once a year to discuss educational matters of mutual interest and to recommend to the General Assembly such policies as are appropriate to encourage the improvement of public education at every level in this State. The meeting in 1987 and every three years thereafter shall be hosted by the University Board of Governors, the meeting in 1988 and every three years thereafter shall be hosted by the State Board of Education, and the meeting in 1989 and every three years thereafter shall be hosted by the State Board of Community Colleges.

(c)   Special Meetings. - Special meetings of the Board may be set at any regular meeting or may be called by the chairman or by the secretary upon the approval of the chairman: Provided, a special meeting shall be called by the chairman upon the request of any five members of the Board. In case of regular meetings and special meetings, the secretary shall give notice to each member, in writing, of the time and purpose of the meeting, by letter directed to each member at his home post-office address. Such notice must be deposited in the Raleigh Post Office at least three days prior to the date of meeting.

(d)   Voting. - No voting by proxy shall be permitted. Except in voting on textbook adoptions, all voting shall be viva voce unless a record vote or secret ballot is demanded by any member, and a majority of those present and voting shall be necessary to carry a motion.

(e) Voting on Adoption of Textbooks. - A majority vote of the whole membership of the Board shall be required to adopt textbooks, and a roll call vote shall be had on each motion for such adoption or adoptions. A record of all such votes shall be kept in the minute book.

(f) Committees. - The Board may create from its membership such committees as it deems necessary to facilitate its business. The chairman of the Board shall with approval of the majority of the Board appoint members to the several committees authorized by the Board and to any additional committees which the chairman may deem to be appropriate.

(g) Record of Proceedings. - All of the proceedings of the Board shall be recorded in a well-bound and suitable book, which shall be kept in the office of the Superintendent of Public Instruction, and open to public inspection.

(h) Rules and Regulations. - The Board shall adopt reasonable rules and regulations not inconsistent herewith, to govern its proceedings which the Board may amend from time to time, which rules and regulations shall become effective when filed as provided by law: Provided, however, a motion to suspend the rules so adopted shall require a consent of two-thirds of the members. The rules and regulations shall include, but not be limited to, clearly defined procedures for electing the officers of the State Board referred to in G.S. 115C-11(a), fixing the term of said officers, specifying how the voting shall be carried out, and establishing a date when the first election shall be held. (1955, c. 1372, art. 2, s. 1; 1959, c. 573, s. 19; 1971, c. 704, s. 3; 1975, c. 699, s. 1; 1981, c. 423, s. 1; 1985 (Reg. Sess., 1986), c. 991, s. 1; 1987 (Reg. Sess., 1988), c. 1102, s. 1; 1989, c. 720; 2003-306, s. 1.)

§ 115C-12. Powers and duties of the Board generally.

The general supervision and administration of the free public school system shall be vested in the State Board of Education. The State Board of Education shall establish policy for the system of free public schools, subject to laws enacted by the General Assembly. The powers and duties of the State Board of Education are defined as follows:

(1) Financial Powers. - The financial powers of the Board are set forth in Article 30 of this Chapter.

(1a) To Submit a Budget Request to the Director of the Budget. - The Board shall submit a budget request to the Director of the Budget in accordance with G.S. 143C-3-3. In addition to the information requested by the Director of the Budget, the Board shall provide an analysis relating each of its requests for expansion funds to anticipated improvements in student performance.

(2) Repealed by Session Laws 1985 (Regular Session, 1986), c. 975, s. 24.

(3), (4) Repealed by Session Laws 1987 (Regular Session, 1988), c. 1025, s. 1.

(5) Apportionment of Funds. - The Board shall have authority to apportion and equalize over the State all State school funds and all federal funds granted to the State for assistance to educational programs administered within or sponsored by the public school system of the State.

(6) Power to Demand Refund for Inaccurate Apportionment Due to False Attendance Records. - When it shall be found by the State Board of Education that inaccurate attendance records have been filed with the State Board of Education which resulted in an excess allotment of funds for teacher salaries in any school unit in any school year, the school unit concerned may be required to refund to the State Board the amount allotted to said unit in excess of the amount an accurate attendance record would have justified.

(7) Power to Alter the Boundaries of City School Administrative Units and to Approve Agreements for the Consolidation and Merger of School Administrative Units Located in the Same County. - The Board shall have authority, in its discretion, to alter the boundaries of city school administrative units and to approve agreements submitted by county and city boards of education requesting the merger of two or more contiguous city school administrative units and the merger of city school administrative units with county school administrative units and the consolidation of all the public schools in the respective units under the administration of one board of education: Provided, that such merger of units and reorganization of school units shall not have the effect of abolishing any special taxes that may have been voted in any such units.

(8) Power to Make Provisions for Sick Leave and for Substitute Teachers. - The Board shall provide for sick leave with pay for all public school employees in accordance with the provisions of this Chapter and shall promulgate rules and

regulations providing for necessary substitutes on account of sick leave and other teacher absences.

The minimum pay for a substitute teacher who holds a teaching certificate shall be sixty-five percent (65%) of the daily pay rate of an entry-level teacher with an "A" certificate. The minimum pay for a substitute teacher who does not hold a teaching certificate shall be fifty percent (50%) of the daily pay rate of an entry-level teacher with an "A" certificate. The pay for noncertified substitutes shall not exceed the pay of certified substitutes.

Local boards may use State funds allocated for substitute teachers to hire full-time substitute teachers.

If a teacher assistant acts as a substitute teacher, the salary of the teacher assistant for the day shall be the same as the daily salary of an entry-level teacher with an "A" certificate.

(9) Miscellaneous Powers and Duties. - All the powers and duties exercised by the State Board of Education shall be in conformity with the Constitution and subject to such laws as may be enacted from time to time by the General Assembly. Among such duties are:

a. To certify and regulate the grade and salary of teachers and other school employees.

b. To adopt and supply textbooks.

c. To adopt rules requiring all local boards of education to implement the Basic Education Program on an incremental basis within funds appropriated for that purpose by the General Assembly and by units of local government. Beginning with the 1991-92 school year, the rules shall require each local school administrative unit to implement fully the standard course of study in every school in the State in accordance with the Basic Education Program so that every student in the State shall have equal access to the curriculum as provided in the Basic Education Program and the standard course of study.

The Board shall establish benchmarks by which to measure the progress that each local board of education has made in implementing the Basic Education Program.

c1. To issue an annual "report card" for the State and for each local school administrative unit, assessing each unit's efforts to improve student performance based on the growth in performance of the students in each school and taking into account progress over the previous years' level of performance and the State's performance in comparison with other states. This assessment shall take into account factors that have been shown to affect student performance and that the State Board considers relevant to assess the State's efforts to improve student performance. As a part of the annual "report card" for each local school administrative unit, the State Board shall award, in accordance with G.S. 115C-83.15, an overall numerical school achievement, growth, and performance score on a scale of zero to 100 and a corresponding performance letter grade of A, B, C, D, or F earned by each school within the local school administrative unit. The school performance score and grade shall reflect student performance on annual subject-specific assessments, college and workplace readiness measures, and graduation rates. For schools serving students in any grade from kindergarten to eighth grade, separate performance scores and grades shall also be awarded based on the school performance in reading and mathematics respectively. The annual "report card" for schools serving students in third grade also shall include the number and percentage of third grade students who (i) take and pass the alternative assessment of reading comprehension; (ii) were retained in third grade for not demonstrating reading proficiency as indicated in G.S. 115C-83.7(a); and (iii) were exempt from mandatory third grade retention by category of exemption as listed in G.S. 115C-83.7(b). The annual "report card" for high schools shall also include measures of Advanced Placement course participation and International Baccalaureate Diploma Programme participation and Advanced Placement and International Baccalaureate examination participation and performance.

c2. Repealed by Session Laws 1995 (Regular Session, 1996), c. 716, s. 1.

c3. To develop a system of school building improvement reports for each school building. The purpose of school building improvement reports is to measure improvement in the growth in student performance at each school building from year to year, not to compare school buildings. The Board shall include in the building reports any factors shown to affect student performance that the Board considers relevant to assess a school's efforts to improve student performance. Local school administrative units shall produce and make public their school building improvement reports by March 15, 1997, for the 1995-96 school year, by October 15, 1997, for the 1996-97 school year, and annually thereafter. Each report shall be based on building-level data for the prior school year.

c4. To develop guidelines, procedures, and rules to establish, implement, and enforce the School-Based Management and Accountability Program under Article 8B of this Chapter in order to improve student performance, increase local flexibility and control, and promote economy and efficiency.

d. To formulate rules and regulations for the enforcement of the compulsory attendance law.

e. To manage and operate a system of insurance for public school property, as provided in Article 38 of this Chapter.

In making substantial policy changes in administration, curriculum, or programs the Board should conduct hearings throughout the regions of the State, whenever feasible, in order that the public may be heard regarding these matters.

(9a), (9b) Repealed by Session Laws 2005-458, s. 1, effective October 2, 2005.

(9c) Power to Develop Content Standards and Exit Standards. - The Board shall develop a comprehensive plan to revise content standards and the standard course of study in the core academic areas of reading, writing, mathematics, science, history, geography, and civics. The Board shall involve and survey a representative sample of parents, teachers, and the public to help determine academic content standard priorities and usefulness of the content standards. A full review of available and relevant academic content standards that are rigorous, specific, sequenced, clear, focused, and measurable, whenever possible, shall be a part of the process of the development of content standards. The revised content standards developed in the core academic areas shall (i) reflect high expectations for students and an in-depth mastery of the content; (ii) be clearly grounded in the content of each academic area; (iii) be defined grade-by-grade and course-by-course; (iv) be understandable to parents and teachers; (v) be developed in full recognition of the time available to teach the core academic areas at each grade level; and (vi) be measurable, whenever possible, in a reliable, valid, and efficient manner for accountability purposes.

High school course content standards shall include the knowledge and skills necessary to pursue further postsecondary education or to attain employment in the 21st century economy. The high school course content standards also shall be aligned with the minimum undergraduate course requirements for admission to the constituent institutions of The University of North Carolina. The Board may develop exit standards that will be required for high school graduation.

The Board also shall develop and implement an ongoing process to align State programs and support materials with the revised academic content standards for each core academic area on a regular basis. Alignment shall include revising textbook criteria, support materials, State tests, teacher and school administrator preparation, and ongoing professional development programs to be compatible with content standards. The Board shall develop and make available to teachers and parents support materials, including teacher and parent guides, for academic content standards. The State Board of Education shall work in collaboration with the Board of Governors of The University of North Carolina to ensure that teacher and school administrator degree programs, ongoing professional development, and other university activity in the State's public schools align with the State Board's priorities.

(10) Power to Provide for Programs or Projects in the Cultural and Fine Arts Areas. - The Board is authorized and empowered, in its discretion, to make provisions for special programs or projects of a cultural and fine arts nature for the enrichment and strengthening of educational opportunities for the children of the State.

For this purpose, the Board may use funds received from gifts or grants and, with the approval of the Director of the Budget, may use State funds which the Board may find available in any budget administered by the Board.

(11) Power to Conduct Education Research. - The Board is authorized to sponsor or conduct education research and special school projects considered important by the Board for improving the public schools of the State. Such research or projects may be conducted during the summer months and involve one or more local school units as the Board may determine. The Board may use any available funds for such purposes.

(12) Duty to Provide for Sports Medicine and Emergency Paramedical Program. - The State Board of Education is authorized and directed to develop a comprehensive plan to train and make available to the public schools personnel who shall have major responsibility for exercising preventive measures against sports related deaths and injuries and for providing sports medicine and emergency paramedical services for injuries that occur in school related activities. The plan shall include, but is not limited to, the training,

assignment of responsibilities, and appropriate additional reimbursement for individuals participating in the program.

The State Board of Education is authorized and directed to develop an implementation schedule and a program funding formula that will enable each high school to have a qualified sports medicine and emergency paramedical program by July 1, 1984.

The State Board of Education is authorized and directed to establish minimum educational standards necessary to enable individuals serving as sports medicine and emergency paramedical staff to provide such services, including first aid and emergency life saving skills, to students participating in school activities.

(13) Power to Purchase Liability Insurance. - The Board is authorized to purchase insurance to protect board members from liability incurred in the exercise of their duty as members of the Board.

(14) Duty to Provide Personnel Information to Local Boards. - Upon request, the State Board of Education and the Department of Public Instruction shall furnish to any county or city board of education any and all available personnel information relating to certification, evaluation and qualification including, but not limited to, semester hours or quarterly hours completed, graduate work, grades, scores, etc., that are on that date in the files of the State Board of Education or Department of Public Instruction.

(15) Duty to Develop Noncertified Personnel Position Evaluation Descriptions. - The Board is authorized and directed to develop position evaluation descriptions covering those positions in local school administrative units for which certification by the State Board of Education is not normally a prerequisite. The position evaluation descriptions required in this subdivision are to be used by local boards of education as the basis for assignment of noncertified employees to an appropriate pay grade in accordance with salary grades and ranges adopted by the State Board of Education. No appropriations are required by this subdivision.

(16) Power with Regard to Salary Schedules. - The Board shall provide for sick leave with pay for all public school employees in accordance with the provisions of this Chapter and shall promulgate rules and regulations providing for necessary substitutes on account of sick leave and other teacher absences.

a. Support personnel refers to all public school employees who are not required by statute or regulation to be certified in order to be employed. The State Board of Education is authorized and empowered to adopt all necessary rules for full implementation of all schedules to the extent that State funds are made available for support personnel.

b. Salary schedules for the following public school support personnel shall be adopted by the State Board of Education: school finance officer, office support personnel, teacher assistants, maintenance supervisors, custodial personnel, and transportation personnel. The Board shall classify these support positions in terms of uniform pay grades included in the salary schedule of the State Human Resources Commission.

By the end of the third payroll period of the 1995-96 fiscal year, local boards of education shall place State-allotted office support personnel, teacher assistants, and custodial personnel on the salary schedule adopted by the State Board of Education so that the average salary paid is the State-allotted amount for the category. In placing employees on the salary schedule, the local board shall consider the education, training, and experience of each employee, including experience in other local school administrative units. It is the intent of the General Assembly that a local school administrative unit not fail to employ an employee who was employed for the prior school year in order to implement the provisions of this sub-subdivision. A local board of education is in compliance with this sub-subdivision if the average salary paid is at least ninety-five percent (95%) of the State-allotted amount for the category at the end of the third payroll period of the 1995-96 fiscal year, and at least ninety-eight percent (98%) of the State-allotted amount for the category at the end of the third payroll period of each subsequent fiscal year. The Department of Public Instruction shall provide technical assistance to local school administrative units regarding the implementation of this sub-subdivision.

c. Salary schedules for other support personnel, including but not limited to maintenance and school food service personnel, shall be adopted by the State Board of Education. The Board shall classify these support positions in terms of uniform pay grades included in the salary schedule of the State Human Resources Commission. These schedules shall apply if the local board of education does not adopt a salary schedule of its own for personnel paid from other than State appropriations.

(17) Power to Provide for School Transportation Programs. - The State Board of Education is authorized and empowered to promulgate such policies,

rules, and regulations as it may deem necessary and desirable for the operation of a public school transportation system by each local administrative unit in the State. Such policies, rules, and regulations shall include, but are not limited to, fund allocations and fiscal support to assure the effective and efficient use of funds appropriated by the General Assembly in support of the school transportation system. Nothing herein shall be construed to affect in any way or to lessen in any way the full and complete authority of local boards of education to assign pupils to schools in accordance with G.S. 115C-366.

(18) Duty to Develop and Implement a Uniform Education Reporting System, Which Shall Include Standards and Procedures for Collecting Fiscal and Personnel Information. -

a. The State Board of Education shall adopt standards and procedures for local school administrative units to provide timely, accurate, and complete fiscal and personnel information, including payroll information, on all school personnel.

b. The State Board of Education shall develop and implement a Uniform Education Reporting System that shall include requirements for collecting, processing, and reporting fiscal, personnel, and student data, by means of electronic transfer of data files from local computers to the State Computer Center through the State Communications Network.

c. The State Board of Education shall comply with the provisions of G.S. 116-11(10a) to plan and implement an exchange of information between the public schools and the institutions of higher education in the State. The State Board of Education shall require local boards of education to provide to the parents of children at a school all information except for confidential information received about that school from institutions of higher education pursuant to G.S. 116-11(10a) and to make that information available to the general public.

d. The State Board of Education shall modify the Uniform Education Reporting System to provide clear, accurate, and standard information on the use of funds at the unit and school level. The plan shall provide information that will enable the General Assembly to determine State, local, and federal expenditures for personnel at the unit and school level. The plan also shall allow the tracking of expenditures for textbooks, educational supplies and equipment, capital outlay, at-risk students, and other purposes.

e. When practicable, reporting requirements developed by the State Board of Education as part of the Uniform Education Reporting System under this subdivision shall be incorporated into the PowerSchool application or any other component of the Instructional Improvement System to minimize duplicative reporting by local school administrative units.

(19) Duty to Identify Required Reports and to Eliminate Unnecessary Reports and Paperwork. - Prior to the beginning of each school year, the State Board of Education shall identify all reports that are required at the State level for the school year.

The State Board of Education shall adopt policies to ensure that local school administrative units are not required by the State Board of Education, the State Superintendent, or the Department of Public Instruction staff to (i) provide information that is already available on the student information management system or housed within the Department of Public Instruction; (ii) provide the same written information more than once during a school year unless the information has changed during the ensuing period; (iii) complete forms, for children with disabilities, that are not necessary to ensure compliance with the federal Individuals with Disabilities Education Act (IDEA); or (iv) provide information that is unnecessary to comply with State or federal law and not relevant to student outcomes and the efficient operation of the public schools. Notwithstanding the foregoing, the State Board may require information available on its student information management system or require the same information twice if the State Board can demonstrate a compelling need and can demonstrate there is not a more expeditious manner of getting the information.

The State Board shall permit schools and local school administrative units to submit all reports to the Department of Public Instruction electronically.

The State Board of Education, in collaboration with the education roundtables within the Department of Public Instruction, shall consolidate all plans that affect the school community, including school improvement plans. The consolidated plan shall be posted on each school's Web site for easy access by the public and by school personnel.

The State Board shall report to the Joint Legislative Education Oversight Committee by November 15 of each year on the reports identified that are required at the State level, the evaluation and determination for continuing individual reports, including the consideration of whether those reports exceed what is required by State and federal law, and any reports that it has consolidated or eliminated for the upcoming school year.

(19a) Duty to Consolidate Applications for State Funding. - The State Board of Education shall adopt policies to streamline the process for local school administrative units applying for State funding. The policies shall provide for a consolidation of all such applications.

(20) Duty to Report Appointment of Caretaker Administrators and Boards. - Pursuant to G.S. 120-30.9G the State Board of Education shall submit to the Attorney General of the United States within 30 days any rules, policies, procedures, or actions taken pursuant to G.S. 115C-64.4 which could result in the appointment of a caretaker administrator or board to perform any of the powers and duties of a local board of education where that school administrative unit is covered by the Voting Rights Act of 1965.

(21) Duty to Monitor Acts of School Violence. - The State Board of Education shall monitor and compile an annual report on acts of violence in the public schools. The State Board shall adopt standard definitions for acts of school violence and shall require local boards of education to report them to the State Board in a standard format adopted by the State Board. The State Board shall submit its report on acts of violence in the public schools to the Joint Legislative Education Oversight Committee by March 15 of each year.

(22) Duty to Monitor the Decisions of Teachers to Leave the Teaching Profession. - The State Board of Education shall monitor and compile an annual report on the decisions of teachers to leave the teaching profession. The State Board shall adopt standard procedures for each local board of education to use in requesting the information from teachers who are not continuing to work as teachers in the local school administrative unit and shall require each local board of education to report the information to the State Board in a standard format adopted by the State Board.

(23) Power to Adopt Eligibility Rules for Interscholastic Athletic Competition. - The State Board of Education shall adopt rules governing interscholastic athletic activities conducted by local boards of education, including eligibility for student participation. With regard to middle schools and high schools, the rules shall provide for the following:

a. All coaches, school nurses, athletic directors, first responders, volunteers, students who participate in interscholastic athletic activities, and the parents of those students shall receive, on an annual basis, a concussion and head injury information sheet. School employees, first responders, volunteers, and students must sign the sheet and return it to the coach before they can participate in interscholastic athletic activities, including tryouts, practices, or competition. Parents must sign the sheet and return it to the coach before their children can participate in any such interscholastic athletic activities. The signed sheets shall be maintained in accordance with sub-subdivision d. of this subdivision.

For the purpose of this subdivision, a concussion is a traumatic brain injury caused by a direct or indirect impact to the head that results in disruption of normal brain function, which may or may not result in loss of consciousness.

b. If a student participating in an interscholastic athletic activity exhibits signs or symptoms consistent with concussion, the student shall be removed from the activity at that time and shall not be allowed to return to play or practice that day. The student shall not return to play or practice on a subsequent day until the student is evaluated by and receives written clearance for such participation from (i) a physician licensed under Article 1 of Chapter 90 of the General Statutes with training in concussion management, (ii) a neuropsychologist licensed under Article 18A of Chapter 90 of the General Statutes with training in concussion management and working in consultation with a physician licensed under Article 1 of Chapter 90 of the General Statutes, (iii) an athletic trainer licensed under Article 34 of Chapter 90 of the General Statutes, (iv) a physician assistant, consistent with the limitations of G.S. 90-18.1, or (v) a nurse practitioner, consistent with the limitations of G.S. 90-18.2.

c. Each school shall develop a venue specific emergency action plan to deal with serious injuries and acute medical conditions in which the condition of the patient may deteriorate rapidly. The plan shall include a delineation of roles, methods of communication, available emergency equipment, and access to and plan for emergency transport. This plan must be (i) in writing, (ii) reviewed by an athletic trainer licensed in North Carolina, (iii) approved by the principal of the school, (iv) distributed to all appropriate personnel, (v) posted conspicuously at all venues, and (vi) reviewed and rehearsed annually by all licensed athletic trainers, first responders, coaches, school nurses, athletic directors, and volunteers for interscholastic athletic activities.

d. Each school shall maintain complete and accurate records of its compliance with the requirements of this subdivision pertaining to head injuries.

The State Board of Education may authorize a designated organization to apply and enforce the Board's rules governing participation in interscholastic athletic activities at the high school level.

(24) Duty to Develop Standards for Alternative Learning Programs, Provide Technical Assistance on Implementation of Programs, and Evaluate Programs. - The State Board of Education shall adopt standards for assigning students to alternative learning programs. These standards shall include (i) a description of the programs and services that are recommended to be provided in alternative learning programs and (ii) a process for ensuring that an assignment is appropriate for the student and that the student's parents are involved in the decision. The State Board also shall adopt policies that define what constitutes an alternative school and an alternative learning program.

The State Board of Education shall also adopt standards to require that local school administrative units shall use (i) the teachers allocated for students assigned to alternative learning programs pursuant to the regular teacher allotment and (ii) the teachers allocated for students assigned to alternative learning programs only to serve the needs of these students.

The State Board of Education shall provide technical support to local school administrative units to assist them in developing and implementing plans and proposals for alternative learning programs.

The State Board shall evaluate the effectiveness of alternative learning programs and, in its discretion, of any other programs funded from the Alternative Schools/At-Risk Student allotment. Local school administrative units shall report to the State Board of Education on how funds in the Alternative Schools/At-Risk Student allotment are spent and shall otherwise cooperate with the State Board of Education in evaluating the alternative learning programs. As part of its evaluation of the effectiveness of these programs, the State Board shall, through the application of the accountability system developed under G.S. 115C-83.15 and G.S. 115C-105.35, measure the educational performance and growth of students placed in alternative schools and alternative programs. If appropriate, the Board may modify this system to adapt to the specific characteristics of these schools. Also as part of its evaluation, the State Board shall evaluate its standards adopted under this subdivision and make any necessary changes to those standards based on strategies that have been proven successful in improving student achievement and shall report to the Joint Legislative Education Oversight Committee by April 15, 2006 to determine if any changes are necessary to improve the implementation of successful alternative learning programs and alternative schools.

(25) Duty to Report to Joint Legislative Education Oversight Committee. - Upon the request of the Joint Legislative Education Oversight Committee, the State Board shall examine and evaluate issues, programs, policies, and fiscal information, and shall make reports to that Committee. Furthermore, beginning October 15, 1997, and annually thereafter, the State Board shall submit reports to that Committee regarding the continued implementation of Chapter 716 of the 1995 Session Laws, 1996 Regular Session. Each report shall include information regarding the composition and activity of assistance teams, schools that received incentive awards, schools identified as low-performing, school improvement plans found to significantly improve student performance, personnel actions taken in low-performing schools, and recommendations for additional legislation to improve student performance and increase local flexibility.

(25a) [Development of Goals and Annual Report on Improvement in Graduation Rate.] Prior to the 2010-2011 school year, the State Board of Education shall:

a. Develop a growth model establishing annual goals for continuous and substantial improvement in the four-year cohort graduation rate by local school administrative units.

b. Establish as a short-term goal that local school administrative units meet the annual growth model goals for improvement in the four-year cohort graduation rate beginning with the graduating class of 2011 and continuing annually thereafter.

c. Establish as long-term minimum goals statewide four-year cohort graduation rates of seventy-four percent (74%) by 2014; eighty percent (80%) by 2016; and ninety percent (90%) by 2018.

d. Establish as a long-term goal with benchmarks and recommendations to reach a statewide four-year cohort graduation rate of one hundred percent (100%).

The State Board of Education shall report to the Joint Legislative Education Oversight Committee by November 15, 2010, and annually thereafter on the goals, benchmarks, and recommendations described in this section. Such goals, benchmarks, and recommendations shall appropriately differentiate for students with disabilities and other specially identified subcategories within each four-year cohort. The report shall include goals and benchmarks by local school administrative unit, the strategies and recommendations for achieving the goals and benchmarks, any evidence or data supporting the strategies and recommendations, and the identity of the persons employed by the State Board of Education who are responsible for oversight of local school administrative units in achieving the goals and benchmarks.

(25b)　Repealed by Session Laws 2012-142, s. 7.13(d), effective July 1, 2012.

(26)　Repealed by Session Laws 2012-142, s. 7.13(f), effective July 1, 2012.

(27)　Reporting Dropout Rates, Corporal Punishment, Suspensions, Expulsions, and Alternative Placements. - The State Board shall report by March 15 of each year to the Joint Legislative Education Oversight Committee on the numbers of students who have dropped out of school, been subjected to corporal punishment, been suspended, been expelled, been reassigned for disciplinary purposes, or been provided alternative education services. The data shall be reported in a disaggregated manner, reflecting the local school administrative unit, race, gender, grade level, ethnicity, and disability status of each affected student. Such data shall be readily available to the public. The State Board shall not include students that have been expelled from school when calculating the dropout rate. The Board shall maintain a separate record of the number of students who are expelled from school and the reasons for the expulsion.

(27a)　Reducing School Dropout Rates. - The State Board of Education shall develop a statewide plan to improve the State's tracking of dropout data so that accurate and useful comparisons can be made over time. The plan shall include, at a minimum, how dropouts are counted and the methodology for calculating the dropout rate, the ability to track students movements among schools and districts, and the ability to provide information on who drops out and why.

(28)　Duty to Develop Rules for Issuance of Driving Eligibility Certificates. - The State Board of Education shall adopt the following rules to assist schools in their administration of procedures necessary to implement G.S. 20-11 and G.S. 20-13.2:

a. To define what is equivalent to a high school diploma for the purposes of G.S. 20-11 and G.S. 20-13.2. These rules shall apply to all educational programs offered in the State by public schools, charter schools, nonpublic schools, or community colleges.

b. To establish the procedures a person who is or was enrolled in a public school or in a charter school must follow and the requirements that person shall meet to obtain a driving eligibility certificate.

c. To require the person who is required under G.S. 20-11(n) to sign the driving eligibility certificate to provide the certificate if he or she determines that one of the following requirements is met:

1. The person seeking the certificate is eligible for the certificate under G.S. 20-11(n)(1) and is not subject to G.S. 20-11(n1).

2. The person seeking the certificate is eligible for the certificate under G.S. 20-11(n)(1) and G.S. 20-11(n1).

These rules shall apply to public schools and charter schools.

d. To provide for an appeal to an appropriate education authority by a person who is denied a driving eligibility certificate. These rules shall apply to public schools and charter schools.

e. To define exemplary student behavior and to define what constitutes the successful completion of a drug or alcohol treatment counseling program. These rules shall apply to public schools and charter schools.

The State Board also shall develop policies as to when it is appropriate to notify the Division of Motor Vehicles that a person who is or was enrolled in a public school or in a charter school no longer meets the requirements for a driving eligibility certificate.

The State Board shall develop a form for parents, guardians, or emancipated juveniles, as appropriate, to provide their written, irrevocable consent for a school to disclose to the Division of Motor Vehicles that the student no longer meets the conditions for a driving eligibility certificate under G.S. 20-11(n)(1) or G.S. 20-11(n1), if applicable, in the event that this disclosure is necessary to comply with G.S. 20-11 or G.S. 20-13.2. Other than identifying under which statutory subsection the student is no longer eligible, no other details or information concerning the student's school record shall be released pursuant to this consent. This form shall be used for students enrolled in public schools or charter schools.

The State Board of Education may use funds appropriated for drivers education to cover the costs of driving eligibility certificates.

(29) To Issue Special High School Diplomas to Veterans of World War II, Korea, and Vietnam. - The State Board of Education shall issue special high school diplomas to all honorably discharged veterans of World War II, the Korean Conflict, and the Vietnam era who request special diplomas and have not previously received high school diplomas.

(30) Duty to Adopt Model Guidelines and Policies for the Establishment of Local Task Forces on Closing the Academic Achievement Gap. - The State Board shall adopt a Model for local school administrative units to use as a guideline to establish local task forces on closing the academic achievement gap at the discretion of the local board. The purpose of each task force is to advise and work with its local board of education and administration on closing the gap in academic achievement and on developing a collaborative plan for achieving that goal. The State Board shall consider the recommendations of the Commission on Improving the Academic Achievement of Minority and At-Risk Students to the 2001 Session of the General Assembly in establishing its guidelines.

(30a) Duty to Assist Schools in Meeting Adequate Yearly Progress. - The State Board of Education shall:

a. Identify which schools are meeting adequate yearly progress with subgroups as specified in the No Child Left Behind Act of 2001;

b. Study the instructional, administrative, and fiscal practices and policies employed by the schools selected by the State Board of Education that are meeting adequate yearly progress specified in the No Child Left Behind Act of 2001;

c. Create assistance models for each subgroup based on the practices and policies used in schools that are meeting adequate yearly progress. The schools of education at the constituent institutions of The University of North Carolina, in collaboration with the University of North Carolina Center for School Leadership

Development, shall assist the State Board of Education in developing these models; and

d.   Offer technical assistance based on these assistance models to local school administrative units not meeting adequate yearly progress, giving priority to those local school administrative units with high concentrations of schools that are not meeting adequate yearly progress. The State Board of Education shall determine the number of local school administrative units that can be served effectively in the first two years. This technical assistance shall include peer assistance and professional development by teachers, support personnel, and administrators in schools with subgroups that are meeting adequate yearly progress.

(31)   To Adopt Guidelines for Individual Diabetes Care Plans. - The State Board shall adopt guidelines for the development and implementation of individual diabetes care plans. The State Board shall consult with the North Carolina Diabetes Advisory Council established by the Department of Health and Human Services in the development of these guidelines. The State Board also shall consult with local school administrative unit employees who have been designated as responsible for coordinating their individual unit's efforts to comply with federal regulations adopted under Section 504 of the Rehabilitation Act of 1973, as amended, 29 U.S.C. § 794. In its development of these guidelines, the State Board shall refer to the guidelines recommended by the American Diabetes Association for the management of children with diabetes in the school and day care setting and shall consider recent resolutions by the United States Department of Education's Office of Civil Rights of investigations into complaints alleging discrimination against students with diabetes.

The guidelines adopted by the State Board shall include:

a.   Procedures for the development of an individual diabetes care plan at the written request of the student's parent or guardian, and involving the parent or guardian, the student's health care provider, the student's classroom teacher, the student if appropriate, the school nurse if available, and other appropriate school personnel.

b.   Procedures for regular review of an individual care plan.

c.   Information to be included in a diabetes care plan, including the responsibilities and appropriate staff development for teachers and other school personnel, an emergency care plan, the identification of allowable actions to be taken, the extent to which the student is able to participate in the student's diabetes care and management, and other information necessary for teachers and other school personnel in order to offer appropriate assistance and support to the student. The State Board shall ensure that the information and allowable actions included in a diabetes care plan as required in this subdivision meet or exceed the American Diabetes Association's recommendations for the management of children with diabetes in the school and day care setting.

d. Information and staff development to be made available to teachers and other school personnel in order to appropriately support and assist students with diabetes.

The State Board shall ensure that these guidelines are updated as necessary and shall ensure that the guidelines and any subsequent changes are published and disseminated to local school administrative units.

(32) Duty to Encourage Early Entry of Motivated Students into Four-Year College Programs. - The State Board of Education, in cooperation with the Education Cabinet, shall work with local school administrative units, the constituent institutions of The University of North Carolina, local community colleges, and private colleges and universities to (i) encourage early entry of motivated students into four-year college programs and to (ii) ensure that there are opportunities at four-year institutions for academically talented high school students to get an early start on college coursework, either at nearby institutions or through distance learning.

The State Board of Education shall also adopt policies directing school guidance counselors to make ninth grade students aware of the potential to complete the high school courses required for college entry in a three-year period.

(33) Duty to Develop Recommended Programs for Use in Schools on Memorial Day. - The State Board of Education shall develop recommended instructional programs that enable students to gain a better understanding of the meaning and importance of Memorial Day. All schools, especially schools that hold school on Memorial Day, shall instruct students on the significance of Memorial Day.

(34) Duty to Protect the Health of School-Age Children From Toxicants at School. - The State Board shall address public health and environmental issues in the classroom and on school grounds by doing all of the following:

a. Develop guidelines for sealing existing arsenic-treated wood in playground equipment or establish a time line for removing existing arsenic-treated wood on playgrounds and testing the soil on school grounds for contamination caused by the leaching of arsenic-treated wood in other areas where children may be at particularly high risk of exposure.

b. Establish guidelines to reduce students' exposure to diesel emissions that can occur as a result of unnecessary school bus idling, nose-to-tail parking, and inefficient route assignments.

c. Study methods for mold and mildew prevention and mitigation and incorporate recommendations into the public school facilities guidelines as needed.

d. Establish guidelines for Integrated Pest Management consistent with the policy of The North Carolina School Boards Association, Inc., as published in 2004. These guidelines may be updated as needed to reflect changes in technology.

e. Establish guidelines for notification of students' parents, guardians, or custodians as well as school staff of pesticide use on school grounds.

(35) To Encourage Local Boards of Education to Enter into Agreements Regarding the Joint Use of Facilities for Physical Activity. - The State Board of Education shall encourage local boards of education to enter into agreements with local governments and other entities regarding the joint use of their facilities for physical activity. The agreements should delineate opportunities, guidelines, and the roles and responsibilities of the parties, including responsibilities for maintenance and liability.

(36) Duty to Charge Tuition for the Governor's School of North Carolina. - The State Board of Education may implement a tuition charge for students attending the Governor's School of North Carolina to cover the costs of the School.

(37) To Adopt Guidelines for Fitness Testing. - The State Board of Education shall adopt guidelines for the development and implementation of evidence-based fitness testing for students statewide in grades kindergarten through eight.

(38) Repealed by Session Laws 2012-194, s. 55(a), effective July 17, 2012.

(39) Power to Accredit Schools. - Upon the request of a local board of education, the State Board of Education shall evaluate schools in local school administrative units to determine whether the education provided by those schools meets acceptable levels of quality. The State Board shall adopt rigorous academic standards for accreditation after consideration of (i) the standards of regional and national accrediting agencies, (ii) the Common Core Standards adopted by the National Governors Association Center for Best Practices and the Council of Chief State School Officers, and (iii) other information it deems appropriate.

The local school administrative unit shall compensate the State Board for the actual costs of the accreditation process.

(40) To Establish High School Diploma Endorsements. - The State Board of Education shall establish, implement, and determine the impact of adding (i) college, (ii) career, and (iii) college and career endorsements to high school diplomas to encourage students to obtain requisite job skills and to reduce the need for remedial education in institutions of higher education. These endorsements shall reflect courses completed, overall grade point average, and other criteria as developed by the State Board of Education. The State Board of Education shall report annually to the Joint Legislative Education Oversight Committee on the impact of awarding these endorsements on high school graduation, college acceptance and remediation, and post-high school employment rates.

(41) To Establish Career and Technical Education Incentives. - The State Board of Education shall establish, implement, and determine the impact of a career and technical education incentive program as provided under G.S. 115C-156.2. (1955, c. 1372, art. 2, s. 2; art. 17, s. 6; art. 18, s. 2; 1957, c. 541, s. 11; 1959, c. 1294; 1961, c. 969; 1963, c. 448, ss. 24, 27; c. 688, ss. 1, 2; c. 1223, s. 1; 1965, c. 584, s. 20.1; c. 1185, s. 2; 1967, c. 643, s. 1; 1969, c. 517, s. 1; 1971, c. 704, s. 4; c. 745; 1973, c. 236; c. 476, s. 138; c. 675; 1975, c. 686, s. 1; c. 699, s. 2; c. 975; 1979, c. 300, s. 1; c. 935; c. 986; 1981, c. 423, s. 1; 1983, c. 630, s. 1; 1983 (Reg. Sess., 1984), c. 1034, s. 16; 1985, c. 479, s. 55(c)(3); c. 757, s. 145(a); 1985 (Reg. Sess., 1986), c. 975, s. 24; 1987, c. 414, s. 1; 1987 (Reg. Sess., 1988), c. 1025, ss. 1, 3; 1989, c. 585, s. 1; c. 752, s. 65(c); c. 778, s. 6; 1991, c. 529, s. 3; c. 689, s. 196(b); 1991 (Reg. Sess., 1992), c. 880, s. 3; c. 900, s. 75.1(e); 1993, c. 321, ss. 125, 133(a), 139(b); 1993 (Reg. Sess., 1994), c. 769, ss. 19(a), 19.9; 1995, c. 60, s. 1; c. 324, s. 17.15(a); c. 450, s. 4; c. 509, s. 59; 1995 (Reg. Sess., 1996), c. 716, s. 1; 1996, 2nd Ex. Sess., c. 18, ss. 18.4, 18.28(a); 1997-18, s. 15(a), (c)-(e); 1997-221, s. 12(a); 1997-239, s. 1;

1997-443, s. 8.27(a), (e); 1997-443, s. 8.29(o), (u); 1997-507, s. 3; 1998-153, s. 16(b); 1998-212, ss. 9.16(a), 9.23; 1999-237, s. 8.25(d); 1999-243, s. 5; 1999-397, s. 3; 2001-86, s. 1; 2001-151, s. 1; 2001-424, ss. 28.30(e), (f), 31.4(a); 2002-103, s. 1; 2002-126, s. 7.15; 2002-159, s. 63; 2002-178, s. 1(a); 2003-251, s. 1; 2003-419, s. 1; 2005-155, s. 1; 2005-276, ss. 7.18, 9.34(a); 2005-446, s. 1; 2005-458, ss. 1, 2; 2006-75, s. 1; 2006-143, s. 1; 2006-203, s. 30; 2006-260, s. 1; 2009-305, s. 4; 2009-334, s. 1; 2009-451, s. 7.39(a); 2010-31, s. 7.5(c), (g); 2010-111, s. 1; 2010-112, s. 4(a); 2010-161, s. 1; 2011-145, ss. 7.9, 7.13(a); 2011-147, s. 3; 2011-185, s. 9(b); 2011-282, s. 4; 2011-306, s. 3; 2011-379, ss. 2(a), (b), 6(a); 2011-391, s. 14(b); 2012-142, ss. 7.13(d), (f), 7A.3(a); 2012-194, s. 55(a); 2013-1, s. 1(a); 2013-226, ss. 9(e), (f); 2013-360, ss. 8.27(a), 8.28(a), 9.4(c), (d); 2013-382, s. 9.1(c).)

§ 115C-12.1. Training of State Board members.

The State Board of Education shall establish minimum training requirements for members of the State Board of Education. All Board members shall participate in training programs, as required by the State Board. (1991, c. 689, s. 200(c).)

§ 115C-12.2. Voluntary shared leave.

(a)   The State Board of Education, in cooperation with the State Board of Community Colleges and the State Human Resources Commission, shall adopt rules and policies to allow any employee at a public school to share leave voluntarily with an immediate family member who is an employee of a public school, community college, or State agency; and with a coworker's immediate family member who is an employee of a public school, community college, or State agency. For the purposes of this section, the term "immediate family member" means a spouse, parent, child, brother, sister, grandparent, or grandchild. The term includes the step, half, and in-law relationships. The term "coworker" means that the employee donating the leave is employed by the same agency, department, institution, university, local school administrative unit, or community college as the employee whose immediate family member is receiving the leave.

(b)   The State Board of Education shall adopt rules and policies for the voluntary shared leave program to allow an employee at a public school to donate sick leave to a nonfamily member employee of a public school. A donor of sick leave to a nonfamily member recipient shall not donate more than five days of sick leave per year to any one nonfamily member recipient. The combined total of sick leave donated to a recipient from nonfamily member donors shall not exceed 20 days per year. Donated sick leave shall not be used for retirement purposes, and employees who donate sick leave shall be notified in writing of the State retirement credit consequences of donating sick leave. (1999-170, s. 2; 2003-9, s. 2; 2003-284, s. 30.14A(b); 2010-139, s. 2; 2013-382, s. 9.1(c).)

§ 115C-13. Duty to maintain confidentiality of certain records.

Except as otherwise provided by federal law, local boards of education and their officers and employees shall provide to the State Board and to the Superintendent all information needed to carry out their duties. It is unlawful for any member of the State Board of Education, the Superintendent of Public Instruction, or any employee or officer of the State Board of Education or the Department of Public Instruction to disclose any of this information that the local board or its officers or employees could not lawfully disclose. This disclosure is a Class 1 misdemeanor. (1985, c. 757, s. 145(j); 1993, c. 539, s. 880; 1994, Ex. Sess., c. 24, s. 14(c).)

§ 115C-14. Repealed by Session Laws 1987, c. 414, s. 11.

§ 115C-15: Repealed by Session Laws 1997-18, s. 1.

§ 115C-16. Authorization for school uniform pilot program.

The State Board of Education may authorize up to five local school administrative units to implement pilot programs in which students are required to wear uniforms in public schools.

Prior to selecting the pilot units, the State Board of Education shall develop guidelines for local boards of education to use when establishing requirements for students to wear uniforms in public schools. In developing these guidelines, the State Board shall consider (i) ways to promote parental and community involvement in the pilot programs, (ii) relevant State and federal constitutional concerns such as freedom of religion and freedom of speech, and (iii) the ability of students to purchase the uniforms.

Local boards in the pilot units shall establish requirements, consistent with the State Board's guidelines, for students enrolled in any of their schools to wear uniforms at school during the regular school day.

No State funds shall be used for the uniforms. (1995, c. 334, s. 1.)

§ 115C-17. Rulemaking to implement ABC's Plan.

(a) G.S. 150B-21.2(a)(1) shall not apply to proposed rules adopted by the State Board of Education if the proposed rules are directly related to the implementation of this act [1995 (Reg. Sess., 1996), c. 716, s. 18].

(b) Notwithstanding G.S. 150B-21.3(b), a permanent rule that is adopted by the State Board of Education, is approved by the Rules Review Commission, and is directly related to the implementation of this act, shall become effective five business days after the Commission delivers the rule to the Codifier of Rules, unless the rule specifies a later effective date. If the State Board of Education specifies a later effective date, the rule becomes effective upon that date. A permanent rule that is adopted by the State Board of Education that is directly related to the implementation of this act, but is not approved by the Rules Review Commission, shall not become effective.

(c) G.S. 150B-21.4(b1) shall not apply to permanent rules the State Board of Education proposes to adopt if those rules are directly related to the implementation of this act [1995 (Reg. Sess., 1996), c. 716, s. 28].

(d) The State Board of Education shall determine whether a proposed rule is directly related to this act based upon a finding that there is a rational relationship between the proposed rule and specific provisions of this act. A proposed rule may create, amend, or repeal a rule. The State Board shall indicate in the notice of proposed text that the rule is directly related to the implementation of this act and that the Board is proceeding under the authority granted by this act.

(e) The State Board of Education shall provide written notice to all boards of county commissioners and all local boards of education of proposed rules that are directly related to the implementation of this act and that would affect the expenditures or revenues of a unit of local government under G.S. 150B-21.4(b). The notice shall state that a copy of the fiscal note may be obtained from the State Board. (1995 (Reg. Sess., 1996), c. 716, s. 28.)

Article 3.

Department of Public Instruction.

§ 115C-18. Election of Superintendent of Public Instruction.

The Superintendent of Public Instruction shall be elected by the qualified voters of the State in 1972 and every four years thereafter at the same time and places as members of the General Assembly are elected. His term of office shall be four years and shall commence on the first day of January next after election and continue until his successor is elected and qualified.

If the office of the Superintendent of Public Instruction is vacated by death, resignation, or otherwise, it shall be the duty of the Governor to appoint another to serve until his successor is elected and qualified. Every such vacancy shall be filled by election at the first election for members of the General Assembly that occurs more than 30 days after the vacancy has taken place, and the person chosen shall hold the office for the remainder of the unexpired term fixed in Article III, Sec. 7 of the Constitution of North Carolina. When a vacancy occurs in the office and the term expires on the first day of January succeeding the next election for members of the General Assembly, the Governor shall appoint to fill the vacancy for the unexpired term of the office. Upon the occurrence of a vacancy in the office for any of the causes stated herein, the Governor may appoint an interim officer to perform the duties of that office until a person is appointed or elected pursuant to Article III, Sec. 7 of the Constitution of North Carolina to fill the vacancy and is qualified.

The time of the election of the Superintendent of Public Instruction shall be in accordance with the provisions of Article 1 of Subchapter I of Chapter 163 of the General Statutes.

The election, term and induction into office of the Superintendent of Public Instruction shall be in accordance with the provisions of G.S. 147-4. (1981, c. 423, s. 1.)

§ 115C-19. Chief administrative officer of the State Board of Education.

As provided in Article IX, Sec. 4(2) of the North Carolina Constitution, the Superintendent of Public Instruction shall be the secretary and chief administrative officer of the State Board of Education. As secretary and chief administrative officer of the State Board of Education, the Superintendent manages on a day-to-day basis the administration of the free public school system, subject to the direction, control, and approval of the State Board. Subject to the direction, control, and approval of the State Board of Education, the Superintendent of Public Instruction shall carry out the duties prescribed under G.S. 115C-21. (1955, c. 1372, art. 3, s. 1; 1971, c. 704, s. 5; 1981, c. 423, s. 1; 1987 (Reg. Sess., 1988), c. 1025, s. 4; 1995, c. 72, s. 1.)

§ 115C-20. Office and salary.

The Superintendent of Public Instruction shall keep his office in the Education Building in Raleigh, and his salary shall be set by the General Assembly in the Current Operations Appropriations Act. In addition to the salary set by the General Assembly in the Current Operations Appropriations Act, longevity pay shall be paid on the same basis as is provided to employees of the State who are subject to the North Carolina Human Resources Act. (1955, c. 1372, art. 3, s. 2; c. 1374; 1963, c. 1178, s. 2; 1967, c. 1130; c. 1237, s. 2; 1969, c. 1214, s. 2; 1971, c. 912, s. 2; 1973, c. 778, s. 2; 1975, 2nd Sess., c. 983, s. 17; 1977, c. 802, s. 42.15; 1981, c. 423, s. 1; 1983, c. 761, s. 210; 1983 (Reg. Sess., 1984), c. 1034, s. 164; 1987, c. 738, s. 32(b); 2013-382, s. 9.1(c).)

§ 115C-21. Powers and duties generally.

(a) Administrative Duties. - Subject to the direction, control, and approval of the State Board of Education, it shall be the duty of the Superintendent of Public Instruction:

(1) To organize and establish a Department of Public Instruction which shall include such divisions and departments as the State Board considers necessary for supervision and administration of the public school system. All appointments of administrative and supervisory personnel to the staff of the Department of Public Instruction are subject to the approval of the State Board of Education, which may terminate these appointments for cause in conformity with Chapter 126 of the General Statutes, the State Personnel System.

(2) To keep the public informed as to the problems and needs of the public schools by constant contact with all school administrators and teachers, by personal appearance at public gatherings, and by information furnished to the press of the State.

(3) To report biennially to the Governor 30 days prior to each regular session of the General Assembly, such report to include information and statistics of the public schools, with recommendations for their improvement and for changes in the school law.

(4) To have printed and distributed such educational bulletins as are necessary for the professional improvement of teachers and for the cultivation of public sentiment for public education, and to have printed all forms necessary and proper for the administration of the Department of Public Instruction.

(5) To manage all those matters relating to the supervision and administration of the public school system that the State Board delegates to the Superintendent of Public Instruction.

(6) To create a special fund within the Department of Public Instruction to manage funds received as grants from nongovernmental sources in support of public education. Effective July 1, 1995, this special fund is transferred to the State Board of Education and shall be administered by the State Board in accordance with G.S. 115C-410.

(7) Repealed by Session Laws 1995, c. 72, s. 2.

(b) Duties as Secretary to the State Board of Education. - Subject to the direction, control, and approval of the State Board of Education, it shall be the duty of the Superintendent of Public Instruction:

(1) To administer through the Department of Public Instruction, the instructional policies established by the Board.

(1a) Repealed by Session Laws 1995, c. 72, s. 2.

(2) To keep the Board informed regarding developments in the field of public education.

(3) To make recommendations to the Board with regard to the problems and needs of education in North Carolina.

(4) To make available to the public schools a continuous program of comprehensive supervisory services.

(5) To collect and organize information regarding the public schools, on the basis of which he shall furnish the Board such tabulations and reports as may be required by the Board.

(6) To communicate to the public school administrators all information and instructions regarding instructional policies and procedures adopted by the Board.

(7) To have custody of the official seal of the Board and to attest all deeds, leases, or written contracts executed in the name of the Board. All deeds of conveyance, leases, and contracts affecting real estate, title to which is held by the Board, and all contracts of the Board required to be in writing and under seal, shall be executed in the name of the Board by the chairman and attested by the secretary; and proof of the execution, if required or desired, may be had as provided by law for the proof of corporate instruments.

(8) To attend all meetings of the Board and to keep the minutes of the proceedings of the Board in a well-bound and suitable book, which minutes shall be approved by the Board prior to its adjournment; and, as soon thereafter as possible, to furnish to each member of the Board a copy of said minutes.

(9) To perform such other duties as the Board may assign to him from time to time. (1955, c. 1372, art. 2, s. 2; art. 3, ss. 3, 4; 1957, c. 541, s. 11; 1961, c. 969; 1963, c. 448, ss. 24, 27; c. 688, ss. 1, 2; c. 1223, s. 1; 1965, c. 1185, s. 2; 1967, c. 643, s. 1; 1969, c. 517, s. 1; 1971, c. 704, s. 4; c. 745; 1973, c. 476, s. 138; c. 675; 1975, c. 699, ss. 2, 3; c. 975; 1979, c. 300, s. 1; c. 935; 1981, c. 423, s. 1; 1985, c. 479, s. 37; 1987 (Reg. Sess., 1988), c. 1025, ss. 5-8; 1989, c.

752, s. 78(a); 1989 (Reg. Sess., 1990), c. 1066, s. 102; 1991 (Reg. Sess., 1992), c. 812, s. 6(g); c. 1044, s. 22(a); 1993, c. 522, s. 1; 1995, c. 72, s. 2.)

§ 115C-21.1: Repealed by Session Laws 1997-18, s. 2.

§ 115C-22: Repealed by Session Laws 1997-18, s. 3.

§ 115C-23. Reserved for future codification purposes.

§ 115C-24. Reserved for future codification purposes.

§ 115C-25. Reserved for future codification purposes.

§ 115C-26. Reserved for future codification purposes.

Article 4.

Office of the Controller.

§§ 115C-27 through 115C-34: Repealed by Session Laws 1987 (Regular Session, 1988), c. 1025, s. 2.)

Article 5.

Local Boards of Education.

§ 115C-35. How constituted.

(a) The county board of education in each county shall consist of five members elected by the voters of the county at large for terms of four years: Provided, that where there are multiple local school administrative units located within the county, and unless the county board is responsible for appointing members of the board of education of a city administrative unit located within the county, only those voters who reside within the county school administrative unit boundary lines shall be eligible to vote for members of the county board of education. Where the county board is responsible for appointing members of the board of education of a city administrative unit located within the county, the voters residing within that city school administrative unit shall be eligible to vote for members of the county board of education.

The terms of office of the members of boards of education of all school administrative units in this State, who serve on June 25, 1975, shall continue until members are elected and qualified as provided in this section unless modified by local legislation.

(b) No person residing in a local school administrative unit shall be eligible for election to the board of education of that local school administrative unit unless such person resides within the boundary lines of that local school administrative unit. (1955, c. 1372, art. 5, s. 1; 1967, c. 972, s. 1; 1969, c. 1301, s. 2; 1975, c. 855, ss. 1-3; 1981, c. 423, s. 1.)

§ 115C-36. Designation of board.

All powers and duties conferred and imposed by law respecting public schools, which are not expressly conferred and imposed upon some other official, are conferred and imposed upon local boards of education. Said boards of education shall have general control and supervision of all matters pertaining to the public schools in their respective administrative units and they shall enforce the school law in their respective units. (1955, c. 1372, art. 5, s. 18; 1957, c. 262; 1963, c. 425; 1965, c. 1185, s. 1; 1969, c. 517, s. 2; 1981, c. 423, s. 1.)

§ 115C-37. Election of board members.

(a) Method of Election. - The county boards of education shall be elected on a nonpartisan basis at the time of the primary election in 1970 and biennially thereafter. The names of the candidates shall be printed on the ballots without reference to any party affiliation and any qualified voter residing in the county shall be entitled to vote such ballots. Except as otherwise provided herein, the election shall be conducted according to the provisions of Chapter 163 of the General Statutes then governing primary elections.

The terms of office of the members shall be staggered so as nearly equal to one half as possible shall expire every two years.

(b) County Board of Elections to Provide for Elections. - The county board of elections under the direction of the State Board of Elections, shall make all necessary provisions for elections of county boards of education as are herein provided for. The county board of elections of each county shall file with the State Board of Elections a statement specifying the size and method of election of members of its county board of education.

(c) City Board of Education. - The board of education for any city administrative unit shall be appointed or elected as now provided by law. If no provision is now made by the law for the filling of vacancies in the membership of any city board of education, such vacancy may be filled by the governing body of the city or town embraced by said administrative unit. In the event that any such vacancy is not filled in this manner within 30 days, the State Board of Education may fill such vacancy.

(d) Members to Qualify. - Each county board of education shall hold a meeting in December following the election. At that meeting, newly elected members of the board of education shall qualify by taking the oath of office prescribed in Article VI, Sec. 7 of the Constitution.

This subsection shall not have the effect of repealing any local or special acts relating to boards of education of any particular counties whose membership to said boards is chosen by a vote of the people.

(e) Vacancies in Nominations for Membership on County Boards. - If any candidate nominated on a partisan basis shall die, resign, or for any reason become ineligible or disqualified between the date of his nomination and the time for the election, such vacancy caused thereby may be filled by the actions of the county executive committee of the political party of such candidate.

(f) Vacancies in Office. - All vacancies in the membership of the boards of education whose members are elected pursuant to the provisions of subsection (a) of this section by death, resignation, or other causes shall be filled by appointment by the remaining members of the board, of a person to serve until the next election of members of such board, at which time the remaining unexpired term of the office in which the vacancy occurs shall be filled by election.

(g) Eligibility for Board Membership; Holding Other Offices. - Any person possessing the qualifications for election to public office set forth in Article VI, Sec. 6 of the Constitution of North Carolina shall be eligible to serve as a member of a local board of education: Provided, however, that any person elected or appointed to a local board of education, and also employed by that board of education, shall resign his employment before taking office as a member of that board of education.

Membership on a board of education is hereby declared to be an office that, with the exceptions provided above, may be held concurrently with any appointive office, pursuant to Article VI, Sec. 9 of the Constitution, but any person holding an elective office shall not be eligible to serve as a member of a local board of education.

(h) Death or Disqualification of Candidate in Nonpartisan Election. - If a candidate dies or becomes disqualified after the filing period has closed and before the election, and the ballots have not been printed, the county board of elections shall immediately reopen the filing period for five days so that additional candidates may file for election. If the ballots have been printed at the time the board of elections receives notice of the death or disqualification, the board shall reopen the filing period for three days if the board determines it will have time to reprint the ballots before the election.

In the event the board of elections determines that there is not time enough to reopen the filing period for three days and to reprint the ballots, then the ballots shall not be reprinted and the name of the deceased or disqualified candidate shall remain on the ballot. Votes cast for such candidate shall not be considered and the candidates receiving the highest number of votes equal to the number of positions to be filled shall be elected.

(i) The local board of education shall revise electoral district boundaries from time to time as provided by this subsection. If district boundaries are set by local act or court order and the act or order does not provide a method for revising them, the local board of education shall revise them only for the purpose of (i) accounting for territory annexed to or excluded from the school administrative unit, and (ii) correcting population imbalances among the districts shown by a new federal census or caused by exclusions or annexations. After the General Assembly has ratified an act establishing district boundaries, the local board of education shall not revise them again until a new federal census of population is taken or territory is annexed to or excluded from the school administrative unit, whichever event first occurs. After the local board of education has revised district boundaries in conformity with this act, the local board of education shall not revise them again until a new federal census of population is taken or territory is annexed to or excluded from the school administrative unit, whichever event occurs first, except that the board may make an earlier revision of district boundaries it has drawn if it must do so to comply with a court order or to gain approval of a district-revision plan by the U.S. Justice Department under Section 5 of the Voting Rights Act. In establishing district boundaries, the local board of education shall use data derived from the most recent federal census. (1955, c. 1372, art. 5, ss. 2-8; 1967, c. 972, ss. 2-6; 1969, c. 1301, s. 2; 1971, c. 704, s. 6; 1973, c. 1446, s. 1; 1977, c. 662; 1981, c. 423, s. 1; 1985, c. 404; c. 405, ss. 1, 2; 1985 (Reg. Sess., 1986), c. 975, s. 10; 1991, c. 400, s. 1.)

§ 115C-37.1. Vacancies in offices of county boards elected on partisan basis in certain counties.

(a) All vacancies in the membership of county boards of education which are elected by public or local act on a partisan basis shall be filled by appointment of the person, board, or commission specified in the act, except that if the act specifies that appointment shall be made by a party executive committee, then the appointment shall be made instead by the remaining members of the board.

(b) If the vacating member was elected as the nominee of a political party, then the person, board, or commission required to fill the vacancy shall consult with the county executive committee of that party and appoint the person recommended by that party executive committee, if the party executive committee makes a recommendation within 30 days of the occurrence of the vacancy.

(c) Whenever only the qualified voters of less than the entire county were eligible to vote for the member whose seat is vacant (either because the county administrative unit was less than countywide or only residents of certain areas of the administrative unit could vote in the general election for a district seat), the appointing authority must accept the recommendation only if the county executive committee restricted voting to committee members who represent precincts all or part of which were within the territory of the vacating school board member.

(d) (Effective until December 5, 2016) This section shall apply only in the following counties: Alleghany, Brunswick, Graham, Lee, New Hanover, Vance, and Washington.

(d) (Effective December 5, 2016) This section shall apply only in the following counties: Alleghany, Brunswick, Graham, Guilford, Lee, New Hanover, Vance, and Washington. (1981, c. 763, ss. 4, 14; c. 830; 1983, c. 493, s. 1; 1987 (Reg. Sess., 1988), c. 974, s. 5; 1989, c. 497, s. 3; 2009-277, ss. 1, 2; 2013-220, s. 2; 2013-361, s. 2.)

§ 115C-38. Compensation of board members.

The tax-levying authority for a local school administrative unit may, under the procedures of G.S. 153A-92, fix the compensation and expense allowances paid members of the board of education of that local school administrative unit.

Funds for the per diem, subsistence, and mileage for all meetings of county and city boards of education shall be provided from the current expense fund budget of the particular county or city.

The compensation and expense allowances of members of boards of education shall continue at the same levels as paid on July 1, 1975, until changed by or pursuant to local act or pursuant to this section. (1955, c. 1372, art. 5, s. 12; 1975, c. 569, ss. 1-3; 1977, c. 802, s. 39.5; 1981, c. 423, s. 1.)

§ 115C-39. Suspension of duties by State Board.

(a) Repealed by Session Laws 2007-498, s. 1, effective August 30, 2007.

(b) In the event the State Board of Education has appointed an interim superintendent under G.S. 115C-105.39 and the State Board determines that the local board of education has failed to cooperate with the interim superintendent, the State Board shall have the authority to suspend any of the powers and duties of the local board and to act on its behalf under G.S. 115C-105.39. (1955, c. 1372, art. 5, s. 13; 1981, c. 423, s. 1; 1995 (Reg. Sess., 1996), c. 716, s. 5; 2007-498, s. 1.)

§ 115C-40. Board a body corporate.

The board of education of each county in the State shall be a body corporate by the name and style of "The _____ County Board of Education," and the board of education of each city administrative school unit in the State shall be a body corporate by the name and style of "The _____ City Board of Education." The several boards of education, both county and city, shall hold all school property and be capable of purchasing and holding real and personal property, of building and repairing schoolhouses, of selling and transferring the same for school purposes, and of prosecuting and defending suits for or against the corporation.

Local boards of education, subject to any paramount powers vested by law in the State Board of Education or any other authorized agency shall have general control and supervision of all matters pertaining to the public schools in their respective local school administrative units; they shall execute the school laws in their units; and shall have authority to make agreements with other boards of education to transfer pupils from one local school administrative unit to another unit when the administration of the schools can be thereby more efficiently and more economically accomplished. (1955, c. 1372, art. 5, s. 10; 1981, c. 423, s. 1; 1985 (Reg. Sess., 1986), c. 975, s. 24.)

§ 115C-41. Organization of board.

(a) Unless otherwise provided by local law, all local boards of education shall have an organizational meeting no later than 60 days after the swearing in of members following election or appointment and as often thereafter as the board shall determine appropriate. The board may fix the date and time of its organizational meeting. At the organizational meeting the members of all boards shall elect one of their members as chairman for a period of one year, or until his successor is elected and qualified. The chairman of the local board of education shall preside at the meetings of the board, and in the event of his absence or sickness, the board may appoint one of its members temporary chairman. The superintendent of schools, whether a county or city superintendent, shall be ex officio secretary to his respective board. He shall keep the minutes of the meetings of the board but shall have no vote: Provided, that in the event of a vacancy in the superintendency, the board may elect one of its members to serve temporarily as secretary to the board.

(b) All local boards of education shall meet on the first Monday in January, April, July, and October of each year, or as soon thereafter as practicable. A board may elect to hold regular monthly meetings, and to meet in special session upon the call of the chairman or of the secretary as often as the school business of the local school administrative unit may require. (1955, c. 1372, art. 5, ss. 9, 11; 1981, c. 423, s. 1; 1983, c. 408.)

§ 115C-42. Liability insurance and immunity.

Any local board of education, by securing liability insurance as hereinafter provided, is hereby authorized and empowered to waive its governmental immunity from liability for damage by reason of death or injury to person or property caused by the negligence or tort of any agent or employee of such board of education when acting within the scope of his authority or within the course of his employment. Such immunity shall be deemed to have been waived by the act of obtaining such insurance, but such immunity is waived only to the extent that said board of education is indemnified by insurance for such negligence or tort.

Any contract of insurance purchased pursuant to this section shall be issued by a company or corporation duly licensed and authorized to execute insurance contracts in this State or by a qualified insurer as determined by the Department of Insurance and shall by its terms adequately insure the local board of education against liability for damages by reason of death or injury to person or property proximately caused by the negligent act or torts of the agents and employees of said board of education or the agents and employees of a particular school in a local administrative unit when acting within the scope of their authority. The local board of education shall determine what liabilities and what officers, agents and employees shall be covered by any insurance purchased pursuant to this section. Any company or corporation which enters into a contract of insurance as above described with a local board of education, by such act waives any defense based upon the governmental immunity of such local board of education.

Every local board of education in this State is authorized and empowered to pay as a necessary expense the lawful premiums for such insurance.

Any person sustaining damages, or in case of death, his personal representative may sue a local board of education insured under this section for the recovery of such damages in any court of competent jurisdiction in this State, but only in the county of such board of education; and it shall be no defense to any such action that the negligence or tort complained of was in pursuance of governmental, municipal or discretionary function of such local board of education if, and to the extent, such local board of education has insurance coverage as provided by this section.

Except as hereinbefore expressly provided, nothing in this section shall be construed to deprive any local board of education of any defense whatsoever to any such action for damages or to restrict, limit, or otherwise affect any such defense which said board of education may have at common law or by virtue of any statute; and nothing in this section shall be construed to relieve any person sustaining damages or any personal representative of any decedent from any duty to give notice of such claim to said local board of education or to commence any civil action for the recovery of damages within the applicable period of time prescribed or limited by statute.

A local board of education may incur liability pursuant to this section only with respect to a claim arising after such board of education has procured liability insurance pursuant to this section and during the time when such insurance is in force.

No part of the pleadings which relate to or allege facts as to a defendant's insurance against liability shall be read or mentioned in the presence of the trial jury in any action brought pursuant to this section. Such liability shall not attach unless the plaintiff shall waive the right to have all issues of law or fact relating to insurance in such an action determined by a jury and such issues shall be heard and determined by the judge without resort to a jury and the jury shall be absent during any motions, arguments, testimony or announcement of findings of fact or conclusions of law with respect thereto unless the defendant shall request a jury trial thereon: Provided, that this section shall not apply to claims for damages caused by the negligent acts or torts of public school bus, or school transportation service vehicle drivers, while driving school buses and school transportation service vehicles when the operation of such school buses and service vehicles is paid from the State Public School Fund. (1955, c. 1256; 1957, c. 685; 1959, c. 573, s. 2; 1961, c. 1102, s. 4; 1977, 2nd Sess., c. 1280, s. 3; 1981, c. 423, s. 1; 1985, c. 527.)

§ 115C-43. Defense of board of education members and employees.

(a) Upon request made by or in behalf of any member or employee or former member or employee, any local board of education may provide for the defense of any civil or criminal action or proceeding brought against him either in his official or in his individual capacity, or both, on account of any act done or omission made, or any act allegedly done or omission allegedly made, in the scope and course of his duty as a member of or employee of the local board of education. The defense may be provided by the local board of education by its own counsel, or by employing other counsel, or by purchasing insurance which requires that the insurer provide the defense. Nothing in this section shall be deemed to require any local board of education to provide for the defense of any action or proceeding of any nature.

(b) Any local board of education may budget funds for the purpose of paying all or part of a claim made or any civil judgment entered against any of its members or employees or former members and employees, when such claim is made or such judgment is rendered as damages on account of any act done or omission made, or any act allegedly done or omission allegedly made, in the scope and course of his duty as a member of the local board of education or as an employee. Nothing in this section shall authorize any local board of education to budget funds for the purpose of paying any claim made or civil judgment entered against any of its members or employees or former members and employees if the local board of education finds that such member or employee acted or failed to act because of actual fraud, corruption or actual malice on his part. Any local board of education may budget for and purchase insurance coverage for payment of claims or judgments pursuant to this section. Nothing in this section shall be deemed to require any local board of education to pay any claim or judgment referred to herein, and the purchase of insurance coverage for payment of any such claim or judgment shall not be deemed an assumption of any liability not covered by such insurance contract, and shall not be deemed an assumption of liability for payment of any claim or judgment in excess of the limits of coverage in such insurance contract.

(c) Subsection (b) of this section shall not authorize any local board of education to pay all or part of a claim made or civil judgment entered or to provide a defense to a criminal charge unless (i) notice of the claim or litigation is given to the local board of education prior to the time that the claim is settled or civil judgment is entered and (ii) the local board of education shall have adopted, and made available for public inspection, uniform standards under which claims made, civil judgments entered, or criminal charges against members or employees or former members and employees shall be defended or paid. (1979, c. 1074, s. 1; 1981, c. 423, s. 1.)

§ 115C-44. Suits and actions.

(a) A local board of education shall institute all actions, suits, or proceedings against officers, persons, or corporations, or their sureties, for the recovery, preservation, and application of all money or property which may be due to or should be applied to the support and maintenance of the schools, except in case of the breach of his bond by the treasurer of the county school fund, in which case action shall be brought by the board of county commissioners.

(b) In all actions brought in any court against a local board of education, the order or action of the board shall be presumed to be correct and the burden of proof shall be on the complaining party to show the contrary. (1955, c. 1372, art. 5, s. 14; 1981, c. 423, s. 1.)

§ 115C-45. Judicial functions of board.

(a) Power to Subpoena and to Punish for Contempt. - Local boards of education shall have power to issue subpoenas for the attendance of witnesses. Subpoenas may be issued in any and all matters which may lawfully come within the powers of the board and which, in the discretion of the board, require investigation; and it shall be the duty of the sheriff or any process serving officer to serve such subpoena upon payment of their lawful fees.

Local boards of education shall have power to punish for contempt for any disorderly conduct or disturbance tending to disrupt them in the transaction of official business.

(b) Witness Failing to Appear; Misdemeanor. - Any witness who shall wilfully and without legal excuse fail to appear before a local board of education to testify in any manner under investigation by the board shall be guilty of a Class 3 misdemeanor.

(c) (Applicable to employees employed before July 1, 2014) Appeals to Board of Education and to Superior Court. - An appeal shall lie to the local board of education from any final administrative decision in the following matters:

(1) The discipline of a student under G.S. 115C-390.7, 115C-390.10, or 115C-390.11;

(2) An alleged violation of a specified federal law, State law, State Board of Education policy, State rule, or local board policy, including policies regarding grade retention of students;

(3) The terms or conditions of employment or employment status of a school employee; and

(4) Any other decision that by statute specifically provides for a right of appeal to the local board of education and for which there is no other statutory appeal procedure.

As used in this subsection, the term "final administrative decision" means a decision of a school employee from which no further appeal to a school administrator is available.

Any person aggrieved by a decision not covered under subdivisions (1) through (4) of this subsection shall have the right to appeal to the superintendent and thereafter shall have the right to petition the local board of education for a hearing, and the local board may grant a hearing regarding any final decision of school personnel within the local school administrative unit. The local board of education shall notify the person making the petition of its decision whether to grant a hearing.

In all appeals to the board it is the duty of the board of education to see that a proper notice is given to all parties concerned and that a record of the hearing is properly entered in the records of the board conducting the hearing.

The board of education may designate hearing panels composed of not less than two members of the board to hear and act upon such appeals in the name and on behalf of the board of education.

An appeal of right brought before a local board of education under subdivision (1), (2), (3), or (4) of this subsection may be further appealed to the superior court of the State on the grounds that the local board's decision is in violation of constitutional provisions, is in excess of the statutory authority or jurisdiction of the board, is made upon unlawful procedure, is affected by other error of law, is unsupported by substantial evidence in view of the entire record as submitted, or is arbitrary or capricious. However, the right of a noncertified employee to appeal decisions of a local board under subdivision (3) of this subsection shall only apply to decisions concerning the dismissal, demotion, or suspension without pay of the noncertified employee. A noncertified employee may request and shall be entitled to receive written notice as to the reasons for the employee's dismissal, demotion, or suspension without pay. The notice shall be provided to the employee prior to any local board of education hearing on the issue. This subsection shall not alter the employment status of a noncertified employee.

(c)   (Applicable to employees employed on or after July 1, 2014) Appeals to Board of Education and to Superior Court. - An appeal shall lie to the local board of education from any final administrative decision in the following matters:

(1)   The discipline of a student under G.S. 115C-390.7, 115C-390.10, or 115C-390.11;

(2)   An alleged violation of a specified federal law, State law, State Board of Education policy, State rule, or local board policy, including policies regarding grade retention of students;

(3)   The terms or conditions of employment or employment status of a school employee; and

(4)   Any other decision that by statute specifically provides for a right of appeal to the local board of education and for which there is no other statutory appeal procedure.

As used in this subsection, the term "final administrative decision" means a decision of a school employee from which no further appeal to a school administrator is available.

Any person aggrieved by a decision not covered under subdivisions (1) through (4) of this subsection shall have the right to appeal to the superintendent and thereafter shall have the right to petition the local board of education for a hearing, and the local board may grant a hearing regarding any final decision of school personnel within the local school administrative unit. The local board of education shall notify the person making the petition of its decision whether to grant a hearing.

In all appeals to the board it is the duty of the board of education to see that a proper notice is given to all parties concerned and that a record of the hearing is properly entered in the records of the board conducting the hearing.

The board of education may designate hearing panels composed of not less than two members of the board to hear and act upon such appeals in the name and on behalf of the board of education.

An appeal of right brought before a local board of education under subdivision (1), (2), or (4) of this subsection may be further appealed to the superior court of the State on the grounds that the local board's decision is in violation of constitutional provisions, is in excess of the statutory authority or jurisdiction of the board, is made upon unlawful procedure, is affected by other error of law, is unsupported by substantial evidence in view of the entire record as submitted, or is arbitrary or capricious. (1955, c. 1372, art. 5, ss. 15-17; 1971, c. 647; 1981, c. 423, s. 1; 1993, c. 539, s. 881; 1994, Ex. Sess., c. 24, s. 14(c); 2001-260, s. 1; 2001-500, s. 6; 2011-282, s. 5; 2013-360, s. 9.6(c).)

§ 115C-46. Powers of local boards to regulate parking of motor vehicles.

(a)   Any local board of education may adopt reasonable rules and regulations with respect to the parking of motor vehicles and other modes of conveyance on public school grounds and may enforce such rules and regulations. A violation of a rule or regulation concerning parking on public school grounds is an infraction punishable by a penalty of not more than ten dollars ($10.00) unless the regulation provides that the violation is not punishable as an infraction. Rules and regulations adopted hereunder shall be made available for inspection by any person upon request.

(b)   Any local board of education may adopt written guidelines governing the individual assignment of parking spaces on school grounds. Such guidelines shall give first priority treatment to the physically handicapped.

(c)   Any local board of education, by rules and regulations adopted hereunder, may provide for the registration of motor vehicles and other modes of conveyance maintained, operated or parked on school grounds. Any local board of education, by rules and regulations adopted hereunder, may provide for the issuance of stickers, decals, permits or other indicia representing the registration status of vehicles or the eligibility of vehicles to park on school grounds and may prohibit the forgery, counterfeiting, unauthorized transfer or unauthorized use of them.

(d)   Any motor vehicle parked in a parking lot on school grounds, when such lot is clearly designated as such by a sign no smaller than 24 inches by 24 inches prominently displayed at each entrance thereto, in violation of the rules and regulations adopted by the local board of education, or any motor vehicle otherwise parked on school grounds in violation of the rules and regulations adopted by the county or city local board of education, may be removed from school grounds to a place of storage and the registered owner of that vehicle shall become liable for removal and storage charges. Any person who removes a vehicle pursuant to this section shall not be held liable for damages for the removal of the vehicle to the owner, lienholder or other person legally entitled to the possession of the vehicle removed; however, any person who intentionally or negligently damages a vehicle in the removal of such vehicle, or intentionally or negligently inflicts injury upon any person in the removal of such vehicle, may be held liable for damages. (1979, c. 821; 1981, c. 423, s. 1; 1981 (Reg. Sess., 1982), c. 1239, s. 2; 1983, c. 420, s. 3; 1985, c. 764, s. 37; 1989, c. 644, s. 4.)

§ 115C-46.1. Limitation on the use of public funds.

A local board of education shall not use public funds to endorse or oppose a referendum, election or a particular candidate for elective office. (2010-114, s. 1.5(c).)

§ 115C-46.2. Probation officer visits at school; limitations.

(a)   Except as provided in this section, probation officers are not authorized to visit students during school hours on school property.

(b)   Probation officers of the Section of Community Corrections of the Division of Adult Corrections, when working as a part of the Section's School Partnership Program, may visit students during school hours on school property with prior authorization by school administrators. For purposes of this section, "authorization" includes requests for assistance from guidance counselors or school resource officers.

(c) Each local board of education shall develop policies and guidelines for coordinating with probation officers of the Section of Community Corrections of the Division of Adult Corrections in the planning and scheduling of school visits as provided in this section, utilizing existing administrative capacity to manage scheduling. Visits shall be conducted in a private area designated for such use and located away from contact with the general student population. The probation officer shall not initiate direct contact with a student while the student is in class or between classes. Initial contact with the student shall be made by a school administrator or other designated school employee, who shall direct the student to a private area to meet with the probation officer. (2011-145, s. 19.1(k); 2012-149, s. 6.)

§ 115C-47. Powers and duties generally.

In addition to the powers and duties designated in G.S. 115C-36, local boards of education shall have the power or duty:

(1) To Provide an Adequate School System. - It shall be the duty of local boards of education to provide adequate school systems within their respective local school administrative units, as directed by law.

(2) To Exercise Certain Judicial Functions and to Participate in Certain Suits and Actions. - Local boards of education shall have the power and authority to exercise certain judicial functions pursuant to the provisions of G.S. 115C-45 and to participate in certain suits and actions pursuant to the provisions of G.S. 115C-44.

(3) To Divide Local School Administrative Units into Attendance Areas. - Local boards of education shall have authority to divide their various units into attendance areas without regard to district lines.

(4) To Regulate Extracurricular Activities. - Local boards of education shall make all rules and regulations necessary for the conducting of extracurricular activities in the schools under their supervision, including a program of athletics, where desired, without assuming liability therefor; provided, that all interscholastic athletic activities shall be conducted in accordance with rules and regulations prescribed by the State Board of Education.

(5) To Fix Time of Opening and Closing Schools. - The time of opening and closing the public schools shall be fixed under G.S. 115C-84.2.

(6) To Regulate Fees, Charges and Solicitations. - Local boards of education shall adopt rules and regulations governing solicitations of, sales to, and fund-raising activities conducted by, the students and faculty members in schools under their jurisdiction, and no fees, charges, or costs shall be collected from students and school personnel without approval of the board of education as recorded in the minutes of said board; provided, this subdivision shall not apply to such textbooks fees as are determined and established by the State Board of Education. All schedules of fees, charges and solicitations approved by local boards of education shall be reported to the Superintendent of Public Instruction.

(7) To Accept and Administer Federal or Private Funds. - Local boards of education shall have power and authority to accept, receive and administer any funds or financial assistance given, granted or provided under the provisions of the Elementary and Secondary Education Act of 1965 (Public Law 89-10, 89th Congress, HR 2362) and under the provisions of the Economic Opportunity Act of 1964 (Public Law 88-452, 88th Congress, S. 2642), or other federal acts or funds from foundations or private sources, and to comply with all conditions and requirements necessary for the receipt, acceptance and use of said funds. In the administration of such funds, local boards of education shall have authority to enter into contracts with and to cooperate with and to carry out projects with nonpublic elementary and secondary schools, community groups and nonprofit corporations, and to enter into joint agreements for these purposes with other local boards of education. Local boards of education shall furnish such information as shall be requested by the State Board of Education, from time to time, relating to any programs related or conducted pursuant to this subdivision.

(8) To Sponsor or Conduct Educational Research. - Local boards of education are authorized to sponsor or conduct educational research and special projects approved by the Department of Public Instruction and the State Board of Education that may improve the school system under their jurisdictions. Such research or projects may be conducted during the summer months and the board may use any available funds for such purposes.

(9) To Assure Accurate Attendance Records. - When the governing board of any local school administrative unit shall have information that inaccurate school attendance records are being kept, the board concerned shall immediately investigate such inaccuracies and take necessary action to

establish and maintain correct records and report its findings and action to the State Board of Education.

(10) To Assure Appropriate Class Size. - It shall be the responsibility of local boards of education to assure that the class size requirements set forth in G.S. 115C-301 for kindergarten through third grade are met. Any teacher who believes that the requirements of G.S. 115C-301 have not been met shall make a report to the principal and superintendent, and the superintendent shall immediately determine whether the requirements have in fact not been met. If the superintendent determines the requirements have not been met, he or she shall make a report to the next local board of education meeting. The local board of education shall take action to meet the requirements of the statute. If the local board cannot organizationally correct the exception, it shall immediately apply to the State Board of Education for additional personnel or a waiver of the class size requirements, as provided in G.S. 115C-301(g).

Upon notification from the State Board of Education that the reported exception does not qualify for an allotment adjustment or a waiver under provisions of G.S. 115C-301, the local board, within 30 days, shall take action necessary to correct the exception.

At the end of the second month of each school year, the local board of education, through the superintendent, shall file a report with the State Board of Education, in a format prescribed by the State Board of Education, describing the organization of each school, the duties of each teacher, and the size of each class. As of February 1 each year, local boards of education, through the superintendent, shall report all exceptions to individual class size maximums that exist at that time.

In addition to assuring that the requirements of G.S. 115C-301 are met, each local board of education shall also have the duty to provide an adequate number of classrooms to meet the requirements of that statute.

(11) To Determine the School Calendar. - Local boards of education shall determine the school calendar under G.S. 115C-84.2.

(12) (For final effective date, see notes) To Implement the Basic Education Program. - Local boards of education shall implement the Basic Education Program in accordance with rules adopted by the State Board. This implementation shall include provision for the efficient teaching of the course content required by the standard course of study.

(12) (For future effective date, see notes) To Implement the Basic Education Program. - Local boards of education shall implement the Basic Education Program in accordance with rules adopted by the State Board. This implementation shall include provision for the efficient teaching of the course content required by the Basic Education Program.

(13) To Elect a Superintendent. - The local boards of education shall elect superintendents subject to the requirements and limitations set forth in G.S. 115C-271.

(14) To Supply an Office, Equipment and Clerical Assistance for the Superintendent. - It shall be the duty of the various boards of education to provide the superintendent of schools with an office, equipment and clerical assistance as provided in G.S. 115C-277.

(15) To Prescribe Duties of Superintendent. - The local boards of education shall prescribe the duties of the superintendent as subject to the provisions of G.S. 115C-276(a).

(16) To Remove a Superintendent, When Necessary. - Local boards of education shall remove a superintendent for cause, pursuant to the provisions of G.S. 115C-274(a).

(17) To Employ Assistant Superintendent and Supervisors. - Local boards of education have the authority to employ assistant superintendents and supervisors pursuant to the provisions of G.S. 115C-278 and 115C-284(g).

(18) To Make Rules Concerning the Conduct and Duties of Personnel. - Local boards of education, upon the recommendation of the superintendent, shall have full power to make all just and needful rules and regulations governing the conduct of teachers, principals, and supervisors, the kind of reports they shall make, and their duties in the care of school property.

Prior to the beginning of each school year, each local board of education shall identify all reports, including local school required reports, that are required at the local level for the school year and shall, to the maximum extent possible, eliminate any duplicate or obsolete reporting requirements and consolidate remaining reporting requirements. No additional reports shall be required at the local level after the beginning of the school year without the prior approval of the local board of education.

Prior to the beginning of each school year, each local board of education shall also identify software protocols such as NC Wise that could be used to minimize repetitious data entry by teachers and shall make them available to teachers.

Each local board of education shall appoint a person or establish a local paperwork control committee to monitor all reports and other paperwork required of teachers by the central office and to monitor teachers' access to software protocols that minimize repetitious data entry.

(18a) To Adopt Rules and Policies Limiting the Noninstructional Duties of Teachers. - Local boards of education shall adopt rules and policies limiting the noninstructional duties assigned to teachers. A local board may temporarily suspend the rules and policies for individual schools upon a finding that there is a compelling reason the rules or policies should not be implemented. These rules and policies shall ensure that:

a. Teachers with initial certification are not assigned extracurricular activities unless they request the assignments in writing and that other noninstructional duties assigned to these teachers are minimized, so these teachers have an opportunity to develop into skilled professionals;

b. Teachers with 27 or more years of experience are not assigned extracurricular activities unless they request the assignments in writing and that other noninstructional duties assigned to these teachers are minimized, so these teachers have an opportunity to informally share their experience and expertise with their colleagues;

c. The noninstructional duties of all teachers are limited to the extent possible given federal, State, and local laws, rules, and policies, and that the noninstructional duties required of teachers are distributed equitably among employees.

(19) To Approve the Assignment of Duties to an Assistant Principal. - Local boards of education shall permit certain duties of the principal to be assigned to an assistant or acting principal pursuant to the provisions of G.S. 115C-289.

(20) To Provide for Training of Teachers. - Local boards of education are authorized to provide for the training of teachers as provided in G.S. 115C-300.

(21) It is the duty of every local board of education to provide for the prompt monthly payment of all salaries due teachers and other school officials and employees, and of all current bills and other necessary operating expenses. All salaries and bills shall be paid as provided by law for disbursing State and local funds.

The local board shall determine salary schedules of employees pursuant to the provisions of G.S. 115C-273, 115C-285(b), 115C-302.1(i), and 115C-316(b).

The authority for boards of education to issue salary vouchers to all school employees, whether paid from State or local funds, shall be a monthly payroll prepared on forms approved by the State Board of Education and containing all information required by the State Board of Education. This monthly payroll shall be signed by the principal of each school.

(22) To Provide School Food Services. - Local boards of education shall provide, to the extent practicable, school food services as provided in Part 2 of Article 17 of this Chapter.

(23) To Purchase Equipment and Supplies. - Local boards shall contract for equipment and supplies under G.S. 115C-522(a) and G.S. 115C-528.

(24) Purchase of Activity Buses with Local Capital Outlay Tax Funds. - Local boards of education are authorized to purchase activity buses with local capital outlay tax funds, and are authorized to maintain these buses in the county school bus garage. Reimbursement to the State Public School Fund shall be made for all maintenance cost including labor, gasoline and oil, repair parts, tires and tubes, antifreeze, etc. Labor cost reimbursements and local funds may be used to employ additional mechanics so as to insure that all activity buses owned and operated by local boards of education are maintained in a safe mechanical condition. Replacement units for activity buses shall be financed with local funds.

(25) To Secure Liability Insurance. - Local boards of education are authorized to secure liability insurance, as provided in G.S. 115C-42, so as to waive their immunity for liability for certain negligent acts of their employees.

(25a) To Reimburse the Additional Cost of Automobile Liability Coverage for School Social Workers Required to Transport Students. - Unless a local board of education otherwise provides for liability insurance coverage of a school social worker who is required to transport students under G.S. 115C-317.1, a local board of education may require a school social worker who is required to transport students as provided under G.S. 115C-317.1 to increase the liability limits or add a business-use rider, or both, on that employee's personal automobile liability insurance policy for the purpose of transporting students within the course of that employee's work duties, only if the board reimburses the employee for the additional premium charged, up to the maximum additional amount charged to a person with up to two points assessed under the Safe Driver Incentive Plan pursuant to G.S. 58-36-65, for the increased liability limits or the added rider, or both.

(26)   If a local board of education provides access to its buildings and campus and the student information directory to persons or groups which make students aware of occupational or educational options, the local board of education shall provide access on the same basis to official recruiting representatives of the military forces of the State and of the United States for the purpose of informing students of educational and career opportunities available in the military.

(27)   Repealed by Session Laws 1987, c. 571, s. 2.

(28)   To Enter Lease Purchase and Installment Purchase Contracts. - Local boards may enter into lease purchase and installment purchase contracts as provided in G.S. 115C-528.

(28a)   To Enter Guaranteed Energy Savings Contracts for Energy Conservation Measures. - Local boards may purchase energy conservation measures by guaranteed energy savings contracts pursuant to Part 2 of Article 3B of Chapter 143 of the General Statutes.

(29)   To Authorize the Observance of a Moment of Silence. - To afford students and teachers a moment of quiet reflection at the beginning of each day in the public schools, to create a boundary between school time and nonschool time, and to set a tone of decorum in the classroom that will be conducive to discipline and learning, each local board of education may adopt a policy to authorize the observance of a moment of silence at the commencement of the first class of each day in all grades in the public schools. Such a policy shall provide that the teacher in charge of the room in which each class is held may announce that a period of silence not to exceed one minute in duration shall be observed and that during that period silence shall be maintained and no one may engage in any other activities. Such period of silence shall be totally and

completely unstructured and free of guidance or influence of any kind from any sources.

(29a) To Require the Display of the United States and North Carolina Flags, and to Require the Recitation of the Pledge of Allegiance. - Local boards of education shall adopt policies to (i) require the display of the United States and North Carolina flags in each classroom, when available, (ii) require that recitation of the Pledge of Allegiance be scheduled on a daily basis, and (iii) provide age-appropriate instruction on the meaning and historical origins of the flag and the Pledge of Allegiance. These policies shall not compel any person to stand, salute the flag, or recite the Pledge of Allegiance. If flags are donated or are otherwise available, flags shall be displayed in each classroom.

(29b) To Ensure Freedom of Religion. - No local board of education shall have a policy of denying, or that effectively prevents participation in, prayer in public schools by individuals on a voluntary basis, except when necessary to maintain order and discipline. No local board of education shall encourage or require any person to participate in prayer or influence the form or content of any prayer in public schools. This subdivision shall not be construed to direct any local board of education to take any action in violation of the Constitutions of North Carolina or the United States.

(30) To Appoint Advisory Councils. - Local boards of education are authorized to appoint advisory councils as provided in G.S. 115C-55.

(31) Local boards of education shall determine the hours of employment for teacher assistants. The Legislative Commission of Salary Schedules for Public School Employees shall include in its report to the General Assembly recommendations regarding hours of employment for teacher assistants and other employees.

(32) To Refer All Students Who Drop Out of the Public Schools to Appropriate Services. - Local boards of education shall refer all students who drop out of the public schools to appropriate services. When appropriate public school services such as extended day programs are available, the local boards shall refer the students to those services. When appropriate public school programs are not available or are not suitable for certain students, the local board shall refer the students to the community college system or to other appropriate services.

(32a) To Establish Alternative Learning Programs and Develop Policies and Guidelines. - Each local board of education shall establish at least one alternative learning program and shall adopt guidelines for assigning students to alternative learning programs. These guidelines shall include (i) a description of the programs and services to be provided, (ii) a process for ensuring that an assignment is appropriate for the student and that the student's parents are involved in the decision, and (iii) strategies for providing alternative learning programs, when feasible and appropriate, for students who are subject to long term suspension or expulsion. In developing these guidelines, local boards shall consider the State Board's standards developed under G.S. 115C-12(24).

The General Assembly urges local boards to adopt policies that prohibit superintendents from assigning to any alternative learning program any professional public school employee who has received within the last three years a rating on a formal evaluation that is less than above standard.

Notwithstanding this subdivision, each local board shall adopt policies based on the State Board's standards developed under G.S. 115C-12(24). These policies shall apply to any new alternative learning program or alternative school that is implemented beginning with the 2006-2007 school year. Local boards of education are encouraged to apply these standards to alternative learning programs and alternative schools implemented before the 2006-2007 school year.

Local boards shall assess on a regular basis whether the unit's alternative schools and alternative learning programs comply with the State Board's standards developed under G.S. 115C-12(24) and whether they incorporate best practices for improving student academic performance and reducing disruptive behavior, are staffed with professional public school employees who are well trained and provided with appropriate staff development, are organized to provide coordinated services, and provide students with high quality and rigorous academic instruction.

(33) Local boards of education shall have sole authority to select and procure supplementary instructional materials, whether or not the materials contain commercial advertising, pursuant to the provisions of G.S. 115C-98(b).

(33a) To Approve and Use Textbooks Not Adopted by State Board of Education. - Local boards of education shall have the authority to select, procure, and use textbooks not adopted by the State Board of Education as provided in G.S. 115C-98(b1).

(34) To Encourage the Business Community to Facilitate Student Achievement. - Local boards of education, in consultation with local business leaders, shall develop voluntary guidelines relating to after-school employment. The guidelines may include an agreement to limit the number of hours a student may work or to tie the number of hours a student may work to his academic performance, school attendance, and economic need. The General Assembly finds that local boards of education do not currently have information regarding how many of their students are employed after school and how many hours they work; the General Assembly urges local boards of education to compile this critical information so that the State can determine to what extent these students' work affects their school performance.

Local boards of education shall work with local business leaders, including local chambers of commerce, to encourage employers to include and adopt as part of their stated personnel policies time for employees who are parents or guardians to attend conferences with their children's teachers.

The Superintendent of Public Instruction shall provide guidance and technical assistance to the local boards of education on carrying out the provisions of this subdivision.

(34a) To Encourage High School to Work Partnerships. - Each local board of education shall encourage high schools and local businesses to partner, specifically target students who may not seek higher education, and facilitate high school to work partnerships. Local businesses shall be encouraged to work with local high schools to create opportunities for students to complete a job shadow, internship, or apprenticeship. Students may also be encouraged to tour the local business or clinic, meet with employees, and participate in career and technical student organizations. Waiver forms may be developed in collaboration with participating businesses for the protection of both the students and the businesses.

Each local board of education shall encourage high schools to designate the Career Development Coordinator or other designee of the local Career and Technical Education administrator to be the point person for local businesses to contact. If the person selected is a teacher, the teacher shall work with the principal and the local Career and Technical Education administrator to find time in the school day to contact businesses and develop opportunities for students. The high school shall include a variety of trades and skilled labor positions for students to interact with and shadow and shall encourage students who may be interested in a job-shadowing opportunity to pursue and set up the job shadow.

Each local board of education shall develop a policy with provisions for students who are absent from school while doing a job shadow to make up the work. Students shall not be counted as absent when participating in these work-based learning opportunities or in Career and Technical Education student organization activities. Local boards may determine maximum numbers of days to be used for job-shadowing activities.

(35) To produce school building improvement reports. - Each administrative unit shall produce school building improvement reports for each school building in the local school administrative unit, in accordance with G.S. 115C-12(9)c3.

(36) To Report All Acts of School Violence. - Local boards of education shall report all acts of school violence to the State Board of Education in accordance with G.S. 115C-12(21).

(37) To purchase group accident and health insurance for students. - Local boards of education may purchase group accident, group health, or group accident and health insurance for students in accordance with G.S. 58-51-81.

(38) To Establish School Improvement Teams. - Local boards shall adopt a policy to ensure that each principal has established a school improvement team under G.S. 115C-105.27 and in accordance with G.S. 115C-288(l) and that the composition of the team complies with G.S. 115C-105.27(a). Local boards shall direct the superintendent or the superintendent's designee to provide appropriate guidance to principals to ensure that these teams are established and that the principals work together with these teams to develop, review, and amend school improvement plans for their schools.

(39) To Adopt Policies Related to Student Retention Decisions. - Local boards shall adopt policies related to G.S. 115C-45(c) that include opportunities for parents and guardians to discuss decisions to retain students.

(40) To adopt emergency response plans. - Local boards of education shall, in coordination with local law enforcement agencies, adopt emergency response plans relating to incidents of school violence. These plans are not a public record as the term "public record" is defined under G.S. 132-1 and shall not be subject to inspection and examination under G.S. 132-6.

(41) To Encourage Recycling in Public Schools. - Local boards of education shall encourage recycling in public schools and may develop and implement recycling programs at public schools.

(42) Recodified as G.S. 115C-375.3 by Session Laws 2005-22, s. 3(a), effective April 28, 2005.

(43) Local boards of education are encouraged to adopt policies that require superintendents to assign to the core academic courses, in seventh through ninth grades, teachers who have at least four years' teaching experience and who have received within the last three years an overall rating on a formal evaluation that is at least above standard.

(44) Recodified as G.S. 115C-375.4 by Session Laws 2005-22, s. 4(a), effective April 28, 2005.

(45) To Report Certain Incidents of Seclusion and Restraint. - Local boards of education shall maintain a record of incidents reported under G.S. 115C-391.1(j)(4) and shall provide this information annually to the State Board of Education.

(46) At the discretion of the board, to adopt policies and procedures authorizing schools that operate programs under G.S. 115C-307(c) to utilize unlicensed health care personnel to perform the technical aspects of medication administration to students. If adopted, the policies and procedures shall be consistent with the requirements of Article 9A of Chapter 90 of the General Statutes and shall include the following:

a. Training and competency evaluation of medication aides as provided for under G.S. 131E-270.

b. Requirements for listing under the Medication Aide Registry as provided for under G.S. 131E-271.

c. Requirements for supervision of medication aides by licensed health professionals or appropriately qualified supervisory personnel consistent with Articles 5, 6, 10, and 16 of Chapter 131E of the General Statutes.

(47) To Address the Use of Pesticides in Schools. - Local boards of education shall adopt policies that address the use of pesticides in schools. These policies shall:

a. Require the principal or the principal's designee to annually notify the students' parents, guardians, or custodians as well as school staff of the schedule of pesticide use on school property and their right to request notification. Such notification shall be made, to the extent possible, at least 72 hours in advance of nonscheduled pesticide use on school property. The notification requirements under this subdivision do not apply to the application of the following types of pesticide products: antimicrobial cleansers, disinfectants, self-contained baits and crack-and-crevice treatments, and any pesticide products classified by the United States Environmental Protection Agency as belonging to the U.S.E.P.A. Toxicity Class IV, "relatively nontoxic" (no signal word required on the product's label).

b. Require the use of Integrated Pest Management. As used in this sub-subdivision, "Integrated Pest Management" or "IPM" means the comprehensive approach to pest management that combines biological, physical, chemical, and cultural tactics as well as effective, economic, environmentally sound, and socially acceptable methods to prevent and solve pest problems that emphasizes pest prevention and provides a decision-making process for determining if, when, and where pest suppression is needed and what control tactics and methods are appropriate.

(48) To Address Arsenic-Treated Wood in the Classroom and on School Grounds. - Local boards of education shall prohibit the purchase or acceptance of chromated copper arsenate-treated wood for future use on school grounds. Local boards of education shall seal existing arsenic-treated wood in playground equipment or establish a time line for removing existing arsenic-treated wood on playgrounds, according to the guidelines established under G.S. 115C-12(33). Local boards of education are encouraged to test the soil on school grounds for contamination caused by the leaching of arsenic-treated wood.

(49) To Address Mercury in the Classroom and on School Grounds. - Local boards of education are encouraged to remove and properly dispose of all bulk elemental mercury, chemical mercury, and bulk mercury compounds used as teaching aids in science classrooms, not including barometers. Local boards of education shall prohibit the future use of bulk elemental mercury, chemical mercury compounds, and bulk mercury compounds used as teaching aids in science classrooms, not including barometers.

(50) To Address Exposure to Diesel Exhaust Fumes. - Local boards of education shall adopt policies and procedures to reduce students' exposure to diesel emissions.

(51) To Ensure that Schools Provide Information Concerning Cervical Cancer, Cervical Dysplasia, Human Papillomavirus, and the Vaccines Available

to Prevent These Diseases. - Local boards of education shall ensure that schools provide parents and guardians with information about cervical cancer, cervical dysplasia, human papillomavirus, and the vaccines available to prevent these diseases. This information shall be provided at the beginning of the school year to parents of children entering grades five through 12. This information shall include the causes and symptoms of these diseases, how they are transmitted, how they may be prevented by vaccination, including the benefits and possible side effects of vaccination, and places parents and guardians may obtain additional information and vaccinations for their children.

(52)   To Ensure That Certain Students Receive Information Annually on Lawfully Abandoning a Newborn Baby. - Not later than August 1, 2008, local boards of education shall adopt policies to ensure that students in grades nine through 12 receive information annually on the manner in which a parent may lawfully abandon a newborn baby with a responsible person, in accordance with G.S. 7B-500.

(53)   To Encourage Programs for Successful Transition Between the Middle School and High School Years. - Local boards of education are encouraged to adopt policies to implement programs that assist students in making a successful transition between the middle school and high school years. The programs may include Ninth Grade Academies, programs to effectively prepare eighth grade students for the expectations and rigors of high school, early warning systems to flag students not ready for ninth grade and develop plans for those students, mentoring programs that pair upperclassmen with incoming students, and graduation plans for students who have fallen behind and are off track for graduation.

(54)   To Increase Parental Involvement in Student Achievement and Graduation Preparation. - Local boards of education are encouraged to adopt policies to promote and support parental involvement in student learning and achievement at school and at home and to encourage successful progress toward graduation. These policies may include strategies to increase school communications with parents regarding expectations for students and student progress, graduation requirements, and available course offerings, to provide increased opportunities for parental involvement in schools, and to create an environment in the schools conducive for parental involvement.

(55)   To Reduce Suspension and Expulsion Rates and Provide for Academic Progress During Suspensions. - Local boards of education are encouraged to adopt policies and best practices to reduce suspension and expulsion rates and

to provide alternative learning programs for continued academic progress for students who have been suspended.

(56) To Notify Parents or Legal Guardians of Students Alleged to be Victims of Acts Required to be Reported to Law Enforcement and the Superintendent. - Local boards of education shall adopt a policy on the notification to parents or legal guardians of any students alleged to be victims of any act that is required to be reported to law enforcement and the superintendent under G.S. 115C-288(g).

(57) To adopt a code of ethics. - Local boards of education shall adopt a resolution or policy containing a code of ethics, as required by G.S. 160A-86.

(58) To Inform the Public About the North Carolina School Report Cards Issued by the State Board of Education. - Each local board of education shall ensure that the report card issued for it by the State Board of Education receives wide distribution to the local press or is otherwise provided to the public. Each local board of education shall ensure that the overall school performance score and grade earned by each school in the local school administrative unit for the current and previous four school years is prominently displayed on the Web site of the local school administrative unit. If any school in the local school administrative unit is awarded a grade of D or F, the local board of education shall provide notice of the grade in writing to the parent or guardian of all students enrolled in that school.

(59) To Encourage Student Voter Registration. - Local boards of education are encouraged to adopt policies to promote student voter registration. These policies may include collaboration with county boards of elections to conduct voter registration and preregistration in high schools. Completion and submission of voter registration forms shall not be a course requirement or graded assignment for students.

(60) Repealed by Session Laws 2012-194, s. 55(a), effective July 17, 2012.

(61) To Provide a Safe School Environment. - Local boards of education may enter into an agreement with the sheriff, chief of police of a local police department, or chief of police of a county police department to provide security at the schools by assigning volunteer school safety resource officers who meet the selection standards and criteria developed by the head of the appropriate local law enforcement agency and the criteria set out in G.S. 162-26 or G.S. 160A-288.4, as appropriate. (1955, c. 1372, art. 5, ss. 18, 28, 30, 33; art. 6, s.

6; art. 17, s. 7; c. 1185; 1959, c. 1294; 1963, c. 425; c. 688, s. 3; 1965, c. 584, ss. 4, 6; c. 1185, s. 1; 1969, c. 517, s. 2; c. 538; 1973, c. 770, ss. 1, 2; c. 782, s. 31; 1975, c. 150, s. 1; c. 965, s. 3; 1977, c. 1088, s. 4; 1981, c. 423, s. 1; c. 901, s. 1; 1983 (Reg. Sess., 1984), c. 1019, s. 2, 1; c. 1034, s. 16; 1985, c. 436, s. 1; c. 479, ss. 55(c)(4), 55(c)(6); c. 637; c. 757, s. 145(i); 1985 (Reg. Sess., 1986), c. 975, ss. 3, 11; c. 1014, s. 58; 1987, c. 340; c. 414, s. 2; c. 571, s. 2; c. 738, s. 182; 1987 (Reg. Sess., 1988), c. 1025, ss. 9, 15; c. 1086, s. 89(b); 1989, c. 585, s. 2; c. 752, s. 65(b); 1989 (Reg. Sess., 1990), c. 1074, s. 23(b); 1991, c. 706, s. 1; 1991 (Reg. Sess., 1992), c. 900, s. 75.1(f); 1993, c. 114, s. 1; c. 321, s. 139(c); 1993 (Reg. Sess., 1994), c. 716, s. 2; c. 775, s. 5; 1995, c. 455, s. 1; c. 497, ss. 1, 2; 1995 (Reg. Sess., 1996), c. 716, ss. 11, 12, 17; 1997-443, s. 8.38(j)-(l); 1998-194, s. 3; 1998-202, s. 12; 1999-96, s. 7; 1999-237, s. 8.25(a); 1999-373, s. 3; 1999-397, s. 4; 1999-456, s. 35; 2000-67, s. 8.18(b); 2000-140, s. 77; 2001-424, s. 28.17(c); 2001-500, s. 3; 2001-512, s. 12; 2002-103, s. 2; 2002-178, s. 3; 2003-147, s. 4; 2004-118, s. 2; 2004-203, s. 72(b); 2005-22, ss. 3(a), 4(a); 2005-205, s. 5; 2005-276, s. 10.40D(f); 2005-355, s. 2; 2005-446, s. 3; 2006-137, s. 1; 2006-143, s. 2; 2007-59, s. 1; 2007-126, s. 1; 2009-223, s. 1; 2009-330, ss. 1, 2; 2009-403, s. 2; 2009-410, s. 2; 2009-451, s. 7.28; 2009-541, s. 29(a); 2011-91, s. 1; 2011-145, s. 7.13(b), (w); 2011-185, s. 9(a); 2011-379, s. 3; 2011-391, s. 14(b); 2012-142, s. 7A.3(b); 2012-194, s. 55(a); 2013-360, ss. 8.37(a), 8.45(c); 2013-363, s. 3.3(b); 2013-381, s. 12.1(h).)

§ 115C-48. Penalties for certain conduct.

(a) Members of local boards of education are criminally liable for certain conduct as provided in G.S. 14-234.

(b) Members of local boards of education are civilly liable for certain conduct as provided in G.S. 115C-441. (1981, c. 423, s. 1; 1995, c. 509, s. 60; 2001-409, s. 4.)

§ 115C-49: Repealed by Session Laws 1995, c. 501, s. 1.

§ 115C-50. Training of board members.

(a) All members of local boards of education, whether elected or appointed, shall receive a minimum of 12 clock hours of training annually. The 12 clock hours of training may include the ethics education required by G.S. 160A-87.

(b) The training shall include but not be limited to public school law, public school finance, and duties and responsibilities of local boards of education.

(c) The training may be provided by the North Carolina School Boards Association, the School of Government at the University of North Carolina at Chapel Hill, or other qualified sources at the choice of the local board of education. (1991, c. 689, s. 200(d); 2006-264, s. 29(h); 2009-403, s. 3.)

Vision Books Order Form

Fax Orders:	1-980-299-5965
Phone Orders:	1-704-898-0770
E-mail Orders:	www.visionbooks.org
Mail Orders:	Vision Books, LLC P.O. Box 42406 Charlotte, NC 28215

Shipp To:
Name_____
Address_____
City_____State_____Zip_____
Phone_____Fax_____
Email_____@_____

Bill To: We can bill a third party on your behalf.
Name_____
Address_____
City_____State_____Zip_____
Phone___(_____)_____Fax_____
Email_____@_____

Pamphlet Number ($15.00 Each)	Qty	Total Cost
_____	_____	_____
_____	_____	_____
_____	_____	_____
_____	_____	_____
_____	_____	_____
_____	_____	_____
_____	_____	_____
Full Volume Set 1-92	**92 Pamphlets**	**1,380.00**

Free Shipping Shipping & Handling on Full Volume Orders
Add $1.00 Shipping & Handling per pamphlet $_____

Total Cost $_____

Thank you for your support. Management!

DID YOU ENJOY THIS BOOK?

Vision Books, LLC would like to hear from you! If you or someone you know has been fasely imprisoned, we would like to hear your story. If the 'North Carolina Criminal Law and Procedure' has had an effect in your life or if you have suggestions, we would like to hear from you. Send your letters to:

Vision Books, LLC
Attn: Staff Writers
P.O. Box 42406
Charlotte, NC 28215
Email: staff@visionbooks.org

Order Additional Copies:

Fax Orders:	1-980-299-5965
Phone Orders:	1-704-898-0770
E-mail Orders:	www.visionbooks.org
Mail Orders:	Vision Books, LLC P.O. Box 42406 Charlotte, NC 28215

www.ingramcontent.com/pod-product-compliance
Lightning Source LLC
Chambersburg PA
CBHW051628170526
45167CB00001B/109